Stop the Killing

Stop the Killing

How to End the
Mass Shooting Crisis

Katherine Schweit

ROWMAN & LITTLEFIELD
Lanham • Boulder • New York • London

Published by Rowman & Littlefield
A wholly owned subsidiary of The Rowman & Littlefield Publishing Group, Inc.
4501 Forbes Boulevard, Suite 200, Lanham, Maryland 20706
www.rowman.com

6 Tinworth Street, London SE11 5AL, United Kingdom

British Library Cataloguing in Publication Information Available

Library of Congress Cataloging-in-Publication Data

Names: Schweit, Katherine W., author.
Title: Stop the killing : how to end the mass shooting crisis / Katherine Schweit.
Description: Lanham : Rowman & Littlefield, [2021] | Includes bibliographical
   references and index.
Identifiers: LCCN 2020057500 (print) | LCCN 2020057501 (ebook) | ISBN
   9781538146927 (cloth) | ISBN 9781538146934 (ebook)
Subjects: LCSH: Mass shootings—United States.
Classification: LCC HV6536.5 .S39 2021 (print) | LCC HV6536.5 (ebook) | DDC
   364.4—dc23
LC record available at https://lccn.loc.gov/2020057500
LC ebook record available at https://lccn.loc.gov/2020057501

Contents

Preface

A NEW LEGAL FRONTIER IN SCHOOL SHOOTINGS

Just after this book went to press, a fifteen-year-old boy in Michigan was charged with killing four and wounding seven at Oxford High School, not far from my birthplace, Detroit. Many from my large Irish Catholic family still live nearby.

Some would say another week, another shooting. But I knew immediately this was different and called my publisher. This was worth stopping the presses for—literally—I told her. We are witnessing a new and aggressive battle plan in the war on mass shootings. It's a pendulum swing some say may go too far; but maybe not.

I'm talking about the criminal charges filed against the alleged shooter as well as his parents.

The day after the November 30, 2021, shooting, the Oakland County prosecutor filed not only murder charges against the accused but also charges he committed an act of terrorism. A few days later, the prosecutor charged the boy's parents with the most serious charges ever levied at parents in a school shooting: four counts of involuntary manslaughter.

The boy faces life in prison. If convicted, the parents face fifteen years each. The couple's combined bonds total $1 million. They are all destined to spend Christmas in matching jumpsuits but separate cells.

These charges made this a stop-the-presses event, and as a former prosecutor, I appreciate its watershed nature. We have been struggling to find the right pieces of the puzzle that will stop this terrible rise in mass killings. And now, new pieces are on the board. Accused shooters have never faced charges for terrorizing students and school officials.

Now, going forward, every prosecutor will consider bringing a charge of terrorism if their state law allows. And though this happened in Michigan, the impact will ripple across a country ravaged as active shooters clocked somewhere north of sixty incidents for 2021, a 50 percent increase from the record high in 2020.

But let me back up.

This is what happened that day and how these extraordinary charges came to be. I'm writing this in the days after charges have been filed and the lengthy legal process is just beginning. That said, I'll tell you what we know based on information released in charging documents and from statements by the prosecutor, law enforcement, and witnesses.

Sometime after noon on Tuesday, November 30, 2021, a high school sophomore allegedly walked from a boys' bathroom inside his school and began shooting at students in the hallway of Oxford High School, 30 miles north of Detroit's city limit, 8 Mile Road. An announcement went out over the school intercom that there was an active shooter in the school.

The 1,800 students were trained in a version of Run. Hide. Fight.® and quickly barricaded themselves in rooms. They knew to block the doors to bar the shooter from entering. Many followed the run protocol, fleeing the school, at times at the urging of teachers.

Undeterred, the shooter continued to pull the trigger as he pointed at students, a teacher, and blocked doors attempting to hit people behind them. He fired about thirty rounds in five minutes, ended four lives, wounded seven, and changed an entire community forever.

The all-to-familiar police response followed, and within minutes a shooter was in police custody, willingly handing over his gun with seven rounds still in the weapon and other ammunition still unspent.

The next day, the alleged shooter was charged as an adult with twenty-four separate criminal charges. These included four counts of first-degree murder, seven counts of assault with intent to murder, and twelve counts of possession of a firearm in the commission of a felony.

But unlike charges filed against school shooters in the past, this fifteen-year-old also was charged with one count of committing an act of terrorism. Michigan state law allows a person to be charged with an act of terrorism if the action is intended to intimidate or coerce a civilian population. Michigan had adopted the law in the wake of the September 11, 2001, terrorist attacks. No federal criminal charge currently exists for domestic terrorism. The added charge was appropriate, the sheriff and prosecutor agreed, because people who weren't hit by bullets were still terrorized.

A search of the teen's home and personal belongings seemed to verify he had planned well ahead, prosecutor Karen McDonald said in announcing the charges against the teen. The shooter had recorded two messages on his phone the night before talking about killing students and had written similar things out.

It was "absolutely premeditated," McDonald said, spelling out some details at her press conference. This wasn't an impulsive act, and a "mountain" of evidence will back up the charges.

Replying to a reporter, McDonald indicated her office was considering charges against the parents and might announce charges "shortly." Responsible gun ownership must include securing guns, and we must hold accountable those who fail to secure a gun they own, she said.

As I watched the press conference, I heard her say what is said at every press conference after a shooting: "We have watched school shootings unfold across this country for far too long," McDonald lamented. "Sadly, the national spotlight is shining today on our community. We send our kids to school. We think they are going to be safe. If the incident yesterday is not enough to revisit our gun laws, I don't know what is."

DID SHE REALLY DO THAT?

But where other prosecutors might be a bit all hat and no cattle, McDonald put actions behind her words. Two days later, she filed charges against the parents as details emerged that seemed incredible. Among the most revealing, if found to be true:

- The fifteen-year-old boy and his father had gone to a gun shop to buy the gun for the boy on a Black Friday sale just four days before the shooting.
- The boy posted a picture of himself that day with his new gun that he then used at the range with his mother.
- His mother posted online the next day about her son's "new Christmas present."
- The next school day, a Monday, a teacher saw the boy searching for ammunition online and reported the behavior.
- A school counselor spoke to the boy but did not receive a return call after leaving a voicemail message for the parents.
- The same day the mother sent a text to her son that read: "LOL I'm not mad at you. You have to learn not to get caught."
- The next day, a teacher photographed a drawing on a paper found on the boy's desk. The prosecutor described the drawing at her press conference as a semiautomatic handgun, pointing at the words, "The thoughts won't stop. Help me." In another section of the note was a drawing of a bullet, with the following words above that bullet: "Blood everywhere." Between the drawing of the gun and the bullet is a drawing of a person who appears to have

been shot twice and to be bleeding. Below that figure is a drawing of a laughing emoji. Further down the drawing are the words, "My life is useless." And to the right of that are the words, "The world is dead."

- The same day, a Tuesday, the boy and his parents were called to a counselor's office and, though the details of that conversation have not been publicly disclosed, the parents apparently agreed to seek counseling for their son but resisted taking him home that day.
- The boy returned to class and, shortly after, allegedly emerged from the boys' bathroom and began firing his weapon.
- About five minutes later, police arrived, and the boy was arrested.
- About a half hour after the shooting occurred, as the media began reporting on the shooting, the mother texted her son begging him, "Don't do it."
- Seemingly sharing the same concern, the father went home to check on the whereabouts of the gun and called police when he discovered it was missing, telling police his son might be the shooter.

No information released by the time of publication of this book verified whether the school knew the family had purchased a gun for the boy. The same is true of anyone asking where the gun was located or asking to search the boy, his locker, or his backpack the day of the shooting.

The day the parents were charged, their attorneys allegedly reported their clients would turn themselves in at 4 p.m. But by 3 p.m., those interviewing me on cable news had turned their questions from asking me to explain the charges against the parents to asking me how the FBI and law enforcement would go about apprehending individuals who might be on the run. Four o'clock came and went, but the parents did not show up in court. Fearing the two had fled, the US Marshals issued a BOLO notice—be on the lookout—and joined by the FBI and Oakland County Fugitive Apprehension Team as a massive manhunt ensued.

Relying on a tip, the Detroit Police led an arrest team taking the couple into custody at about 1:30 a.m. the next day. They were hidden inside an empty warehouse in downtown Detroit, three miles and eight minutes from the Canadian border. Police told the news media they had withdrawn $4,000 in cash from a bank account the previous afternoon.

Pleadings and the court hearings will shine more light on what really happened with the parents both before and after the shooting. Either way, the parents clearly understood the serious nature of the charges. At their arraignment the next day, the father's legal counsel included the weather-worn and experienced attorney who had represented convicted sex offender Larry Nassar. Nassar, accused of sexually molesting more than 200 gymnasts, spent eighteen years as the team doctor for the US women's national gymnastics team until he was convicted of multiple counts involving child pornography, sexual assault, and evidence tampering.

I'll be watching and listening to the legal battles. Some of that is the nerdy lawyer in me, but most of it is a pensive watch over how these new ways to charge shooters and their enablers will play out.

Lawyers recognize perhaps more than most that if the terrorism prosecution charge is successful, any person shooting in a public place could face similar terrorism charges in the future, regardless of whether their bullets hit their target. This means that it might be possible to file changes against a shooter even if no one is killed or wounded during a shooting. Charges for even attempting to terrorize might result, as would be allowed under Michigan law.

If parents or their child could face terrorism charges, would parents feel more urgency to keep guns out of their hands and educate children and instill in them the seriousness of the matter? Younger students often consider their actions to be more of a prank, and the older ones may want to get out of taking a history test. But now, these kids are being handcuffed and processed in juvenile court.

I recall when fire departments started charging parents, schools, or businesses when they had to send a truck out on a false alarm. Maybe the terrorism charge in the Michigan shooting will change the minds of those who make even a vague threat to a school full of people.

Perhaps the risk of a terrorism charge on your criminal record will make potential troublemakers pause. When it comes to fines, people take things seriously. When it comes to jail time, people take things even more seriously.

Even when the criminal charges are dropped, many of these kids are being kicked out of school, taking them away from watchful eyes and a stable environment.

In the same way, we'll all be watching with interest for the outcome of the involuntary manslaughter charges against the parents. Will the resulting legal action jolt gun owners into taking more care to safely store their firearms and reach out for assistance faster when they see their child on a pathway to potential violence?

I am often between the very loud voices on either side of the gun debate. Those urging stronger gun control laws and regulations point to safe storage laws for guns as one of their highest priorities. Research has found that more than half of all gun owners store at least one gun unsafely—without any locks or other safe storage measures. And nearly a quarter of all gun owners report storing all their guns in an unlocked location in the home.

I grew up in Michigan, and my cousins had their rifles on a gun rack on their dresser at their Canton farm outside of Detroit. But hundreds of millions more guns are in circulation now, and the days where that should be acceptable have ended. It doesn't matter whether it used to be ok and you wish it could be that way again. It isn't that way now, so it is time to move on.

Most states have some sort of law holding parents responsible for failing to secure a gun when a resulting incident involves their child. I recall a few cases where a parent was convicted of involuntary manslaughter when one of their young children found a loaded gun and used it to kill a sibling. Thankfully, charges like that are rare.

These charges against the parents of the Michigan shooter stretch responsibility for their action a bit, extending legal culpability to those who are essentially the enabler.

As a Special Agent for the FBI, I often had a rifle, shotgun, and one or two handguns. All of them had to be secured. I raised two girls by myself and didn't want to take any chances. Both of my kids even learned to shoot.

My younger daughter used to try to convince me to share my gun safe combination. What if a bad guy comes in, she'd say? I know better, understanding that younger children can be taught *gun safety*, but that is completely different from having the *maturity* to make wise decisions with a gun, particularly under duress.

Given the critical state of our nation when it comes to mass shootings, don't we owe it to ourselves to reexamine every possible option for keeping guns out of the hands of people who are struggling with mental wellness?

Now we have a watershed case for when to charge parents. Going forward, parents facing involuntary manslaughter is a reality. Shooters facing a terrorism charge is a reality.

These may not be THE missing pieces to complete the puzzle that will put an end to mass shootings, but I'm anxious to find out whether the new use of these criminal charges turns out to be two of those very valuable corner pieces on our vexing puzzle board.

SO GOES THE STATE, SO GOES THE NATION

In the days following the Oxford shooting, the floodgates opened. Scores of copycat threats followed, the inevitable contagion phenomenon I write about in chapter 2. Similar terrorism and other charges were filed against dozens of middle and high school students all over Michigan who threatened violence, primarily online.

To their credit, students and parents alike heeded the call; thousands called police and school officials, and some used the anonymous tip and text line, OK2SAY. This state-supported tip line allows students to text 652729 or call 855-565-2729 with information. Among the cases:

- A thirteen-year-old Mason Middle School student was arrested for a threat he made against his school. He posted a picture of a firearm on social media with the caption "Mason better watch out." He was the second child charged from that school in a week. He faces a charge of knowingly making a false report of terrorism; a twenty-year felony.

- A fifteen-year-old Orion High School junior was arrested two days after the Oxford shooting and was charged with making terroristic threats. According to police, the boy said he "would shoot up the school if he could get a gun." His school is seven miles from Oxford High School.
- A sixteen-year-old Martin Luther King High School student was charged with making false report of a threat of terrorism.
- Students at two different schools were arrested after they were discovered carrying loaded firearms.
- Two eighth graders from different schools, Pierce Middle School and Oakland Scholars Charter School, were taken into custody after they made statements about bringing guns to school or being school shooters. Both were seen making threatening gestures as if their hand was a gun shooting people.
- Two nine-year-old students from Riverside Elementary School were removed from their school and turned over to their parents when they were found to be in possession of "naughty/nice lists," which contained several names along with the words "alive" and "dead" on each side of the lists.

And these events didn't just occur in Michigan.

Katherine Fung, reporting for *Newsweek* December 3, 2021, found seventy different districts were forced to close 519 schools in the week after the Oxford shooting. These were just the closings identified in seven states— Michigan, Virginia, Pennsylvania, Connecticut, New York, New Jersey, and Georgia. The issues at hand: threats made against the student and staff, guns brought to school, and social media posts urging others to violence.

KEEPING PARENTS OUT OF JAIL

After the wave of arrests, Michigan law enforcement responded aggressively, asking parents to warn their children against copycat threats. The frustrated public exploded with support and a bit of skepticism, hoping these more severe charges might be one way to influence parents—if not shooters—and turn the tide on a seemingly unstoppable rise in mass shootings.

While we await the impact of these serious charges filed by the Oakland County prosecutor, parents are on notice they could face very serious jail time for the actions of their child.

To prevent such actions in your household, I urged a friend of mine to consider these two things.

First, honestly evaluate your child's access to guns, at your home and the houses of friends and family. Don't let your child go to a home without knowing whether there is safe storage for firearms.

Second, I told my friend, begin today having honest and repeated discussions about not only the danger of hoax calls and copycat incidents but also their responsibility to look and listen for those in distress who may be reaching out: those who might commit suicide or be on a pathway to violence.

"Kids are wicked smart and their brains are sponges," a middle school teacher, who happens to also be my daughter, told me. "Give your kids more credit. Stop pushing your own anxieties onto them. Teach them that if another child does or says something abnormal or disturbing, you can't chalk it off to a 'bad day.' Stir the pot and stir it immediately. Worst case scenario, they're mad for a few days. Best case scenario, you saved literal human lives."

"No one wants to train children to respond to violence or notice violent tendencies," she added. "It is sad, but, until the culture that fosters shootings goes away, it's literally a life-or-death decision."

STAYING HOME, COVID, AND FEELING EMPOWERED

I was halfway through my next book when the Oxford shooting happened, compelling me to set it aside. I began to field calls from parents who wanted to let their kids skip school or maybe join the ranks of the home-schooled.

I couldn't give them the hall pass they wanted. Running from the problem of school shootings isn't the answer. Children get support and confide in teachers at times. COVID showed us how tough online learning can be. The absence of a brick-and-mortar experience hindered opportunities to learn empathy and heightened anxiety and depression, my daughter added.

"I think the pandemic taught us that an enormous portion of social etiquette, problem solving, and emotional resilience and regulation is learned outside of the home," she said, while not discounting what is learned in the home. Face-to-face interactions with teachers can have an enormous impact.

"Our sixth graders in the year 2021 are struggling with basic behaviors that are reinforced in fourth and fifth grade, which are the years they missed out on for in-person learning: standing quietly in line, raising your hand, figuring out what questions you need to ask to understand, how to handle confrontation, and being friendly to people you don't like. School offers that built-in, supervised, and tiered social and academic climate that is difficult to find elsewhere."

My daughter's cousin, Meggan, is one of my favorite nieces (I have fifteen!). She has three beautiful children who attend a small Catholic elementary school not far away from Oxford.

She and I had spent a lot of time on the phone after the 2018 Parkland High School shooting in Florida where seventeen were killed and another seventeen injured. For some reason the shooting set off alarm bells in her head. She wondered then whether her children could ever be safe in a school. Maybe she should teach them at home? We talked through the risks and the rewards.

I encouraged my niece to listen to my podcast, also called *Stop the Killing*, which I cohost with my London-based friend Sarah Ferris. In each episode we focus on a shooting, what we learned, and how we might have been able to prevent the next shooter from striking. When our limitations because of the COVID pandemic are behind us, I plan to stop by for a wine-and-friends gathering to talk empowerment.

When I published this book, I wanted to be sure my niece was one of the first to read it, neither of us realizing that just a few months later the book's content would help her through the stress of a shooting not far from her own backyard. When I heard about Oxford, my thought immediately went to her. But when we spoke, my niece said this time around she felt more calm and able to make informed decisions.

"I have friends at larger public schools who, while their school was open, they opted to keep their kids home," she told me. "They were too afraid to send the kids to school. Just too scared. I didn't feel that way. We can't pull our kids from school. If you pull your kids from school, are you going to stop letting them play outside or at a friend's house? A catastrophe can happen to anyone at any time."

She credited her change in attitude to the comfort she feels with her small school community and the effort she had made to educate herself, leaving her more empowered. She is sharing this philosophy now with all of her friends, she explained.

Investing time in reading the book and listening to the podcast, she said, has taught her how to turn away from her fears and "refocus the conversation on learning from the mistakes and then implementing something different or new so we don't repeat the mistakes."

I can almost hear Meggan's anxiety go down as she talks about it. So, while I await the results of the legal action against Oxford shooter and his parents, I am encouraged by those like you who have picked up this book. I hope it helps you to push your fears aside and to empower yourself with facts to help stop the killing.

Acknowledgments

To my beautiful girls, Sarah and Fionna, who encouraged me to write this book and stuck by me through it all.

To honest editing by Bob Barbrow and the patience shown by his lovely wife, Leslie, despite other pressures in their lives. To my longtime friend and advisor, Michael Kortan, whose steady professionalism improved the language in this book immeasurably.

To many at the FBI but most importantly James A. Green, who carried the weight of guiding the FBI's Active Shooter program after I left and brought his knowledge of tactics to further hone how to stop the killings. To my other FBI and law enforcement team members during those critical years after Sandy Hook who made miracles happen and hid all misgivings about my demands: Deb Cryan, Fay Campos, David Knoff, Jerry Castleberry, Dennis Jahnke, Pete Lapp, Michael McElhenny, Kathryn M. Crotts, Ashley Mancik, and, most particularly, Andrew Ames. And to wise guidance from James Yacone and Chris Combs.

To the brave members of state, local, and tribal law enforcement who run toward the danger and risk their lives every day to save others during mass shootings.

To my good friends Jim and Gabrielle Patton, who ignored me so I could meet my deadline and then celebrated with a Negroni when the publisher took charge. For the encouragement and support of those around me, most importantly, Stephanie and Al Miller, Michele Yaroma and Tim McCants, Stavriana Dimopoulos and Farrell Brody, and Allison Adams Bousson.

To Sharon Wray for early guidance, my agent, Elaine Spencer, The Knight Agency, and the team at Rowman & Littlefield Publishing Group.

Finally, to my sister and sparring partner, Maribeth Coulombe, and my dear friend Carol Okamoto, who checked in with me nearly every day in the final months of finishing this book—keeping me laughing, working through challenges, and listening to me prattle on endlessly. Their generosity must be repaid.

Chapter One

A "How-To" Manual

On December 14, 2012, an anxiety-ridden twenty-year-old shot through the front door of Sandy Hook Elementary School and killed twenty children and six women in five minutes.

The shooting, eleven days before Christmas, stunned the world. The news media subsumed Newtown, Connecticut's 27,000 residents, instantly filling area hotels and restaurants to begin the inevitable weeks of memorial services and funerals.

Headlines told the story:

"Our Hearts Are Broken Today"—*Chicago Tribune*
"Beautiful Little Kids"—*Savannah Morning News*
"Evil Visited This Community Today"—*News Journal* (Delaware)
"Massacre of Innocents"—*Republican-American* (Litchfield, Connecticut)
"Why?"—*Vindicator* (Youngstown, Ohio)
"Unthinkable"—*Tampa Bay Times*
"Gunman Massacres 20 Children at School in Connecticut; 28 Dead Including Killer," read the *New York Times*, the page blanketed by a terrifying five-column picture of a teacher leading little students to safety. "Who Would Do This to Our Poor Little Babies?" it said beside a photo of then–President Barack Obama as he addressed the nation just hours after the shooting.

"We've endured too many of these tragedies in the past few years. And each time I learn the news, I react not as a President, but as anybody else would—as a parent,"[1] Mr. Obama said. "The majority of those who died today were children—beautiful little kids between the ages of 5 and 10 years

1

old."[2] Uncharacteristically and visibly overwhelmed, he paused to wipe away tears welling up and take several breaths of air to compose himself. We felt it.

"They had their entire lives ahead of them—birthdays, graduations, weddings, kids of their own." He said that among the fallen were also teachers, "men and women who devoted their lives to helping our children fulfill their dreams. So our hearts are broken today."[3]

"Like most Americans, I believe the Second Amendment guarantees an individual right to bear arms," the president said. "I respect our strong tradition of gun ownership and the rights of hunters and sportsmen. There are millions of responsible, law-abiding gun owners in America who cherish their right to bear arms for hunting or sport or protection or collection. . . . I believe most of them agree that, if America worked harder to keep guns out of the hands of dangerous people, there would be fewer atrocities like the one that occurred in Newtown."[4]

He announced then–Vice President Joseph Biden would lead a task force to pursue an aggressive legislative agenda, increase research efforts, and implement twenty-three executive actions designed to curb gun violence.[5] Vice presidential (VP) staffers were quickly sent out to recruit the teams that would look for solutions.[6]

Within days I joined Mr. Biden's effort, led by his senior policy analyst Maureen Tracy-Mooney; the pressure to find answers was palpable. Little did I know that the following year US Attorney General Eric Holder and I would be discussing our startling findings.

As a special agent with the Federal Bureau of Investigation, I carried a gun. But understanding targeted violence, the kind occurring when an active shooter strikes, was a challenge.

Growing up in Michigan, I handled a gun only a few times and stayed home when classmates went north at the opening of hunting season. Instead, I concentrated on becoming a professional journalist, a bug I never shook after watching the Watergate hearings.

The day after I turned eighteen, I found work at the local daily newspaper, remaining there until I graduated from Michigan State University. A good newspaper job at the *Daily Herald* took me to Chicago, and before long I had added a law degree from DePaul University College of Law.

An offer to clerk for an appellate court judge led me to a prosecutor's job with the Cook County State's Attorney's office. Though I worked primarily drug cases, for a time I shared an office with a felony attorney who handled what we called the "dead baby cases." I admired her tenacity and told her I couldn't imagine not crying all the time if I worked those horrific cases involving dead children.

When I joined the FBI, it came as somewhat of a relief to be working national security matters in their Milwaukee office, looking for terrorists, recruiting sources, and following the money trails. I felt the weight of the responsibility of counterintelligence investigations and the pressure when fate left me in charge as the supervisor of the Wisconsin terrorism response the morning of the September 11, 2001, attacks.

A promotion to the national counterintelligence division took me to Washington, DC; but, in the FBI, an agent works as assigned, and fifteen years into my career, I was reassigned to the Biden effort.

Some saw the issue only as a gun debate. But guns, explored in a later chapter, are a complex matter.[7]

Guns and active shooters are only part of the gun discussion. In 2016, for example, an estimated 39,000 people died by gun deaths in the United States; nearly 60 percent, or 23,000, of those were suicides.[8] Of the 14,000 homicides, seventy-one of those deaths were attributable to incidents where three or more were killed.[9]

But the impact of each of these shootings is tangible and reaches back decades. How far we have come is best exposed in the rarely mentioned 1984 killing of twenty-one and wounding of nineteen, including five children, at a McDonald's restaurant at the Mexico border in San Ysidro, California.

Police appeared helpless as they set a wide perimeter, and they and America, via live television, watched as an unemployed security guard and welder methodically shot hundreds of rounds from a semiautomatic pistol, a shotgun, and an Uzi rifle. Police followed a protocol of "contain and wait," securing the area until sharpshooters and other tactical officers arrived. For nearly an hour, patrons huddled under tables, some trying to talk the shooter out of continuing his rampage. The shooter fired 257 additional rounds in the 62 minutes after police arrived and before a police sharpshooter finally killed him.

Estimates put the cost of gun violence in the United States in the billions of dollars annually. That includes recovery efforts, such as the $600 million price tag for the 2017 Live Nation music festival shooting in Las Vegas where 58 were killed and 489 injured—about $7.8 million for each fatal assault.[10]

Though potential gun legislation debates loomed, our mission at Team Biden focused on what could be done now. The US gun culture exists.

I had spent two years as the FBI's public information officer for our Washington, DC, field office, and that put me in the middle of many crises, including when an active shooter killed a security guard at the US Holocaust Memorial Museum and, nine months later, when two guards were injured in a shooting at the Pentagon.

Leading the FBI in this new effort, I borrowed personnel and set up shop at spare desks in FBI headquarters. And, eighteen months and thirty-five active shooter incidents later, I was sitting in US Attorney General Holder's small conference room in the Robert F. Kennedy Building on Pennsylvania Avenue in Washington, DC, ready to brief him on what we had learned.

The FBI was about to announce that a fourteen-year analysis of active shooter incidents in the United States had found that an average of 6.4 incidents annually from the first half of the study years had increased to 16.4 incidents annually in the second half of the period.[11]

Our public announcement of an increase in shootings, and who was doing the shootings, surely would make news, and it's always good to keep the Department of Justice's main office in the loop.

And before he had even settled into his seat, the Attorney General spoke up. "If these were deaths from terrorist acts, the American public would be outraged," he said. "And I'd be hearing about that." Surprising and sad, Holder said, was who was doing the killings.

FBI research found active shooter incidents nationwide were killing more people, more frequently, in more states, than terrorist attacks had since September 11, 2001.

In fact, the FBI found that, since the September 11, 2001, terrorist attacks, 468 people had died in active shooter incidents and only fourteen were at the hands of foreign-inspired terrorists.[12] The rest were domestic terrorists.

FBI Deputy Director Sean Joyce sat on the side, snacking on a granola bar and leaning back in his chair. "It's a tough situation," he said, shaking his head in agreement without looking up. Nothing left to say.

After the Sandy Hook shooting, the public and media had become obsessed with the question of whether shootings were on the rise. We knew now that the answer was yes.

AMERICANS KILLING AMERICANS

But even as we released the FBI study publicly, the anticipated and collective public outrage failed to materialize.

Cities continued to be synonymous with shootings: El Paso, Dayton, Pearl Harbor, Pensacola, Aurora, Parkland, Jersey City, San Rafael, Tallahassee, and Sutherland Springs.

Businesses, schools, and houses of worship were too: PJ Harrington's Bar and Grill in Pennsylvania, Henry Pratt Company warehouse in Illinois, West Palm Beach VA Medical Center in Florida, Chabad of Poway synagogue in California, Dependable Plumbing in Texas, Walmart Supercenter in Mississippi, Noblesville West Middle School in Indiana, Waffle House in Tennessee.

Lots of cries of *Never again!* rang out, and lots of news stories about how things were going to change circulated, but each shooting brought the same sympathy tweets and pledges of thoughts and prayers. As we continued to track active shooter incidents around the country, we found the country moved from a shooting every month to a shooting every week. Less outrage and less news coverage followed. When fifty-nine people were gunned down by the shooter at the Live Nation country music festival in Las Vegas, we heard *never again*. The following month brought the gut-wrenching news that an eighteen-month-old child was among the twenty-six dead at a Texas church shooting; *never again*.

Now, with twenty years of research on 305 active shooter incidents behind us, the casualty count was 981 dead with 1,696 injured. Nearly a decade after Mr. Holder's blunt analysis, irrefutable evidence has shown that Americans continue to kill Americans, in America, at an increasing rate greater than any foreign terrorist threat.

The job for Team Biden was substantial: dig into every area, and find ways to do a better job of preventing, responding to, and recovering from these shootings.

A TEAM EFFORT

Our Team Biden was an alphabet soup of federal agencies: DHS, FEMA, HHS, DOJ/COPS, FBI, the Department of Education, and others. Each had their own ideas and initiatives, as well as a role in our joint efforts.[13]

We adopted the singular national mantra *Run, hide, fight* to teach civilians to think through their best options when the shooting starts. We delivered massive training programs to teach people how to develop emergency operations plans for their libraries, auto shops, schools, houses of worship, businesses, and hospitals.

At the FBI, we invested $30 million in local and free training for law enforcement to help them learn that the best way to save lives is not to wait but to go directly to the shooter. I convinced reluctant peers to better share resources that were normally only available to our behavioral experts at Quantico. This information, I urged, would help the public better understand what leads up to an individual's decision to commit a shooting and help everyone to recognize people in trouble. We nearly tripled the size of the teams who respond to shooting scenes to support survivors and families of victims. Millions more dollars supported the push for better equipment for responding officers and the sharing of best practices.

The impact of the team was so successful that we were recognized with the Attorney General's Award for Outstanding Contributions to Community

Partnerships for Public Safety.[14] Surely this would reduce the number of shootings, we thought; but it did not.

Today, more shootings result in more fatalities.

It's infuriating.

Where once a few active shooters struck each year, research shows the numbers doubling, then tripling. We saw twenty incidents annually in each of the years 2014, 2015, and 2016. By 2017, it seems the wheels had come off, with a high watermark of thirty shootings and even higher casualty rates. Higher numbers each year, 40 by 2020, and more than 60 expected in 2021. Nearly every week, my social media feeds would light up over the latest shooting, and I would be taking calls from the media, asking how we can end the violence.

After all these years of violence, it is a hopeless cause to some.

But I have come to believe it is not.

THE ANSWER LIES WITHIN

We have the answers to prevention. It's not new laws. It's not the police. It's not someone else's fault.

It's our fault.

But don't quit reading.

Although I admit to feeling a bit like Don Quixote at times, the best prevention experts in the world agree with me. "Mass violence is a pernicious social pathology," the National Council for Behavioral Health reported in 2019. "The good news is that we have the means to limit if not end it. The bad news is that we have not taken the necessary steps to do so. We lack the social and political will, not the knowledge, capacity, or means."[15]

I agree and shout it from the rooftops. We have the tools, and we have done it before. Practicing fire drills has resulted in our ability to say we haven't lost a child to a school fire since 1958 in Chicago. Remember the successful campaign to warn children of *stranger danger*? How about teaching everybody to stop, drop, and roll? Ask someone alive in the 1960s to sing the jingle, *Buckle up for safety, buckle up*. These are just a few of the many successful safety education campaigns that struggled at the start but later became wildly effective and saved lives.

This was the exact thinking behind adopting the national messaging known as Run. Hide. Fight.®—to teach everyone how to think when bullets start flying. Now universities and businesses tweet and text out *Run, hide, fight* when an emergency is underway. It's a nuanced messaged, discussed in more depth in a later chapter, but it is a great message that sticks like oatmeal to the ribs.

Slogans can only take us so far, though. Action is needed.

Individual citizens have the largest responsibility to own this fix, whether a parent, business leader, neighbor, coworker, cleric, school superintendent, classmate, library administrator, service member, human resources worker, or government worker. This applies too to those charged with security responsibilities. They are at the tip of the spear, developing plans for active shooter responses, workplace violence prevention, and emergency operations. Armed with the latest data and best practices, they can inspire the change.

INFORMATION OVERLOAD

We have the means to get us to our pot of gold: stopping the killings. Tremendous information is out there for the asking, but those doing the planning and training may have trouble finding it. Why is that?

It may be because typing "active shooter" into your Google search engine comes back with 100 million hits. A search for "threat assessment training" returns 200 million hits, and a search for "threat assessment," 300 million hits. Where to start?

The noise and clutter of the internet provides an overwhelming and ever-increasing amount of raw, unvetted information. Articles and opinion pieces blur editorial lines as everyone offers well-intentioned but, at times, misinformed or outdated information. That's actually what inspired me to write this book. I have an advanced degree in wading through all of those materials.

Few could envision today's internet in 1966, when an active shooter spent 96 minutes killing people from the twenty-eighth floor of the University of Texas campus tower. The World Wide Web was in its infancy. Wikipedia was still three years away in 1999 when two teenagers launched their morning attack at their high school in Colorado. Government agencies were years from posting any useful resources for public consumption, leaving newspapers, television news, and opinion pieces as the primary ways the public would learn anything.

The extraordinary burst of information available via the internet may seem like a blessing. With a computer in every hand, it would seem that we have a bounty of resources ripe for the picking. But with so much information available, we are actually drowning in it. Trying to sift through it all takes time, and hiring someone to do it is expensive. For school districts, businesses, houses of worship, and nonprofit organizations, cash is always in short supply. For parents and the public in general, the task is nearly insurmountable. This book consolidates all that clutter and provides a how-to look at data-driven research and the way forward.

STOP LOOKING FOR A SINGLE ANSWER

Equally fatal to the effort to stop active shooters and other targeted violence is a focus on a single solution. We are in a meme, Post-it, sound-bite kind of world right now, and messages must fit into 280 characters. Not helping is the persistent view that there must be a single solution such as:

- Take away the guns.
- Put up more security at businesses.
- Arm teachers and security at houses of worship.
- Provide better mental health solutions.
- Improve anonymous reporting systems.
- Get rid of violent video games.
- Find more good guys with guns.
- Place more police in schools.

A single answer doesn't work because there isn't a single reason why these shootings continue to be on the rise. Complex challenges rarely have a single solution.

A former director of the Centers for Disease Control and Prevention told the *Washington Post* in the early months of the 2020 COVID-19 pandemic, "People keep asking me, 'What's the one thing we have to do?' . . . The one thing we have to do is to understand that there is not one thing. We need a comprehensive battle strategy, meticulously implemented."[16]

Stopping targeted violence, including active shooters, takes a comprehensive battle strategy that very much requires the public on the battlefield. This book will identify and explain errors in some of the common theories. It will review the breadth of the problem and send readers on a path to develop their own safety plans, and it will examine how to provide life-saving training, change policies, and ultimately save lives. There isn't room for everything here, but particular attention has been paid to prevention efforts as we all try to tip the scale toward ending the killings.

STARTING AT GO

In the FBI, our efforts initially focused on finding ways to help law enforcement. Our team set out to speak to dozens of first responders, and we pored over detailed police reports from those events we all know by name: Aurora, Columbine, Fort Hood, Sandy Hook, and Oak Creek, Wisconsin.

We listened to parents whose children were killed, survivors who made it out, and our own FBI personnel to consider what went wrong, and what went right, when they responded to Sandy Hook and other shootings.

We visited locations where shootings had occurred, walking the hallways at Virginia Tech, Aurora Theater, Columbine High School, and Los Angeles International Airport.

We spoke to behavioral experts to hear how and what they learned about potential opportunities to intervene when behavioral cues indicated a shooter might strike.

We found that the FBI did do after-action evaluations but, like other police agencies, rarely shared the information, even inside the FBI. No one wants to point out failures. Companies, too, often kept after-action analysis to themselves. Transparent self-evaluation often brings with it the sting of public criticism, and, for many companies, it can mean loss of stock value and consumer support and can bring on lawsuits.

We discovered that the many written reports identified eerily similar problems, all recommending similar changes to prevention, response, and recovery efforts. We saw repeated first responder problems, such as inadequate communications systems and protocols.

We read over and over again about the lack of awareness training for civilians and the complete absence of training on how to spot behavioral concerns. Behavioral experts pushed back, not keen on training civilians in the nuances of their art and afraid that training would include stereotyping and valueless checklists.

In fact, it seemed everybody I interacted with, both in and out of the government, was moving around the same puzzle pieces, looking for the ones that would fit together. But no one was really talking comprehensively to each other.

We began to widely share this information with first responders. But, despite the efforts to train beyond law enforcement, the general population was not around the table working on the puzzle with us.

I spent much of my last years at the FBI speaking to businesspeople, educators, and government and private organizations—addressing groups often numbering in the hundreds—trying to share what we had learned. I was frustrated that so much of what I spoke about seemed new to decision makers, business leaders, emergency managers, security chiefs, school administrators, and so many members of the public.

Though dozens of reliable government websites were going up, filled with consolidated, evidence-based research and best practices, many of those who were charged with the safety of others had never seen the FBI's research or any other federal guidance designed to provide free support. For example, did you know . . .

- Often those who commit targeted violence move on a path that includes visible signs of planning and preparation? These are opportunities to find a shooter before the shooting starts.
- A handful of nationally available anonymous tiplines exist right now that you can share with students, parents, employees, and others who might be afraid to call police about a potential active shooter?
- Millions of federal dollars are used to aid survivors, victims, and their families through a well-coordinated, and long-established, federal, state, and local victim services network? Having knowledge of contact and other information before a disaster can get you national assistance within hours.

And, just in the past few years, additional and extraordinary research has been conducted by academic groups and local and federal agencies. Though posted on websites or offered with a press release, they are hidden in the mire and little talked about.

Plus, there are so many other useful tidbits we've all learned over the years that the public should know, even if they think they don't want to know. For example,

- Although a novice can fire three rounds a second from a handgun, and many more from a semiautomatic weapon, every shooter still has to stop to change magazines. This creates opportunities to flee or overwhelm the shooter.
- When a shooting occurs and you lie down on the pavement, any bullets that hit the ground in your direction can skid great distances across that ground, looking for something or someone to hit. Don't be on the ground.

Though I can't summarize all I have learned in one book, my hope is that this primer will shepherd readers toward hard-to-find best practices as well as a better understanding of current prevention efforts, how to build your personal safety guide, practical advice about what to do if you are at a shooting, and how to help a community repair after a tragedy.

BEFORE, DURING, AND AFTER

To understand the framework, consider that targeted violence is a tragedy with three distinct stages: before, during, and after. These three time periods require different planning and training solutions.

Before requires prevention preparation, which includes looking for signs that potential shooters might display. *During* requires response preparation for both first responders and the public. *After* requires planning to support survivors, families of victims, scene recovery, and continuity of operations for businesses and educational and other organizations.

For those doing the planning, I describe it this way: see figure 1.1, "Before. During. After."

Before		
Prevention	**During**	
•Train everyone, no matter the age, to act with kindness and remain aware.	**Response**	**After**
•Train adults to identify behaviors of concern and watch for stressors that might trigger violence.	•Use the Run Hide Fight/Escape strategy.	**Recovery**
•Develop a response team with decision-making authority, and pre-assign areas of responsiblity.	•Use Stop the Bleed skills to save lives.	•Be part of the law enforcement command post decision making team.
•Engage police and local government in planning.	•Use what is around you to save your life.	•Engage with state- and county-based organizations.
•Assess the physical security of building and grounds.		•Reach out to established resources such as businesses, churches, and school districts in neighboring counties.
•Develop a support plan that includes mutual aid from unaffected communities, companies, and like organizations.		•Protect the privacy of all by seeking guidance from media relations team members in law enforcement and county agencies, and the FBI.
		•Engage pre-established teams to maintain continuity of operations in businesses, re-open schools and churches, and create calm.

Figure 1.1.   Before. During. After.
Katherine Schweit, Schweit Consulting LLC

The general public is the key to success *Before.*

Prevention efforts require learning the signs of targeted violence and the behaviors that show a person may be on a trajectory toward violence. Sharing this information through formal or informal means, marketing campaigns, or other ways increases everyone's knowledge.

Chapters are dedicated to understanding these behavioral cues and setting up threat assessment teams. Businesses, churches, schools, and other organizations also can examine how kindness and inclusion are part of the organizational culture.

Before is also the time to assess physical space and your surrounding area to help identify vulnerabilities. Doing a physical assessment pinpoints security concerns in parking lots, at gates, and where interior and exterior doors and windows may create hidden vulnerabilities.

This book will explore how to conduct a safety assessment and direct you to reliable and free resources to help you make your buildings safer. Few people go to sleep at night with an unlocked door. No one in a city leaves the keys to the car on the dashboard. Safety assessments help identify vulnerabilities.

Separate chapters discuss unique challenges for houses of worship and businesses, the latter being where about half of all active shootings take place.

Because prevention is the ultimate goal, significant portions of this book will explore the tools available to the public so that, if they see something, they will know what, when, and to whom to say something. This is crucial, because everyone has opinions about prevention, but so many are uninformed. We all need to be better informed.

Attitudes and actions are part of prevention. A good cardiologist still cannot predict when a patient might suffer a heart attack, but they can help you watch for warning signs and share risk factors.

Prevention requires knowing what to watch for and also how to answer when questions like these arise:

- What should I think when my child talks about killing and hate?
- Where should I turn when I have a hunch?
- What should supervisors do when they hear about a troubled employee?
- When is intervention by a counselor important?
- What are the legal limits to sharing personal information when I suspect someone of potential violence?
- What behaviors should be concerning to a schoolteacher?
- What do clerics need to think about when they see behavioral changes in a member of their flock?
- Where do guns fit in?
- When is a neighbor's being a busybody a necessary thing?
- When you see something, what do you say, and to whom?

For *Response*, training and the right equipment are vital for first responders. But, right now, training is actually more important for the public, the bystanders who face the immediate threat of injury or death.

Learn what to do if someone is bleeding or has been shot. It can save the life of an injured person, whether from a shooting, a car accident, or an injury on a hike. Organizations can train their personnel in these vital skills, and the public also can get free training. More details are in the training chapters.

Proper training has immeasurable benefits, chief among them instilling confidence and driving away unwarranted fear. Because I think there is never enough training, I also provide a chapter outlining my own technique for teaching the federally endorsed Run. Hide. Fight.®[17] method of protecting yourself during an ongoing act of violence.

Training is different for every age, so in a later chapter I also have gathered the best free online materials to train children as young as preschool age and included some excellent and reasonably priced books parents and teachers can buy or get their school libraries to purchase. These books are designed to help children learn to follow direction in emergencies of any kind, and, don't worry, they don't focus on shootings.

First responders have made good progress on response protocols, but, locally, there are still too many who don't know what is already in place, how to incorporate it into emergency response plans, and how to tap those vital resources.

For *Recovery*, learn and incorporate into planning all the resources and actions that aid communities to return to some sense of calm after an act of targeted violence, allowing a chance to heal. Explore how to reopen businesses and schools, including finding alternate sites to provide continuity of operations.

A chapter dedicated to survivors and victims' families is part of the *Recovery* effort. Among the topics explored are determining who can help find unconscious people in a hospital, locating financial resources to pay for emergency flights and hotel bills, working with first responders, managing the news media, and obtaining assistance from volunteer agencies. Information on laws and corporate policies are detailed, but, foremost, the public and those developing policies and training need to engage. Ultimately, each of us can make change happen.

PERSONAL RESPONSIBILITY

In the weeks and months after September 11, 2001, Americans were laser-focused on their surroundings, galvanized and determined to prevent another attack. Perhaps we were more afraid and therefore more willing to fight to make things better. I know I was, even as a terrorism supervisor.

Fear is not comfortable, but it does make us act. After September 11, Americans called our FBI offices and their local police departments when they saw something suspicious. They stopped officers on patrol if they saw a package unattended. *See Something, Say Something* may not be a rousing battle cry, but it works: Many of these tips resulted in terrorist plots uncovered and foiled, including several in New York City.

Yet Americans have not responded similarly to the mass shooting and active shooter crisis. Since Sandy Hook, we are better prepared to prevent shootings, take action, support survivors, and bring a community back to a sense of normalcy. But prevention methods and preparedness remain the challenge, particularly among the general population.

Understanding and taking responsibility should be on the to-do list for members of the public, including every company owner, board member, policy maker, cleric, principal, administrator, parent, and community leader. It is no longer acceptable to say you are ready because you know the police will show up or someone in your building has an emergency operations plan inside an electronic file never opened or in a dusty binder on a shelf.

As you read the chapters on prevention, behavioral cues, threat assessment, and threat management, remember that we see and know more about one another's day-to-day lives today than ever before. Perhaps we are not seeing the clues because we aren't looking.

Twenty years ago, an active shooter incident occurred every two months. Today, we face one every seven days. The nation's more than 800,000 law enforcement officers cannot stem this tide of destruction without the active engagement of the country's 300 million–plus citizens.[18]

Consider the facts in the case of Texas shooter Devin Kelley. His threatening text messages to a family member preceded what the authorities reported was a domestic situation that spilled over into a church. He had been court-martialed by the US Air Force in 2012 for assaulting his wife and their child.

The Air Force failed to report his court-martial to the FBI's National Instant Criminal Background Check System, which is checked prior to allowing a gun sale to go forward. Subsequently, Kelley bought four weapons in two different states. At one point, Kelley was denied a permit to purchase one gun in Texas, but gun owners in that state do not have to be licensed, and permits aren't required for other guns.

Kelley had undergone mental health counseling, and his military record was rife with warning signs of a propensity for violence, such as pointing a loaded gun at his wife, choking her, and shaking and assaulting his stepson "with a force likely to produce death or grievous bodily harm."[19]

Even after Kelley had made death threats to members of his chain of command, the US Army discharged him for "bad conduct" rather than dishonorably—which would have prevented future gun purchases. At the trailer park where he landed, CNN reported, a neighbor witnessed him punching a dog, which resulted in animal cruelty charges, later dismissed.

His Facebook page included stories and other posts about guns and gun violence. He was fascinated with mass shootings. One friend, who "unfriended" him on Facebook, told CNN that Kelley had often launched public personal attacks against people he knew. Kelley had posted a rifle photo with the caption "She's a bad bitch."

In 2017, Kelley used a semiautomatic rifle to kill twenty-five people and an unborn child at First Baptist Church in Sutherland Springs, Texas.

Incredibly, when the shooting occurred, Kelley was employed as a security guard at Summit Vacation and RV Resort in New Braunfels, Texas—about an hour away from San Antonio. Kelley's neighbor told news reporters there had been sounds of gunfire coming from his property every morning of the week before the church shooting.

It's hard to know for sure where we failed Kelley's victims, but fail we did. Law enforcement routinely derails brittle individuals on the pathway to violence, thanks to their hard work and the vigilance of concerned citizens. But many times, the call is not made. Today, no one has a right to bystander apathy.

OUR ACTION CAN STOP THE KILLINGS

We cannot know what would have absolutely prevented the tragedy in Texas. There are no guarantees. It is important to say that those who saw signs are not responsible for his actions—Kelley is. We each do what we think is right at the time.

But Devin Kelley is not unique.

We know those closest to a person of concern are the most likely to see behavioral changes. One acquaintance told authorities that the Sandy Hook gunman, who methodically planned the attack for at least eighteen months, was fascinated by past shootings. Two years before the shooting, he took a picture of himself with a gun to his head.

After the shooting, investigators discovered a four-by-seven-foot spreadsheet in his room that listed hundreds of mass murders in fine 9-point font, listing the shooters, the weapons used, and the number of people killed. A Connecticut State Police colonel speculated to a group of law enforcement officers three months after the shooting that the spreadsheet would have taken years to prepare.[20]

What is in place in your community to ensure that we teach everyone not to hesitate but to err on the side of over-reporting? Are you training teachers but not students or parents? Is this all left to supervisors, already short-staffed, at your office?

Are there methods in your community to teach people that those who don't want to call the police should contact somebody—a clergy member, a human resources department, a school counselor, or the place where the person works? Does everyone know an anonymous call can save lives?

Who will make the difference? It is the kids linked to each other by gaming systems, the teachers who hear things, the coworkers who see things, the neighbors who think something is not right, and the parents who stay engaged with their kids, their spouses, and their communities. They can prevent future active shootings and mass killings.

Changes in laws and policies are helpful, but better planning, preparation, and training in what to look for is how each of us will come to understand how we can save lives. The public should have been as shocked as Attorney General Holder was in 2014 when he realized we were losing more Americans to active shooters than to terrorists. Tragically, it was not.

To prevent these terrorist acts, Americans need to be as informed and motivated as they were after the morning of September 11.

So let's get started.

Chapter Two

Active Shooters on the Rise

Weeks after the Sandy Hook shooting, our Biden team was meeting in a conference room at the Department of Education in downtown Washington, DC. We could see the US Holocaust Memorial Museum just west of where, four years earlier, I responded when an active shooter killed a guard there.

I could see the expanse of the Potomac River and within days wished I were boating there instead of heading into the hurricane I had entered. Compelled to participate, Education's representative, David Esquith, balked at the whole effort. He didn't want any policies, funding, or prevention efforts to mention "violence," "shootings," "guns," or any other words he considered too violent. His coworkers agreed.

I cringed and spoke. Shootings are violent, David.

Any focus on the rare school shooting would take money from programs such as anti-bullying campaigns, Esquith countered. Besides, he said, the media hype created a false narrative that shootings were on the rise. Fake news.

Point taken. No one in government was actually tracking numbers. The Department of Homeland Security (DHS) defined these shootings, but they weren't counting them. All I could say is that I *thought* Esquith was wrong.

Shouldn't the FBI and Department of Justice (DOJ) have that kind of data?

The New York Police Department and some academics had begun counting in the 1990s. A decade or two later, the media began tallies, most notably *Mother Jones*, the *Washington Post*, and *USA Today*. Lists are good, but they were just that—lists, not an analytical product. Some went back decades and crossed international waters, muddying the view of how to handle today's problems. And worse, everybody's lists were based on something inherently unreliable that made my lawyer instincts shudder—newspapers, the internet, and public sources.

As early White House team meetings dissolved into the same arguments about media mania, the *New York Daily News* ran a full-page photo of the Capitol with oversized block letters: "BLOOD ON YOUR HANDS: As Burials Begin It's Time for DC to Act."

I wasn't sleeping well as pressure mounted for solutions. I took to sleeping with my phone on the bed, and every alert seemed to be news of another shooting. Just a day after the Sandy Hook shooting, a thirty-eight-year-old man with a handgun began shooting in a hospital in Birmingham, Alabama. No one was killed, but three people, including a police officer, were injured before police killed the shooter. Six days later, a forty-four-year-old with two handguns began shooting at citizens in Frankstown Township, Pennsylvania. Three people were killed, and three police officers wounded, before police killed the shooter.

Less than a dozen school days after Sandy Hook, my BlackBerry rattled again to tell me a sixteen-year-old with a shotgun injured two students in a high school science class in Taft, California. An administrator persuaded the shooter to put down the gun.

I asked my counterparts in the FBI's Criminal Investigative Division if they were tracking shootings. Nope. I spoke to our experts collecting uniform crime statistics in our West Virginia criminal justice information facility. Yes, they had data, but it was incomplete—not all police departments reported their information. They weren't counting active shooters.

I wanted to find the data that narrowed the field of shootings to the essences of active shooter situations: an individual actively engaged in killing or attempting to kill in a populated area. We knew that in 2011, for example, firearms were used to murder 8,583 people in the United States. We knew two out of three handgun-related deaths involved suicide. Many violent situations were domestic matters, Hatfield-McCoy–type fights, or part of drug- or gang-related violence. Others were murder-suicide pacts or mercy killings by loved ones.

What we needed didn't exist. We needed to create the data. The FBI could get access to investigative reports from even the smallest, most remote police jurisdictions just by asking. Local police are the best, I had learned while working in the field. We set about the task, not sure of the outcome.

The core of my borrowed team included California Highway Patrol Lieutenant Commander Dave Knoff; Hennepin County, Minnesota, Detective Dennis Jahnke; and FBI team members: Public Affairs Specialist Andrew Ames; Supervisory Intelligence Analyst Deb Cryan; Special Advisor Kathryn M. Crotts; Honors Intern Jessica Seay; and Supervisory Special Agent Michael McElhenny, an agent borrowed from FBI Director Robert Mueller's security detail. A year later we were joined by Supervisory Special Agent

James Green; Round Rock, Texas, Police Department Detective Jerry Castleberry; and Ashley Mancik, now an assistant professor at the University of South Carolina.

To ensure academic rigor, we connected with former Hays County, Texas, Sheriff Don Montague, who had teamed with Terry Nichols, David Burns, John R. Curnutt, and Steve Griffith to create the Advance Law Enforcement Rapid Response Training Center (ALERRT Center) after the Columbine shooting.

The ALERRT Center was using Texas and federal funds to train law enforcement in partnership with Texas State University–San Marcos. Several on his team were set to release research based on open-source information.[1] I liked their methodology, and they helped us settle on a similar methodology that excluded violence resulting from gangs, drugs, residential and domestic disputes, self-defense, hostage situations, and crossfire from other, ongoing criminal acts.[2] Since I wrote the FBI study and Texas State's J. Pete Blair intended for us to author the academic research, we agreed to put both of our names on the report.[3]

For nearly a year, our small, borrowed team culled through hundreds of police records and tracked down responding officers to develop the first analysis ever based on police investigative files. My gratitude goes to the hundreds of FBI agents who traveled to talk to federal, state, local, and tribal law enforcement officers—a group that, as a whole, recognized the importance of this effort and willingly tracked down old files in warehouses and cabinets, just because we asked.

DEFINITIONS

Before the research, we worked the wordplay to ensure we were all using the same terms and definitions. Very quickly, I learned that writing or talking about active shooters would mean figuring out the difference between *active shooter*, *mass killing*, *mass shootings*, and other violence-related terms such as *serial killers* and *mass casualties*. This confusion was making it challenging to have conversations and prompted arguments about improperly used statistics, adding to the difficulty of interpreting numbers for research and training.

So, let's begin with some essential definitions. Many terms are used interchangeably but have different and sometimes overlapping meanings.

An **active shooter** is an individual or individuals actively engaged in killing or attempting to kill people in a populated area. This definition is used by the FBI, DHS, FEMA, and the rest of the federal government and, most notably, only involves firearms incidents. An earlier definition used by DHS included the words *confined and crowded*, but *confined* was excluded by the FBI in its annual research on active shooters because of misunderstanding about whether to include incidents occurring outside of a building. Yes, count them. A shooter running through a parking lot or running through a mall is still actively trying to kill people.[4]

In much the same way, whether or not someone is killed or injured by an active shooter is not a determining factor in whether to count the incident. The shooter still causes the terror, even if they are a bad shot. This explains the terrorism charge against the Oxford shooter. Inclusion is based on whether a person is in public with a firearm trying to kill people and, because it is on-going, the public or law enforcement has a possible opportunity to intercede.

A **mass killing** is "three or more killings in a single incident" as defined by the Investigative Assistance for Violent Crimes Act of 2012, which was signed into law by US President Barack Obama a few weeks after the Sandy Hook killings.[5] This statute also gives the FBI and DHS authority to assist in mass killing investigations at the request of local authorities where the incident occurs in "places of public use" or where attempted or actual mass killings occurred.

Unfortunately, the statute fails to specify whether a deceased shooter should be included in the three. Law enforcement traditionally never includes the perpetrator in the death toll. But the statute calls for three killed, arguably allowing the shooter to be one of the three—perhaps something future legislators can modify. Though law enforcement never includes the killer, some researchers do, leading to further inconsistencies and confusion.

In 2020, DOJ did an exhaustive review of research and interviews with field experts to bridge the divide between researchers and practitioners in hopes of developing a singular definition for **mass shootings**.[6] Authors Basia E. Lopez, Danielle M. Crimmins, and Paul A. Haskins concluded that inconsistent definitions and the lack of a comprehensive database were holding back meaningful research on how to end this type of violence. They found that "a common definition of mass shooting should be broad but not tied to any fixed minimum number of victims" and identified three elements of a **mass shooting**: (1) the discharge of a firearm in (2) "a single, continuous event, within an undefined timeframe," and (3) where there is "an evident premeditated intent to shoot to kill, regardless of the number of actual fatalities or injuries."[7]

So, a **mass shooting** is when an individual or individuals discharge a firearm, with premeditation, killing or attempting to kill multiple people in a single continuous event within an undefined timeframe. An active shooter incident, therefore, is always a mass shooting incident, but not the other way around (e.g., mass shooter incidents that were not active shooter incidents include mass shootings discovered after they are completed, such as the July 2015 killing of nine in a church in Charleston, South Carolina, and the August 2016 killing of five family members in their home in Citronelle, Alabama). Most shootings and mass shootings occur in homes.

Researchers may choose to disaggregate on particular locations, offender characteristics, motivations, the number killed or injured, or the types of weapons used. The family members in Alabama were killed in the privacy of their home, and the church members' deaths were discovered well after the shooter had fled. This is why you may see differences in research.

It is worth correcting a common misconception here—that the FBI uses four or more victims to define the term *mass shooting*. The FBI has not used that number in mass shooting or active shooter research, though many researchers and writers have mistakenly indicated they do, further muddying the definition. The FBI's work on serial killers, mentioned below, notes the number killed is not a part of a definition but rather a criterion some researchers use (specifically noting the common cutoff of four or more). Researchers have taken heed and are currently focused on trying to create more homogeneous terms between the different federal statutes, research efforts, and generic, common, and agreed-upon definitions.

FBI behavioral experts noted that a 1998 federal statute defining a **serial killing** as three or more killed was not so much a definition as it was a way to indicate when federal investigators could provide assistance. In its research on **serial murder**, the FBI chose to define the event as the unlawful killing of two or more victims by the same offender(s) in separate events.[8]

Mass murder has no technical or statutory definition, and it and *mass shootings* are often used interchangeably by the media, writers, and researchers to describe the killing of multiple individuals, whether it involved firearms or violence caused by knives, blunt instruments, vehicles, explosive devices, or other destructive means.

Mass casualty is also not defined, but it is the most expansive, counting the total killed or injured by any means during any human-made or natural disaster.

In 2013 the research arm for the US Congress, Congressional Research Service (CRS), made up its "own definition" to identify what it called **public mass shootings**: "incidents occurring in relatively public places, involving four or more deaths—not including the shooter(s)—and gunmen who select victims somewhat indiscriminately."[9] I don't know of any other researchers using this definition, but I am sure it helped inform Congress members.

Some researchers choose to use the term **active attack** when they want to track active shooter situations but also include incidents where weapons in addition to firearms are used, such as knives and vehicles.

RESEARCH RESULTS

Eighteen months after the Sandy Hook shooting, I was in a DOJ conference room, briefing Attorney General Holder before the public release of "A Study of Active Shooter Incidents in the United States Between 2000 and 2013."[10] It was the first of what resulted in annual releases.[11]

Today, demand for the FBI research is so universally accepted as a base resource for training and further academic research that the US Government Publishing Office added the study to its paper-available library and Amazon republished it on its own in a Kindle edition in 2017.[12]

But at the time, I cared only about moving past the argument of whether the problem was getting worse.

It was.

Shootings, as well as casualties, were on the rise. The FBI identified 160 active shooter incidents that occurred between 2000 and 2013.[13] Even with Sandy Hook on our minds, the raw numbers were startling. We were trending a shooting first every other month, then about every month, and we did not ever expect we would eventually have one a week.[14]

We were hoping that, although shootings were on the rise, casualties might not keep pace, but they did. The 1,043 casualties identified in the study included 486 dead and 557 wounded, keeping a steady pace with a median number killed in each incident at two and the median number wounded at two.

Close proximity to one another inside a building has always resulted in some of the incidents with the highest casualty counts, and not just in educational environments. Consider the movie theater in Aurora, Colorado, in 2012; the crowded dance floor during the Pulse nightclub shooting in Orlando in 2016; and the jam-packed Live Nation music festival in Las Vegas in 2017. Of the shootings, sixty-four incidents, or 40 percent, met the federal definition of mass killing, with three or more victims killed.[15] We learned other details previously unknown.

LOCATIONS

Shootings occurred in forty of the fifty states and the District of Columbia, painting this as a truly American problem. Nearly half of all active shooters identified in the study, 45.6 percent, struck at a place of business. Then, in declining order, 24.4 percent in educational settings, 10 percent in government buildings, 9.4 percent in open spaces, 4.4 percent in residential settings, 3.8 percent in houses of worship, and 2.5 percent in health care facilities.

We were developing better answers for parents who were asking if they could send a child to school or a movie or take them to church. Although spectacularly, and disproportionally, covered by the media, shootings in hospitals, churches, and mosques proved extremely rare.

The press had been asking, *Is anywhere safe anymore?* And I was wondering if I should say aloud that perhaps the risk to schoolchildren is serious but the risk to their parents, grandparents, aunts, and uncles at work is larger.

In about 15 percent of the active shooter incidents, the shooter was moving, traveling to different sites and running or driving to different buildings. A good reminder to yourself and others is that, if you hear of danger, don't let your curiosity push you closer to the shooting locations. You and your companions may walk right into a shooting, as many did in 1984 when twenty-two were killed and nineteen injured during a shooting at a McDonald's in San Ysidro, California. I've seen other incidents where this happened, often with fatal results.

When we matched these locations with the shooters, we also discovered correlations previously unseen. For example,

- An employee is almost exclusively the shooter in places like offices, packing facilities, manufacturing plants, and other businesses not frequented by the public, with many of these incidents occurring on the day a person is fired from a job. In businesses closed to pedestrian traffic, twenty-two of twenty-three shooters were employees or former employees; four had been fired earlier the same day.
- Middle school and high school students are almost exclusively the active shooters in their own schools—five of six middle school shooters, twelve of fourteen high school shooters.

Casting doubt on a longstanding belief that all the shootings are random, more recent FBI research on the shooters found that at least one victim was specifically targeted in 64 percent of the incidents.[16] Where business shootings occurred, risk to management was high. Among the victims, ten owners, supervisors, and managers were killed and another five wounded. In educational settings, more shootings occurred in middle schools, high schools, and colleges and universities, with only a few incidents of shootings at elementary schools.[17] Thankfully, school shootings have tapered off slightly since the initial study, now making up about 20 percent of the incidents.[18]

CITIZEN HEROES

In the sixty-four incidents where the duration of the incident could be determined, nearly 70 percent ended in five minutes or less—and fully half of those in two minutes or less.

The most unexpected but hopeful result in the research: in 21 of the 160 incidents, or 13 percent of the time, an unarmed citizen selflessly made the deeply personal choice to take on an active shooter to successfully and safely disrupt the shooting.

These are unarmed civilians. I'll discuss armed civilians in a later chapter. Citizens are the true first responders, making it all the more important that they be properly educated and trained.

VALIDATION AND SUBSEQUENT RESEARCH

Since the FBI started publishing data in 2014, multiple researchers and news media organizations have compared their own numbers to the FBI's, effectively putting an end to the question of whether these types of incidents were on the rise before and after the Sandy Hook massacre. Public and private research tallies may vary—depending on the types of research methods used—but nearly all conclude active shooter incidents continued to rise dramatically for two decades.

In 2019, the US Secret Service released the National Threat Assessment Center's report on attacks in public places. The Service looked at twenty-eight incidents in 2018 in which three or more people were killed or injured and found twenty had taken place in places of business. The following year, fifteen of the thirty-four incidents occurred in businesses.[19]

A handful of media organizations devoted extensive investigative time and resources to validate each other's work. For example, in 2017, the BBC news service reviewed research by the FBI and *Mother Jones* to validate the increase in active shooting incidents.

The BBC bucketed the numbers this way over the past three decades:

- In the 1980s, the United States averaged eight incidents annually, the worst resulting in 22 killed at a McDonald's restaurant in San Ysidro, California.
- In the 1990s, an average of 23 incidents occurred annually, with 159 dead—this despite an assault weapons ban passed in 1994.
- In the 2000s, an average of 20 incidents occurred annually, taking 171 lives, including 32 at Virginia Tech.

In another look at numbers, the CRS identified 281 deaths in a twenty-nine-year timespan, spanning 1983 through 2012.[20] FBI researchers found nearly four times as many deaths annually, because the FBI and CRS used different methodologies. The CRS used its own definition of *public mass shooting* and only counted incidents where four or more people were killed. The FBI looked at any incident meeting the active shooter definition, whether or not a person was killed or injured.

The numbers aren't as important as the consistent *increase* in the numbers. Both the FBI and the CRS found a steady increase in incidents.

A small number of researchers supported by the firearms industry—not to be confused with staunch supporters of the Second Amendment—disagree.

Relying on gun violence data when discussing only active shooter incidents can be a red herring, too. Many organizations, such as the Brady Campaign to Prevent Gun Violence, have collected helpful and expansive data for years on all types of gun violence.[21] In fact, mass shootings account for only about two-tenths of 1 percent of all homicides, making broad batches of data of limited value.[22]

Everytown for Gun Safety collects broader data, specifically on school violence. This is valuable but, if misapplied to an argument, can cause confusion. For example, in 2014, CNN had to drastically publicly alter a report on school gun violence after mistakenly using the Everytown for Gun Safety data when referring to active shooter situations.[23]

To stop the killings by active shooters, we need to keep our magnifying glasses focused on this specific type of mass shooting.

POLICY IMPLICATIONS FOR
TRAINING AND MITIGATION STRATEGIES

The FBI baseline research provided data immediately to assist leaders, emergency planners, finance officers, human resource personnel, and others developing protocols and training for active shooter incidents.

In schools, nearly a third of shootings occurred on a Monday, a pattern future researchers could look to when considering stressors. Perhaps violence is bubbling up from family difficulties, stress over schoolwork, or other matters that could be mitigated.

At colleges and universities, nearly half the shootings occurred on a Friday. The FBI found no patterns in the other days of the week or in the time of the year.

School shootings have the most varied locations for attacks, including before and after school, in the cafeteria, from cars, and in hallways. The Columbine High School shooters' first victims were outside at the back of the school.

Despite this, many schools and districts persist in training just to lock-down, which is only the *hide* portion of the federal direction. A later chapter explores my concern that school and district administrators may be hesitant to provide meaningful training in all aspects of Run. Hide. Fight.®, putting their personnel and students at added risk.

A surge in law enforcement training has catapulted nearly every officer into a position where they should be able to respond to an active shooter incident. This is particularly important, as FBI research found at least one officer was killed or wounded 46.7 percent of the time when law enforcement had to engage a shooter.

Even now, this FBI research is practically unknown to most citizens and the policy makers who decide what equipment police should carry—this despite the increasing concern people have about their own safety.

In both Gallup polls and Pew Research Center surveys, Americans routinely respond that they believe the current year was more violent compared to the year before.[24] People say violent crime has steadily increased since 2008.[25]

But has it really?

According to both FBI data and DOJ surveys conducted by the Bureau of Justice Statistics (BJS)—police data collected from the nation's 18,000 law enforcement departments—violent crime declined 49 percent between 1993 and 2017. In 2020, the FBI reported that in 2019 alone there was a 4 percent decline in crime.[26]

So, why all the hysteria over these types of shootings?

Probably because feeling safe and being safe are two different things. Despite the fact that violent crime has declined dramatically, active shooter incidents—these unique types of mass shooting incidents that are so shocking and unexpected—are our Achilles' heel. But we have a growing body of knowledge to change that.

CONTAGION EFFECT AND THE MEDIA'S RESPONSIBILITY

When I was working on this chapter, I was watching news about a horrific shooting rampage in northern California. There, a man had killed his wife and some neighbors, six in total, and then shot up a school while trying to get inside before alert neighbors shot at him and chased him in a car and, ultimately, police arrested him. Shootings are so commonplace now that the California shooting hardly merited a lead story in any news cycle.

In some ways I was kind of happy when that happened. I know that admission may seem startling. But a frightening addendum to this whole problem is the growing body of evidence that *too much* news coverage not only conflates a sense of how many shootings happen but, in fact, actually has a causal impact on the frequency of shootings—what's known as a *contagion effect*.

The responsibility lies not only with the new media but with those who talk to the news media so freely. Research has shown the contagion or copycat effect is real. One shooting prompts another shooter to commit violence.

Media research began in earnest after the disquieting killing of children at Sandy Hook. It was 24-hour, wall-to-wall digital and print coverage of outrage everywhere. Particularly after Sandy Hook, the language the media used to report shootings changed. The media began tallying incidents with extensive stories, presenting context and accompanying interviews with experts who provided explanations.

At the same time, headlines and televised news stories began reporting shootings in aggregate form—how many shootings occurred each month or year and with matching colorful charts tallying the number dead.

Newscasters sat in front of full-screen images using descriptors like the *worst*, or *most*, or *highest*. They compared the shootings to numbers in the last month or year and to other shooters. They reported on who left manifestos and evidence of desktop searches—such as the Columbine High School shooters, and who sent notes or text messages talking about wanting to be remembered as the best.

Researchers had already established that more suicides occurred when the news covered suicide deaths. This coverage prompted academia, and media organizations themselves, to consider whether the news coverage itself was actually part of the problem.

Michael Jetter, from the University of Western Australia, and Jay K. Walker, from Old Dominion University, discussed the effects of media coverage on mass shootings after analyzing three years of coverage on ABC's *World News Tonight* that came on the heels of the Sandy Hook shooting.[27]

Researchers concluded that, in the four to ten days after a shooting, approximately three additional shootings occurred.

"Our findings consistently suggest that media coverage systematically *causes* future mass shootings. . . . Using our benchmark estimation, a simple back-of-the-envelope calculation suggests that 58 percent of all mass shootings between January 1, 2013, and June 23, 2016, are explainable by news coverage," they wrote. "Our findings suggest that decreasing the amount of television coverage shooters receive could limit further tragedies" (emphasis in original).[28]

In 2015, similar findings were reported by a team from Arizona State and Northeastern Illinois universities: Sherry Towers, Andres Gomez-Lievano, Maryam Khan, Anuj Mubayi, and Carlos Castillo-Chavez.[29] Their research found "an effect lasting approximately 13 days" after coverage of similar firearms-related mass shootings.

Taking that to heart, the media is doing something about it. The *Columbia Journalism Review* (*CJR*), the heart and home of journalism contemplation, initiated its own effort to manage news coverage.[30] *CJR* has set up teams to evaluate how to provide balanced reporting but, importantly, also find ways to *cover* the news without *being* the news.

"Research increasingly tells us that our coverage of mass shootings has implications for public health," journalists Katherine Reed and Miles Kohrman noted in announcing the project. "Shooters crave attention and infamy; several modern killers have idolized and sought out information about those who came before them. One murderer mailed videos and documents to a national news station, knowing that the materials would be publicized. Another kept a spreadsheet in which he compared body counts from previous high-profile shootings."

Coverage that puts killers in the spotlight makes an implicit promise to those on the edge of committing mass violence. Adam Lankford, a criminologist at the University of Alabama who has studied the contagion effect of mass shootings, puts it like this: "Many of these at-risk individuals recognize that murdering large numbers of men, women, or children will guarantee them fame. They believe their names and faces will adorn newspapers, television, magazines, and the Internet—and unfortunately, they are right."[31]

Current trends add support to these studies. In the weeks after a Dayton, Ohio, shooting in 2019, United States authorities arrested at least twenty-eight people accused of threatening acts of mass violence.[32]

Reporter Kasey Cordell too explored this very concern in her insightful April 2019 piece in *5280 Magazine*. Founded in Denver in 1983, the magazine is well suited to exploring this question, with its office just 14 miles from Littleton, Colorado, the home of Columbine High School.

"Beyond the reporting challenges involved in understanding a perpetrator's motives, some newsrooms might be genuinely unaware of the media contagion effect," she wrote. "And those that are aware face a hypercompetitive environment in which they're vying for readers or viewers or clicks and worry that if they don't share the news, a competitor will, and they'll lose audience share. That premise assumes Americans want wall-to-wall coverage of the perpetrator."[33]

Cordell offered rules of thumb for reporters that include limiting the use of the shooter information and photographs, as well as references to anniversary dates; providing mental health support and training to reporters covering incidents; and refraining from overly simplifying a shooter's motivation.

CJR's guidelines for media coverage will be a welcome addition to prevention efforts.

Chapter Three

Who and Why

My elder daughter was nearing the end of her junior year in high school when we heard the news about the Virginia Tech massacre. Two of her former schoolmates were among the thirty-two dead, just four hours from our front door. Then . . . unfathomable . . . we learned the shooter had lived just a few blocks away from our house and graduated from her high school. It was April 16, 2007.

As quickly as law enforcement was able to identify who did the shooting, everyone wanted to know why.

National news reporters scoured the neighborhood, looking for anything they hadn't yet reported. Satellite trucks surrounded the school, snarling traffic and blocking entrances. Students and faculty, already filled with the anxieties of state testing and college entrance exams, struggled through the last few weeks wearing a pall of *why*?

Hadn't the shooter been one of those regular neighborhood kids who walked across the street from his townhouse to McDonald's for a Coke or just to hang in the parking lot? What was different about this college senior? Had anyone suspected anything in all those years? Had anyone noticed things while he was here in high school?

My daughter wrote about the morose atmosphere inside her school for her dad's newspaper in Chicago, the *Daily Herald*. She documented the candlelight vigils for the shortened lives of a one-time athlete and aspiring theater star.

As was happening in Blacksburg, Virginia, my community began the long process of coping. Scholarship funds were set up to remember. The victims' names and the Tech colors were cathartically painted on the huge rocks in front of school.

I was an FBI agent but first a parent. I struggled to explain why to my kids, a high school student and a sixth grader. Why would somebody do this to fellow classmates?

I heard explanations—or maybe the word is *guesses*—as to why. They are not unfamiliar.

Violent tendencies missed, they said after Virginia Tech. Bullying, they warned, after the Sparks Middle School shooting in Sparks, Nevada. Bad parenting, copycats, and the media, many said after the Sandy Hook shooting. Too many guns, they decried after the Parkland shooting in Florida. And, by the time El Paso and Dayton were forever linked in the summer of 2019, violent video games and kids with mental health problems were the reasons-of-the-day. It was a bit like a game of Whac-A-Mole, where each shooting involved different fixes on which to focus.

Every bar, backyard barbecue, and lunchroom discussion on the topic of *why* seems to cluster on these theories. Research, however, has chipped away at these guesses, and now we have better facts about shooters, whom they target, and why they may target certain victims.

Shooter motivations, as I noted, can be elusive. Why does one person who was fired from a job just go home and commiserate with friends while another goes home and comes back with a gun?

Some may find it easier to use these shorthand reasons to comfort those in mourning or to provide sound bites to the news. But the most skilled behavioral experts rarely speak to the media for just this reason: dispelling stereotyping, profiling, and even myths can't be done easily on a 20-second news interview.

Several years ago an FBI behavioral team did their own myth-busting about serial murders by exploring and challenging longstanding and persistent but erroneous assumptions.[1] They noted that Hollywood and media talking heads molded these myths through sensational and often inaccurate depictions of Ted Bundy, Jack the Ripper, the Green River Killer, and others.

Law enforcement, too, fell victim to anecdotal inaccuracies and myths while looking for sensational characters that *fit the mold*. A few of the common and persistent myths documented:

- Serial killers are all dysfunctional loners. False.
  Truth: The majority of serial killers are not reclusive social misfits who live alone. They are not monsters and may not appear strange. Many serial killers hide in plain sight within their communities. Serial murderers often have families and homes, are gainfully employed, and appear to be normal members of the community. Because many serial murderers blend in so effortlessly, law enforcement and the public oftentimes overlook them.

- Serial killers are all White males. False.
  Truth: Contrary to popular belief, serial killers span all racial groups. There are White, Black, Hispanic, and Asian serial killers. The racial diversification of serial killers generally mirrors that of the overall US population.
- Serial killers are insane, are evil geniuses, have debilitating mental conditions, and yet are extremely clever and intelligent. False.
  Truth: Serial killers suffer from a variety of personality disorders, including psychopathy, antisocial personality, and others. Most, however, are not adjudicated as insane under the law. The media has created a number of fictional serial killer *geniuses* who outsmart law enforcement at every turn. Like other populations, however, serial killers range in intelligence from borderline to above-average levels.

Similar mistaken assumptions have plagued our effort to look for mass shooters, including active shooters.

Consider these two often-repeated erroneous "facts" about active shooters.

- All active shooters are loners. False.
  Truth: The most comprehensive research done to date says just the opposite. The FBI scoured through police investigative files on sixty-three active shooters where information about the shooters included medical documents, business and school files, and interviews with shooters, friends, and family. Every shooter either lived with someone or had significant in-person or online social interactions.[2] In fact, 68 percent lived with someone else. These aren't kids living in their parents' basement. Research established that 64 percent of those shooters over the age of 18 lived with someone else.
- Active shooters are just unemployed social outcasts. False.
  Truth: Of those eighteen and older, 44 percent were employed, and another 13 percent were students, disabled, or retired. Most active shooters, 57 percent, were single at the time of the offense, but it is worth recognizing that people without an intimate partner may more easily fly under the radar. Bystanders might simply overlook their behaviors. Marital status was otherwise found to be quite insignificant, with 13 percent married, 13 percent divorced, 11 percent partnered but not married, and 6 percent separated.

FINDING SHOOTERS BEFORE THEY STRIKE

Threat assessment teams (TATs), detailed in a future chapter, gather information about a person who may be planning violence, and then the team devises methods to prevent the violence. Often while people are busy buttonholing people into categories—gamers, loners, teens, veterans—the threat assessment process is stymied. Looking for the next potential shooter requires dismissal of these preconceived notions, including guesses based on ignorance or political or social biases.

Since the Virginia Tech shooting, critical evidence-based research assures me that I could give my daughter a better answer today than I'd been able to back in 2007.

One thing we know for sure is that we are missing the boat if we categorize large swaths of individuals because of who they are and what they do. Blaming White teenage boys with mental health problems who are forever playing video games in their parents' basements is just . . . wrong.

To aid in understanding what kind of person commits these crimes, it helps to discard erroneous stereotypes and fallacies. I'll explore some of these categories, focusing on the most-often-repeated characteristics mentioned after a shooting occurs.

Video Gaming

A link between violent video games and increases in aggression and violence has been documented, but multiple research efforts have found that to look for potential killers in the gaming world is often a perilous and fruitless effort. This requires a more complicated and nuanced discussion.

For example, can anyone use gaming as a predictive factor on a TAT when more than 90 percent of US children play video games of some kind? If taking into account only adolescents, that figure rises to 97 percent of people between the ages of twelve and seventeen, according to the American Psychological Association.[3] And 2018 research identified women as 45 percent of all gamers in the United States.[4]

Further, the majority of targeted violence worldwide occurs in the United States, although video game consumption is dwarfed here by international play. In 2020, North America had an estimated 200 million people playing video games, while the Asia Pacific region had 1.5 billion video gamers.[5]

Viewed alone, playing video games is a valueless predictor of any future violent action. When Monday morning quarterbacks mention video games, they are likely just struggling to assign blame instead of looking for real causes. But as you will see with each category, this stabbing at the air prevents us from developing effective methods to find the next shooter.

Criminal History and Violent Behavior

The FBI found that many active shooters had struggled to control their tempers when agitated, including those who'd had prior brushes with the law or previously committed violent acts. More than 60 percent of those found in the FBI's research had a history of acting in an abusive, harassing, or oppressive way (e.g., bullying). A full 35 percent had adult criminal convictions prior to the event, with 16 percent engaging in intimate partner violence and 11 percent engaging in stalking-related conduct.[6]

That may sound like we should look for criminals. But look at the numbers again. This research shows a majority of active shooters have no criminal history at all. TATs can't dismiss anyone based on lack of a pronounced violent criminal history.

Age, Gender, and Ethnicity

Demographic information can prove useful if not dispositive, but it is of limited value when it comes to age. In the past twenty years, active shooters in the United States have ranged from a twelve-year-old who killed and wounded people at his middle school to a White supremacist who killed one person and then died at age 89 after being shot in the head by one of the three guarding the entrance at the Holocaust Memorial Museum in Washington, DC.

The varied ages have held consistent, said FBI Special Agent Steven B. Bennett, who also took a turn at overseeing the agency's research and active shooter program. Of the 308 shooters whose ages could be identified from the 2000 to 2019 data, the average age was 35 years old, and the median age was 32.

Gender data tell us that only a few females have participated in active shooter incidents. The FBI's research I coauthored on active shooters identified only two females among 161 shooters during a fourteen-year period. Both were involved in shootings on college campuses.[7]

Though most active shooters are male, women are just as capable of committing targeted violence. To focus only on men ignores half the population, behavioral experts warn. Another benefit to looking beyond gender can be seen in situations where two or more conspire to commit violence. Friends and married teams conspiring present a good opportunity to catch leaked or mistakenly leaked details. Two or more working together are always more likely to conduct observable behaviors of concern as they plan and prepare.

Active shooters are often immediately assumed to be White, but that too is supposition without foundation. In line with official US Census data that tallies about 61 percent of the population as "White," including "White Hispanics," the FBI identified 63 percent of the shooters as White.[8]

Mental Health

The relationship between mental health and violence is one of the most challenging to understand and explain.

Prominent politicians and elected officials, even an uninformed former president, were quick to blame mental health and violent video games in public statements issued following four shootings in a week during the summer of 2019.

The nightmare started with three killed and fifteen injured by a nineteen-year-old at a Gilroy, California, food festival, followed by two killed by a former employee at a Walmart in Mississippi, then twenty more killed and twenty-six injured by a twenty-one-year-old at a Walmart in El Paso, Texas, and, finally, less than 24 hours later, nine killed and twenty-seven injured by a twenty-three-year-old shooting outside a popular bar in an often safe area in Dayton, Ohio.

Mentally deranged or mentally ill, the talking heads and politicians said all week.

Blaming mental instability for every shooting is an easy trap to fall into. I've had plenty of conversations that start with, "Hey how can they not be mentally deranged when they are doing that?" Next time you hear that, remember these details.

Mental health can be a potential factor, yes, but consistent research fails to correlate mental health issues and the likelihood of mass violence with any certitude. Several analyses of mental health matters and violence have been conducted with the US Secret Service looking at this particular kind of public violence.

The US Secret Service evaluated twenty-seven incidents that occurred in 2018 where violence happened in public spaces and three or more people were killed or harmed through the use of vehicles or weapons.[9] The Secret Service concluded, "most [shooters] had histories of criminal charges, mental health symptoms and/or illicit substance use or abuse." They estimated two-thirds of the attackers had experienced symptoms related to mental health issues prior to their attacks, identifying ten as suffering from depression, ten from psychotic symptoms (paranoia, delusion, and hallucinations), and eight having suicidal thoughts. Note that suicide potential was included, a factor some may not equate with potential violence.

After drawing this conclusion, researchers qualified their statements significantly, acknowledging that individuals who are *not* mentally ill commit the most violence. And they also acknowledged that their information regarding the mental health status of the shooters in the twenty-seven incidents examined was coming secondhand, from open sources.

Open-source information is inherently less reliable because it's gleaned from publicly available documents such as newspapers, aggregate websites, and television interviews. At times, this can include aftermath news stories where neighbors describe what they see or hear, often opining that the shooter was mentally ill, sick, or not right in the head.

I don't point this out to slight the Secret Service. They noted themselves the limitations of this resource. Nearly all research in this area—including academic research—has been conducted using publicly available documents. After a tragedy, it is the interviews with friends, coworkers, classmates, and neighbors that are preserved through media to make up a majority of the available information about a shooter's past.

But neighbors who only wave to each other from the driveway are not necessarily good barometers of a person's temperament and mental state. They may live nearby but likely don't know what their neighbor is thinking or capable of doing or when the person changes. Yet they are the ones most often interviewed because they fill the news story when tragedy happens.

Information also is lacking because many shooters commit suicide, taking their secrets to the grave. Few shooters make it to trial or leave writings that can be evaluated.

A summary of shooter mental health records has been included in a few thorough after-action reports or state-directed investigative reports. This occurred after shootings at Virginia Tech in 2007 and at the Los Angeles International Airport in 2013. But even when mental health professionals participate in these post-incident investigations, they often have limited information from which to draw while making their best estimate about a shooter's mental state.

Recognizing these limitations, Secret Service researchers concluded, "mental illness, alone, is not a risk factor for violence" and recommended that prevention models include mental wellness programs.

FBI behavioral experts, too, would have been limited in their investigation but for the FBI's ability to access reports painstakingly prepared and provided by cooperating police departments. With this direct access, the FBI, for the first time, could evaluate actual medical information included about the active shooters identified in the FBI's initial study.

Behavioral experts were able to identify sufficient information to evaluate sixty-three shooters and found 25 percent had an atypical behavior or were diagnosed with a mental illness. Those diagnosed with atypical behaviors included one diagnosed with an autism spectrum disorder, one with a developmental disorder, and one with something undefined and only described as "other." Of the mental health diagnoses, most involved something you or someone around you may be under care for and managing. This included twelve with a mood disorder (e.g., a type of depression or bipolar disorder), four with an anxiety disorder, three with a psychotic disorder, and two with a personality disorder.

Compared to the population as a whole, these numbers are negligible. This prompted FBI behavioral experts to call mental health no more than a "slight" factor relative to predicting potential active shooters.

> In light of the very high lifetime prevalence of the symptoms of mental illness among the U.S. population, formally diagnosed mental illness is not a very specific predictor of violence of any type, let alone targeted violence. . . . Some studies indicate that nearly half of the U.S. population experiences symptoms of mental illness over their lifetime, with population estimates of the lifetime prevalence of diagnosable mental illness among U.S. adults at 46%, with 9% meeting the criteria for a personality disorder. . . . Therefore, absent specific evidence, careful consideration should be given to social and contextual factors that might interact with any mental health issue before concluding that an active shooting was "caused" by mental illness. In short, declarations that all active shooters must simply be mentally ill are misleading and unhelpful.[10]

Nearly echoing those findings, in 2019 the National Council for Behavioral Health called the correlation a "modest link" and warned that grouping those who perpetrate mass violence into a subset of people with mental health problems will unnecessarily impact "millions of harmless, nonviolent people recovering from treatable mental health conditions."[11]

Having a psychiatric diagnosis is neither necessary nor sufficient as a risk factor for committing an act of mass violence, the Council noted, adding that mental distress brought about by negative family or employment dynamics and personal relationship instability plays a more significant role.

The wide expanse of contributors came to this conclusion after meeting together to weigh volumes of information from researchers and real-life practitioners. Those contributing included academics and business professionals, advocacy groups, policy makers, the Substance Abuse and Mental Health Services Administration, and those in the federal departments of Justice and Health and Human Services. Though several years in the making, the Council report was hastily released just days after the fourth shooting in August 2019, in great part to quell the growing speculation that mental illness was the major contributing factor.

Domestic Partner Violence

Research in the last ten years has strengthened our understanding of violence committed against intimate partners and violence against family members when it involves a larger plan to murder people. FBI research on active shooters found that often family and friends, former lovers, bosses, or coworkers are among the first victims. In the FBI research, about 10 percent of the shootings targeted family members—many the first to die. Another 10 percent were estranged from current wives or girlfriends.[12]

Several forward-leaning organizations have put together more comprehensive research in the area of domestic gun violence. One, Everytown for Gun Safety, which looked at shootings during the two-year period spanning 2015 to 2017, found that more than half of the shooters had a record of domestic violence in their background. In some cases, the shooter killed an intimate partner or family member first before the shooting in public. Their data also revealed that, in more than half of mass shootings over the past decade, the shooter shot a current or former intimate partner or family member as part of the rampage.[13]

This is consistent with information from the Department of Justice, Bureau of Justice Statistics, that estimates 45 percent of all female homicide victims over a six-year period were killed by an intimate partner.[14]

Military Service

If we were tagging those dealing with mental health issues as an indicator of potential mass shooters—which we are not—we could also mistakenly assign risk to being in the US military. FBI researchers found 24 percent of the shooters studied had at least some military experience. But know that, at any given time, the United States has about 2.4 million active duty and reserve personnel worldwide and tens of millions who have retired or left service. With such a wide pool, this too cannot be looked to as a predictive factor.

Employees and Students

Age may be of limited value by itself but, when additional facts are included, it assists in predicting where an active shooter might attack. The intimate partner data above is supportive of that. Educational settings, too, are another area where the data can reveal potential shooters.

A quarter of all active shooters strike in an educational environment. Nearly every middle school and high school shooter was a student at the affected school. In rare cases, the students had graduated or left a year or two earlier. Elementary school shooters, however, are generally at the school looking for an intimate partner. That places middle school shooters most often in the 11- to 14-year-old age range and high school students most often in the 14- to 19-year-old age range.

Though society may be quick to blame teens and younger people for most active shootings, one in three is committed by a person between the ages of thirty and forty. So it makes sense that, in the past twenty years, nearly 45 percent of all active shooter incidents have occurred in places of business.[15]

Researchers were surprised to find another factor when it came to shootings in businesses. Where shootings occurred at businesses closed to pedestrian traffic—factories, dentist offices, manufacturing plants, and other closed environments—the shooter was almost always an employee. At shooting locations where the public frequented—shopping centers, groceries, bookstores, and big box stores—the shooter was almost never an employee of the targeted business.

For example, in twenty-three incidents that occurred in businesses generally closed to pedestrian traffic, twenty-two of the shooters were employed or previously employed at the business. The sole shooter not employed by a business had a relationship with a current employee.[16]

The most telling statistic I took away from my study was that, of those twenty-two shooters, fourteen were current employees, four employees had been fired the day of the shooting, three were former employees, and one was a suspended employee.

Follow-up research by the behavioral team showed that, overall, more than three out of four shooters were found to have a connection with the place they attacked. This is in direct opposition to the view that the location for this type of shooting is generally just random.[17]

WHERE STRESS HAPPENS

With all we've learned, it may still be tempting to take the easy route and blame mass shootings on mental illness, outcasts, those who are isolated, teen gamers, or unemployed loners. But in reality, potential shooters might be your coworkers, your neighbors, your boss, the guy who sits across from you in the office, the woman in the pew next to you at church, and the kid who plays football with your teenage son—or his dad. The people perpetrating these horrific acts every day are the people around us and our families. This is the reason that TATs, detailed later, are so valuable. Teams weigh information they receive against each individual.

Mental health can come into play as part of the analysis in threat assessments, and, in fact, it was identified as the most common "stressor" among factors evaluated by FBI researchers.[18] Stressors are situations we might all encounter, but, in the cases of these shooters, the stressors had "more than a minimal amount of adverse impact" on them.

Successful shooters faced an average of 3.6 stressors each in the year before they attacked, according to FBI researchers.[19] The most common stressors, in descending order after mental health, included financial strain, job-related matters, conflicts with friends and peers, marital problems, and abuse of alcohol or illicit drugs.

Consider how mental health stressors played a role, but clearly not the only role, in the fate of the youngest shooter, the twelve-year-old middle school student mentioned above.

In October of 2013, Jose Reyes was a Las Vegas seventh grader who still played with toy soldiers at home. His parents owned and ran a popular restaurant where Jose had begun working when he was ten, learning to cook, count change, and help customers. His parents were known to be attentive and loving. The boy was well-known and well-liked among the customers. Jose earned As and Bs in school.

An eleven-year-old friend said the two rode bikes, watched MTV shows together, and had fun with video games, which Jose more often than not won. Jose's classmates and friends said he usually had a smile on his face. He played violin.[20]

But school was sometimes a challenge. His parents said his slight lisp caused classmates to tease him, and once, when he spilled water on his pants, classmates mocked him for wetting his pants and being "gay," his parents later told the media.[21]

The morning of the shooting, Jose asked to take his BB gun to school and had put it in his backpack. His mother declined, saying he needed a note from his teacher, and took it from his backpack before he exited her car for school.

They were unaware he also had taken a 9-mm handgun from the cereal cupboard above the refrigerator. The gun had not been locked in a case, and the parents said they hadn't known that Jose knew it had been secreted there.

When the mother returned home, she noticed the missing handgun and called her husband and then police. The call came too late.

As soon as he arrived at school, Jose walked behind school to the playground and pulled out the handgun. A popular math teacher and Marine Corps veteran of the war in Iraq fairly quickly approached him. "Don't make me do this," one witness reported hearing Jose say.[22] The boy raised the gun, shooting the teacher point-blank in the chest, killing him.

As the shooting became apparent, a call to 911 was made, but the school intercom did not work, so no one could be warned. Jose walked around behind the school, passing by some students and shooting others. He raised the gun toward students he could see inside windows. Video footage shows him stopping once to replace an empty magazine.

To one group he'd left alone he said, "You ruined my life; now I am going to ruin yours."[23] After injuring two other students, he then raised the gun to his own head and killed himself.

When asking why this happened or how to stop the next Jose, what clues should we look for?

This shooting didn't occur because of Jose's age, ethnicity, education level, or love of typical kid video games, which subsequent investigation disclosed. He had been diagnosed on the autism spectrum and prescribed medication, as thousands of others might be. By all accounts his family was close and loving.

We don't know what triggered Jose to act this day, but the 1,300-page post-shooting report laid bare a life too short and perhaps signs missed by family, friends, and school officials.[24]

Jose's parents said his birth had been difficult, causing developmental and emotional delays. He didn't speak until he was five.[25] Officials had been concerned his move to middle school might be difficult, as he'd had trouble coping at times. Jose thought people were picking on him, a special education teacher opined. But she did not think that was true. The investigation revealed he had gathered some pictures of the Columbine shooters and searched internet sites involving violence.

School faculty had no knowledge of bullying.

Investigators discovered that, three weeks before the shooting, Reyes was among those students who saw two films depicting bullying in school that prompted the victim to turn to violence. In one, a bullied boy pulls a gun from his backpack and shoots another student. At the end of the film, the actor laments about going back in time to change things in the past.[26]

Consider the parallel language in one of the two notes that police found neatly handwritten in a spiral notebook in Jose's backpack. One to his family seemed to blame himself. One to the people at school seemed to lay fault at their feet.[27]

Dear mom and dad I'm sorry about all this is because some of my family and friends hate me but I understand. What I did this shooting is not because of the shooting games, bullying or other stuff is because of the past causes there some bad things in the past cause of me. And now I'm just a monster. But I want to say my last words I will go back to the past and fix everything so it can be the a [sic] great past. And the shooting of sparks middle school never should have happen. I wish I can be a smart and a better kid so I can be the better son in our family. But if you hate me and my family doesn't love me it's ok. I know I'm that I'm just an idiot. But I love you and I wish the past would be good and better someday.

And the second note:

Dear teachers and students today is the day when I kill you bastards for the embarressment [sic] that you did. You say mean things in school. That I'm gay.

That I'm lazy. Stupid. Idiot and also say I pee my pants and also stealing my money. Well that all ends. Today I will get revenge on the students and teachers for ruinning [sic] *my life . . . And right now this school will now come to an end your death will be rising when I shoot you. Have a great death at school.*[28]

These notes provide insight but not certainty into the stressors Jose faced. Threat assessment experts and law enforcement experts agree that stress can trigger violence. Other likely triggers include financial and job-related stress, mental health challenges, and conflicts with family, friends, and domestic partners.

In personal lives, sometimes the triggering event is the death of a friend or family, a broken engagement, a suitor's rejection, or physical or emotional abuse. In a job, it might be a lost promotion, retirement, a firing, or even the successes of another perceived as less deserving. In school, being kicked out of school, a rejection from a boyfriend or girlfriend, or an inability to meet parental expectations can be a trigger.

The National Council on Behavioral Health's research on mass violence perpetrators is instructive on the need to look both at behaviors and aspects of a person's life, avoiding profiling and stereotypes.

After a terrible shooting, sometimes investigators are able to pinpoint a motivation previously undetected. These motivations may include an attacker's wish to gain notoriety, a desire to copy another shooter, or a plan to prove loyalty to a terrorist group or another person. Rarely is this kind of motivation leaked in time to prevent a shooting. Instead, the success of finding shooters is identified in behaviors of concern and the characteristics of the individual involved.

"Characteristics of an individual perpetrator often cut across demographic, sociologic, cultural and occupational groups," authors concluded in the National Council for Behavioral Health report.

A general profile emerges of males who are often hopeless, harboring grievances that are frequently related to work, finances or interpersonal relationships; who feel victimized and relate to others whom they perceive to be similarly mistreated; who are indifferent to life and often subsequently die by suicide; who plan and prepare for their attack, and who often share information about the attack with others, though often not with the intended victim. . . . Among such individuals are those who exaggerate and personalize slights and misfortunes, and others whose anger and fear stems from symptoms of psychosis. Still others act out of a misguided desire to end the financial/physical/mental suffering of loved ones, as well as themselves.[29]

IDENTIFYING SHOOTERS

One good call by law enforcement in recent years is the decision to stop naming or glamorizing shooters. Though law enforcement has to identify and document who the shooter is—in research, for example—leaders have moved aggressively to leave the names of the shooters out of the public domain altogether. Exceptions may occur. Maybe a shooter got away and police are looking for a suspect. In general, less information is better.

This lesson was learned from the mistakes made after the Columbine shooting in 1999. At that time, the news media and, in fact, all of Hollywood seemed obsessed with the two involved teens. Magazine cover stories and made-for-TV movies turned them into cult heroes, as evidenced by the trails of endless research done by subsequent shooters and the taped-up hero-worship clippings gathered into evidence from other shooters' bedroom walls.

Today I still cringe when I see the news media publicly post a picture of a shooter—and, even worse—past shooters. I appreciate they have a job to do. I was once a journalist, and I agree they must be an avenue of truth and the record. But in the production and studio control rooms, and in the editing rooms, I urge producers and their teams to think cautiously about the impact of a photo displayed. Picture it displayed on multiple large-screen HD televisions in Walmart. If law enforcement isn't searching for the shooter, drop their picture to a corner and use it as little as possible. Consider cutting it from segments, or substitute a picture of the location, the neighborhood street sign, or city hall with the officials responding.

The same applies to pictures of the weapons and ammunition. This is standard fare for a society governed more and more by what we see than by what we hear. Still, photos of shooters, weapons, and ammunition give the shooter exactly what they wanted and likely encourage others on the same path to perceived glory.

The advocates for not naming or glamorizing a killer are admirable and should continue their quest. I hope we are pretty much past that, as we have seen substantial changes in the way shootings are covered these past five years. The media's introspection is a critically important brick in the prevention wall. It's encouraging that the media recognizes the role it can play.

But in this media- and social media–crazed world, I fear memories are short-lived and we will soon be watching Netflix specials on shooters again.

I could be wrong. I hope I am.

Chapter Four

Grievance Collectors and Understanding Violence

Prevention begins with knowing who to look for and then finding the right place to share that information.

Research in the past few years has given us better road maps and helped dispel some old theories and myths. And experts have become—well—experts at sharing what they have learned along the way. And while we are better at sharing, we haven't really shared enough to let the public as a whole understand their role and how they can help find potential shooters.

We know, for example, that these still are common misconceptions:

- Shooters just snap. False.
  Truth: A person who "snaps" does not commit targeted violence. Targeted violence is planned. The misconception that there was no opportunity to observe warning signs is simply wrong and, worse, sometimes may be an excuse voiced by someone who looked the other way.
- The shooter just had mental issues, and the attack couldn't have been stopped. False.
  Truth: The large majority of people with diagnosable mental illness are not violent, and having a psychiatric diagnosis is neither necessary, nor sufficient, as a risk factor for committing an act of mass violence.[1]

You will see that friends, family, teachers, classmates, workmates, and others similarly situated are our best hope. But sometimes those very people are the ones who hold back from sharing what they may have seen or learned.

Teachers will wait out a troubling student, passing them to the next class or grade. The Virginia Tech shooter had been kicked out of his English class for repeatedly writing disturbing and fatalistic papers. The shooter had had troubles in high school, but that information was never passed on when he began his university studies four hours away.

Parents who can't manage a child sometimes pass them off to another relative—a grandmother, for example—who may be less equipped to intercede. This can allow behaviors of concern to be overlooked despite the best of intentions of family and friends.

Sometimes people look at a list of warning signs but just don't believe it could happen to those around them. When I was a prosecutor in Chicago, I often heard family members defending their husband, daughter, uncle, or whomever as simply incapable of having committed the crime for which they were charged.

"I've known him a long time, and he has never done anything violent," they would say. "I don't think he could ever hurt anyone." Others are quick to dismiss threats of violence by reasoning with themselves, saying "He says things like that all the time" or "He's just like that."

It is true that the closer we are to a person, the more difficult it is for us to gauge them honestly and the likelier we are to dismiss accelerating behavioral concerns. Those closest also may be desensitized to the person's repeated actions.

Sometimes leaning on a profile as a crutch allows a person to dismiss concerns by saying a person they observed just doesn't fit that mold.

But to ascertain who might become an active shooter or commit targeted violence, we have to accept a willingness to understand that what we see and hear may be a pattern of *behaviors* that might lead a person to act out violently. That's the analysis law enforcement and mental health professionals perform daily.

The latest research has given us a more vivid picture of who we are looking for and helps us all to see what may be right in front of our eyes. It's good to note here that understanding the language used by professionals is key. This has been a stumbling block among the various professions fighting targeted violence. Medical personnel use their terms, and law enforcement uses different terms. Mental health professionals and academia aren't on the same page language-wise, and researchers and journalists, too, use many different terms.

I'll *italicize* some specific language and provide definitions where needed:

- *behaviors of concern*—observable, identifiable behaviors that a person exhibits while progressing on a pathway to violence.
- *pathway to violence*—a series of sequential steps indicating that an individual is progressing toward an act of targeted violence (see the discussion below).
- *targeted violence*—violent incidents involving an identifiable subject who possesses the intent and potential to cause harm to an identifiable target.

- *grievance*—the cause of someone's distress or reason for complaint and resentment that fuels feelings of being wronged, translating into behaviors related to a sense of mission, destiny, loss, or desire for revenge.
- *grievance collector*—a person carrying grievances whose brittleness moves them on a pathway to violence.

A person who may commit *targeted violence* is often described as a person on a *pathway to violence*. This person displays a concerning pattern of *behaviors of concern*. When people are on this *pathway to violence*, their behaviors, or actions, can be very visible if you keep an eye out.

Let's assume our potential shooter is named Joe.

Clues on how to watch for Joe's *behaviors of concern* can begin with what we know about Joe and his circumstances. It's important not to look at a single behavior while ignoring the rest.

Often, people on a *pathway to violence* may have a *real or perceived grievance*—a grievance that may have its origins inside the office, back at their house, with the people in their school or university, or a combination of these.

Joe may feel pushed around by a neighbor who always parks his truck in front of Joe's house. Joe may be a teenager who believes he made the perfect prom proposal only to be turned down. Joe may believe that he missed out on a promotion because his company hired somebody to fill a supervisor spot—maybe somebody younger, older, or of a different gender, color skin tone, ethnicity, or religion.

When things don't go as Joe wants, he adds that grievance to a mental list he begins to carry around with him. He is becoming a *grievance collector*.

Joe carries that grievance list with him to the office, to school, and even to church on Sunday. He may begin to add to his burgeoning list stressors such as financial trouble, personal relationship problems, and stress over caretaking or a job.

As Joe's list becomes more substantial, it becomes a very important part of his life, because now his primary purpose is to be a *grievance collector*. Now he sees the world stacking up against him. The grocer is always out of his favorite cereal. That teacher is against him because she took a grade away from him for missing classes. That lady at the gas station cut in front of him to get to "his" pump.

Joe may not appreciate that he has become a *grievance collector* even if those around him begin to see it.

Does Joe's collection of grievances mean violence will result? Not necessarily. Plenty of people lose out on promotions, get turned down for prom, or suffer setbacks without becoming violent. But, for any number of reasons, some of the Joes of the world are more brittle or more fragile.

Joe the grievance collector's list gets longer. Pretty soon, he begins to blame others for making him carry around that long list. They "make" him carry that list, and he doesn't like it. These grievance collectors develop the idea that only violence can resolve their situation.

UNDERSTANDING VIOLENCE

Violence fits generally into two categories: impulsive or reactive violence, and predatory or planned violence.

Impulsive or reactive violence is just what it sounds like. It is an emotionally based response to a perceived and imminent threat. This might be a violent response by somebody who believes they are going to be raped or killed, or it could be generated in a person in the midst of committing other violence. It could be a violent response prompted by fear of harm to one's child. It might even be a violent reaction against a person whom they fear will disclose embarrassing or unlawful conduct.

The second kind of violence—predatory or planned violence—is the basis for targeted violence, the type of violence that results in an active shooter situation. This helps to explain why individuals who commit targeted violence don't just *snap*. They are grievance collectors.

Two eminent researchers, Calhoun and Weston, explained how a person's ideas turn into planned violence using this commonly referred-to visual; see figure 4.1, "Grievance Collectors."[2]

They postulate that, before becoming violent, an individual moves through these predictable steps from developing their *grievance*, whether real or perceived, to an *ideation* of that grievance, to *research and planning*, and *preparation*. Then action occurs: *breaching* the target's security to *attack*.[3]

Once a person has developed a grievance, whether real or perceived, they take time to plan and prepare for an attack. These stages may vary from hours and days to weeks and months, or longer.

Few grievances result in a violent outcome. But when a person becomes a grievance collector, it is more likely one or more of those grievances might result in violence. Recognizing grievances as both real and perceived helps us to understand why someone commits targeted violence against another based on misinformation. Perhaps the woman who pulled up to the pump at the gas station in front of Joe did not even see Joe's car. Likely the teacher was not singling Joe out for missing classes and in fact every other student suffered the same grade loss for being absent.

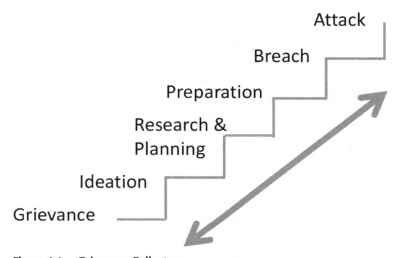

Figure 4.1. Grievance Collectors
Calhoun, F., & Weston, S. (2016). *Threat Assessment and Management Strategies: Identifying the Howlers and Hunters*, 2nd ed. Boca Raton, FL: CRC.

Because Joe's grievance may be based on a perceived slight, not a real one, it's important that those in authority—teachers, human resources personnel, bosses, parents, and family—think of how their interactions are viewed by the Joes of the world.

The second step, ideation, is a fifty-cent word that simply means "the act of having an idea." Think of a cartoon where a light bulb appears above someone's head. The grievance collector suddenly thinks about how to respond, get even, or fix things.

This ideation leads grievance collectors to consciously begin to analyze how they might move from being the victim to the person in charge. They begin the process of thinking through how they can do something to those who have wronged them.

Grievances come in many forms. The grievance collector may have a grievance much more complex than a lost opportunity to pump gas or to use a prime parking space in front of the house. The grievance collector's concerns might be more worldly, such as perceived injustices done by climate change deniers or by people pursuing a political ideology.

Depending on the federal and local laws in place, these individuals might be charged as terrorists for their actions. Hundreds of violent acts over the last decade involve terrorists who acted out grievances. Some are people who believe their race, religion, or rights are under attack.

Are those violent individuals different from the active shooter who enters their local restaurant and begins firing on patrons? No, not when it comes to a *pathway to violence*. No matter the *grievance*, the pathway still reveals the most valuable points at which to intercede—research, planning, and preparation. No matter the motivation, the research, planning, and preparation stages are an opportunity for others to hear and see behaviors and actions and catch a person before disaster strikes.

Violence Rarely Occurs in a Vacuum

Every experienced law enforcement officer can recount interview after interview after a crime in which a neighbor or an across-the-room office mate offered some version of "I knew it was him," "She was acting strange," and "Now that you mentioned it, I did notice . . ."

Research shows that at the time when people should say something, they often digress into a ***truth-default theory***, explaining away any concerns. Professor Tim Levine at the University of Alabama at Birmingham coined this term to describe how people presume others to be honest because they either don't think of deception as a possibility or they don't have enough information to prove that what they see or hear is false.[4]

Canadian journalist and author Malcolm Gladwell, in his 2019 book, *Talking to Strangers*,[5] provides good examples of people relying on a truth-default theory—tending to believe people and excuse away potential anomalies—which led to disasters. A resulting active shooter incident is perhaps the ultimate disaster.

Consider public information available about the Las Vegas Live Nation concert shooter. He brought five suitcases to his room on September 25th, seven on the 26th, two on the 28th, six on the 30th, and two on October 1st—obtaining extensive assistance multiple times from hotel bellhops—and, at times, he used a service elevator.

Constantly remind yourself and others not to be too quick to explain away concerns, hunches, and those nagging feelings in the pit of the stomach about the Joes of the world.

Joe's planning is more than just intent. It involves the steps to carry out a shooting or other violent attack. This may include surveillance, determining victim schedules, hanging pictures and headlines of past shooters, finding transportation, testing security procedures, buying weapons, and increased target practice. Sometimes the planning is less visible, like writing in journals and tracking other mass killings via the internet.

FBI researchers found that 42 percent of shooters studied spent one to six months planning their attack and another 18 percent of the shooters spent six months or more.[6] The research, authored by James Silver of Worcester State University and Andre Simons and Sarah Craun from their time at the FBI, provides unique and valuable insight on shooters from previously unreleased details in police investigative files.

Catching a potentially violent person during this middle stage gives investigators and counselors a chance to intercede, react to a person's actions, see changes in their behavior, and, hopefully, prevent a crime from occurring. This applies equally whether the person involved ultimately faces a serious criminal charge, such as terrorism, or is charged with committing a lesser crime, if the violent act is prevented.

Now let's go back to Joe, the *grievance collector*, and consider what might be in our prevention toolbox.

A prevention toolbox has three different steps, each of which must be accessed in succession; see figure 4.2, "Threats: From Discovery to Management." Without the first step, we can't get to the second. Without the second, we can't get to the third.

Figure 4.2.   Threats: From Discovery to Management
Katherine Schweit, Schweit Consulting LLC

The first step begins by identifying what to look for as well as who should do the looking. We hope people who are near the Joes of the world can identify Joe's *behaviors of concern*. Sometimes these behaviors are referred to as *pre-incident indicators*.

The second step is knowing whether and when behaviors should be reported and whom to tell. Often, *bystanders* later interviewed say they didn't know whom to tell.

The third step is managing the Joes of the world—sometimes a one-time event but more likely an ongoing process. This step ideally is carried out by a mixture of family, friends, and a skilled team of professionals who take the information they have and conduct both an initial ***threat assessment*** and ongoing ***threat management***.

Threat assessment and *threat management* can be complicated—as you will see in the next two chapters—but they comprise the most effective and valuable prevention tools available. Scads of books have been written about threat assessment and threat management and an equal number of professionals work just in this area; so consider this a primer only.

Each step is fraught with its own challenges. Consider these thoughts:

* The best people in a position to know something are family, friends, peers, and coworkers. They also are the most likely to see something and not say something.
* People often think small pieces of information are not relevant, though they are generally wrong about that, failing to understand that we often are trying to put together a puzzle and need every little piece.
* Many employers often would rather dismiss troublesome employees than spend time trying to help them. They are passing along potential problems.
* Overburdened law enforcement, health care providers, and educators don't always absorb general or specific threat information from the public that could be passed to a well-functioning threat assessment team.

With these challenges in mind, let's look at the first step here, before moving on to the other two steps in the next chapter.

STEP ONE: LOOKING FOR BEHAVIORS OF CONCERN

Consider who should be looking for behaviors of concern and what behaviors they should be observing.

The first question has the only easy answer in this book. Who should be looking? The answer is—everybody. This is the genesis and genius of "See Something, Say Something."

With 300 million–plus people in the United States and less than a million law enforcement officials of any kind looking for clues, "See Something, Say Something" is really the job of the public.

"See Something, Say Something" was created by the New York City Transit Authority after the September 11, 2001, terrorist attacks in the United States and has been the most successful effort, hands down, for engaging the public to better prevent terrorist attacks in the country.

Research by the Mineta Transportation Institute (MTI) at San Jose State University, released in 2018, found that "See Something, Say Something" prevented between 10 and 14 percent of the potential attacks on public surface transportation.[7] Other research supports similar conclusions, and it is worth noting that support for the MTI effort came from the departments of Transportation and Homeland Security.[8]

MTI's comprehensive researched tracked 5,372 suspicious situations on public surface transportation worldwide since 1970, seeking to identify terrorist activities. These situations primarily involved the reporting of suspicious packages, including vehicles; however, in other cases suicide bombers were stopped.

In a 180-degree turnaround from the time before the September 11, 2001, terrorist attacks, looking for suspicious packages is now ingrained in the US psyche. Still-somewhat-limited research on averted attacks also validates the need to be on the lookout for not only suspicious objects but also suspicious communications.

Leakage

Words themselves and other communication, too, can telegraph intended violence, occurring more often than one might expect. This is called *leakage*.

Leakage is an accidental or gradual escape of information to a third party that reveals clues related to thinking, planning, or executing an act of targeted violence.

Where shooters have a specific target, FBI researchers found more than half delivered a direct threat or confronted their target, 95 percent of the time in person. Researchers found 56 percent of the time the shooter *leaked* an intent to commit a violent act to a third party. When the shooter was age 17 or younger, the percentage was a staggering 88 percent.[9]

"The leaked intent to commit violence was not always directed at the eventual victims of the shooting; in some cases what was communicated was a more general goal of doing harm to others, apparently without a particular person or group in mind," the FBI noted.

Leaking can be in the form of spoken or written words, or even visual indicators. It's helpful to be on the lookout for all three.

Spoken leakage may be in the form of a threat told directly to another student, perhaps to scare that person or test out whether the leaker can incite through threats. It could be less subtle or even an implied intention, such as a warning to a coworker or classmate that it's time for the boss "to see what he did to Joe."

Written leakage—posts that say things like "Everybody better stay away from school tomorrow" or emails threatening individuals—can be equally specific and directed at a wider group of people who may see the concerning behavior.

Equally concerning might be threats such as the intent to bring a weapon to school or work the next day. The idea is so commonplace now that "Don't come to school tomorrow" is in urban dictionaries and endless memes on the internet.

Leakage can be subtler, demonstrated by escalating indications of intolerance and language that signals an intent to "get even" or "fix" things or "make someone pay." This kind of leakage can be written or spoken.

Written leakage might appear in seemingly fictional stories about "other people" or in homework assignments. The Virginia Tech shooter submitted violent writings, obscene poetry, and disturbing papers to his professors. They were so disturbing one professor eventually had him stop coming to class and continue his work through self-study.

In November of 2019, Los Angeles police arrested a thirteen-year-old boy who allegedly threatened to shoot students at his middle school, and, in a subsequent check, LAPD seized an assault-style rifle with a high capacity magazine during a search of his house. During the search, police found a hand-drawn map of his middle school and a list naming specific students and staff members.[10]

The same week, police arrested another teenager after he posted pictures of himself on social media posing with a gun and bullets and talking about a possible attack at a high school in Palmdale, California, police told the *Washington Post*.

This third kind of leakage may appear online with unexplained photographs (e.g., a gun muzzle pointed at people, pictures in the background) dropped on Facebook, YouTube, Instagram, Twitter, Snapchat, Reddit, Tik-Tok, WhatsApp, and FB Messenger. Perhaps not as commonly, other likely locations include image and message boards like 4chan and 8chan, as well as WeChat, Pinterest, LinkedIn, and Discord. Each year new platforms provide new opportunities to see leakage but also require more diligence to encourage viewers to understand and share what they see.

Leakage often occurs when two or more conspire to commit an attack. The US Department of Justice's Office of Community Oriented Policing Services and the National Police Foundation looked at 102 attacks where half were averted, finding that the fifty-one completed attacks all had single attackers. In all, researchers found thirty (58.8 percent) of the averted attacks were planned by a single individual.[11] "This difference may indicate that the presence of additional perpetrators increases the likelihood of the plot being discovered," authors Peter Langman and Frank Straub wrote. Chances are, based on this and other research of prior attacks, most Joes of the world are going it alone.

Behaviors of Concern

Those around Joe—friends, family, peers, and coworkers—are by far in the best position to confront the reality that Joe may be a *person of concern*.

At least one person noticed a concerning behavior in the lives of *every* active shooter researched by the FBI as it delved into the precursor events of sixty-three active shooter incidents in the United States between 2000 and 2013.[12]

"[O]n average, people from three different groups noticed concerning behavior for each active shooter," researchers found. The most likely to see the concerning behaviors:

- Fellow classmates noticed concerning behaviors 92 percent of the time.
- Spouses and domestic partners, 87 percent of the time.
- Teachers and school staff, 75 percent of the time.
- Family members, 68 percent of the time.
- Coworkers, 40 percent of the time.

Law enforcement identified concerning behaviors 25 percent of the time, supporting the notion that the police are often the last to know.

You might fear these concerning behaviors are too subtle to detect, but, in fact, 95 percent of the time the shooters' own words were one of the identified behaviors. The number is worth repeating: Of the 63 shooters in the FBI study, 61 communicated verbally to at least one person some type of concerning behavior.

Concerning behaviors that involved physical action were observed 86 percent of the time. This could be increased drug abuse or risk-taking behavior. It might be an increase in aggressive behavior or a significant change in school or work performance. One in five had observable, contextually inappropriate behaviors involving a firearm.

You might doubt your ability to identify behaviors of concern, but anybody who has every raised a child knows that gut feeling you get when you're hearing a lie. You may not know the truth, but you know you're not hearing it. Trust your gut.

Behaviors don't appear on some checklists; that's just profiling. *Profiling* is making a determination based on general characteristics or past behaviors—assumptions based on a person's clothes, race, gender, job, or more. Tagging someone as a danger because their clothing indicates a religious belief or because they speak a different language is profiling and won't help locate behaviors of concern.

One concerning behavior may be a problem in and of itself, or several together may raise that concern. Professionals are the best equipped to sift the wheat from the chaff, but they can't do that if they only hear about some of the concerns.

Brittle People

Assessing each person independently is essential because words and actions alone don't tell us what is going on inside someone's head.

Consider these two coworkers as illustrative.

Jesse and Kelly work together, party pretty hard, and have hung out together since they joined the company the same day five years earlier. They instigate the weekend fun and are known to hustle at work. But in June when Kelly is promoted, Jesse is passed over. Jesse changes.

Suddenly, Jesse starts using steroids and skipping blood pressure medication. By the end of the month, Jesse is coming to work late and not engaging very much. Word is that Jesse told people in the break room that the boss ruined his life.

The details of Jesse's life at that moment in June are reason to be concerned and should be reported to someone.

Not everyone who misses a promotion is on a pathway to violence. But Jesse is not just a person who missed a promotion. Jesse has become a *grievance collector*.

Some people are more *brittle*, FBI behavioral experts noted in a 2017 monograph on targeted attacks. **Brittle people** are struggling to deal with the stressors in their lives, and they perceive that they are losing that struggle.

If Jesse is a brittle person, he may have a hard time coping and may not be able to deal with even a minor setback, let alone what he may perceive as having happened to him.

"They are exceptionally brittle, unable to withstand slights, rejections, or offenses both minor and otherwise," FBI behavioral experts wrote. "Time and again, targeted violence offenders have claimed to be persecuted and alienated from their peers, family, and the world at large, viewing themselves as outsiders and not part of a larger social network."[13]

About 40 percent of the active shooters tracked by the FBI in the past twenty years have committed suicide, ending their attack. Consider then how a *brittle* person, who may be suicidal, can also become homicidal.

WHAT ARE WE LOOKING FOR?

In 2017 the FBI released an informative guide that shares, in plain English, the critical concerning behaviors that may show a person is on a pathway to violence. The guide, awkwardly titled "Making Prevention a Reality: Identifying, Assessing, and Managing the Threat of Targeted Violence," helps identify behaviors that may lead to violence.[14]

Here are some obvious, and not so obvious, examples of concerning behaviors—not a checklist—that have been identified by the FBI that can be used to guide you and train others:

- Sudden withdrawal from life patterns, such as absence from work without explanation, retreating to temporary quarters, or failing to appear for appointments normally kept.
- Recent and significant personal loss or humiliation, whether real or perceived, such as a death, breakup, or divorce, or loss of a job, status, or self-image.
- Recent acts of novel or experimental aggression, including trespass, animal cruelty, or vandalism.
- Any effort to physically approach an apparent target or close associates, evidence of items left for the target to find even if they appear benign (e.g., flowers), evidence of surveillance without approach, or attempts to breach or circumvent security measures.
- Direct or indirect communication or threats using multiple methods of delivery, including email, facsimile, hand-delivered note, and text message, which escalate in frequency or intensity or which demonstrate that actual surveillance has occurred (e.g., "She looked frustrated when she left the coffee shop in her green coat at 6:23 a.m.").
- Sudden changes in social media behaviors, including but not limited to use of encryption, decrease in postings, increase in postings, and novel use of different platforms, all of which might include leakage that portends future action.
- Drastic changes in appearance, such as a shaved head, an unkempt appearance, sudden weight change, poor hygiene, or uncharacteristically large or multiple tattoos; may also include contextually inappropriate law enforcement or military costuming.
- Intense interest in or fascination with previous shooting incidents or mass assaults where the interest would be contextually inappropriate, and may include identification with perpetrators of violence, in particular, mass violence, whether the perpetrator is real or fictional.
- Recent acquisition of weapons, ammunition, personal protective gear, tactical clothing, or other items, when that indicates a departure from the individual's normal pattern.
- Recent escalation in target practice and weapons training also may be a concern for one who already owns weapons and ammunition.

- Recent interest in explosive devices, or acquisition of components to construct a device.
- Sudden cessation of medications or active substance abuse.
- Sudden onset of reckless sexual, financial, or other behaviors, or giving away of possessions that may suggest a lack of concern for future consequences.
- Statements or behaviors that seem to indicate suicidality, end-of-life planning, or an interest in destructiveness toward the world at large.
- Preparation of a "statement" or farewell writing, to include manifestos, videos, notes, web blogs, emails, or blogs.

Atypical or Contextually Inappropriate Behavior

It may seem challenging to know what to report, but look back and notice that nearly every example above includes a word such as *sudden*, *recent*, or *drastic*. We are all looking for **atypical behaviors** or **contextually inappropriate behaviors** not typical for that particular person. These may be *pre-incident behaviors.*

These *contextually inappropriate* behaviors are easier for friends, family, and coworkers to spot. If you know a person's **baseline behavior**, you will be able to identify *atypical behavior*. Someone who goes to 9:30 a.m. church services every single Sunday but doesn't show up one Sunday is displaying *atypical* or *contextually inappropriate* behavior. If you pay for your gasoline every time in credit but then one time pay with cash, that is *contextually inappropriate* behavior for you. Missed mass and cash for gas aren't likely a concern when it comes to finding potential active shooters, but other actions might be more telling.

Consider an example.

Because Audrey shoots at the range every Saturday, that is contextually appropriate for Audrey. But then you hear Audrey is suddenly going to the range three days a week, shooting longer, and has purchased new weapons and a couple cases of ammunition to try out. Ammunition is expensive.

That doesn't mean that Audrey is going to shoot up a school or church. But it does make it worth asking Audrey's friends or family, or even the police, to check in on Audrey. Maybe Audrey is practicing for a big shooting competition coming up. But maybe Audrey just broke up with a significant other and has been writing papers about death in English class. Maybe Audrey has said she doesn't care about much anymore. Maybe Audrey is beginning to spiral down and needs some support from the community.

We may never know if helping Audrey through some tough time averted a potential attack, but we can hope that if it was a possibility, the intervention was wise. The true answer is that no one can know, but every act of kindness shapes the future.

Professional security officials, including law enforcement, have a whole additional view of subtle behaviors they may see that might indicate a threat is imminent, including a person's increasing stress level, active deception, and detachment from the environment.

These security professionals also are looking for people who ask probing details about operations, site locations, access opportunities, or employees. Good training in this area is available and essential for any security professional. But proceed cautiously with expensive training that doesn't teach your security people to see each person as an individual, and avoid training that relies on profiling or checklists.

With such a broad array of behaviors, it's easy to appreciate how critical it is to train as many people as possible in these matters and why it's helpful to have others besides family take a more earnest and arm's-length look at a person's behaviors. A threat assessment team, which I'll talk about in the next two chapters, is a good place to send all this information. This formalized team has a better collective eye, and more training, to assess whether a person's behaviors should be a concern.

Motivation

Finally, when looking for people who might commit targeted violence, don't get sidetracked by ***motivation***. Motivation is something people in the news talk about to fill airtime. I know; I've done it. When any major crime occurs, law enforcement works backward, checking with family and friends to see what has happened in a person's life that might have caused them to commit a crime, and the public often calls this the offender's motivation.

A potential attacker may be *motivated* by many things—a need to be perceived as powerful or even a desire to become part of the cultural narrative in the news. Expending energy on assessing motivation distracts from efforts to intercede. And motivation isn't always so obvious. To this day, the motivation behind the Live Nation shooter in Las Vegas is unknown.[15] Sixty people dead, approximately 1,000 shots fired, and 800 injured—knowing the motivation won't change that.

No matter the *motivation*, it is only by discovering *concerning behaviors* that opportunities to prevent a disaster materialize. Though *motivations* may vary, it is observing *what* an individual is *doing* and *how* they go about preparing to act violently that can help you anticipate and prevent a tragedy.

In the next chapter, we'll move on to steps two and three, looking at what and where to report, as well as what is done with that information.

Chapter Five

Reporting, Assessing, and Managing Threats

Now let's go back to Joe the *grievance collector* and consider the next two steps in the prevention toolbox that focus on what to do with all that information, including how to get people to report in a timely fashion and how to develop systems to capture the information and do something with it.

STEP TWO: REPORTING BEHAVIORS OF CONCERN TO THE RIGHT PLACE

This second step is where most people seem to make mistakes and later regret it. That happens when someone commits a violent act but those nearby have remained silent. In the aftermath, they are left wondering if they could have done more.

When to Report

So, let's look at when people do or don't share. Even though reporting should occur as soon as possible, silence or hesitation may occur for a number of reasons.

Some people fear getting a stranger or acquaintance in trouble. Some hope others will report so they can "stay out of it."

Some fear interacting with the police.

Some don't want to get involved because they worry others will think they are snitching or interfering in someone else's business.

Some seem to want a guarantee that what they report is important or will make a difference, kind of like waiting around to see what happens after you call in a car accident.

Some don't report because they think the physical security at a building will protect those inside. This is wrong. Many times, a shooter targets where they work, go to school, or pray. Other times the location is open to the public. These **insider threats** may be discussed in **workplace violence** training at your office.

The bottom line is, rarely is an arrest made immediately, so people need to report and trust the system.

Reporting is a particularly difficult challenge for friends and family, those with the best access to information. Often, it's difficult to get to a discussion about *when* to report, because friends and family frequently aren't willing to report at all, putting a fatal flaw into the prevention toolbox. They deny the possibility that their loved one could turn violent. They make excuses for his misconduct, her "strange" behavior, and even for their unusual antisocial or violent reactions to situations. She's just having a bad day, they say. He's having a tough time. He's never done anything like that before. She could never do anything bad.

However, research validates that those who commit suicide often target family members and their closest friends during violent acts. This may be because the shooter is angry with them; at other times it might be that the shooter seems to want to spare them the notoriety and pain that will follow.

Sometimes people choose to report but only after they have slept on it or given someone time to cool off. Delays can be fatal. It's easy to fall into the excuse trap.

I once reached out to local police on an urgent matter after discovering a stalker was trolling a neighborhood child who would leave her empty house each morning to walk to school alone. The stalker had contacted the child in the middle of the night, providing identifying information about her house. The petrified child reached out to my daughter, but would only talk to me if I promised not to tell her mom. The little girl was relieved when we took her to school and the school resource officer intervened. The mother called later in the day and yelled at me, saying the ordeal was embarrassing to her. It surprises me how adults will worry more about what others might think than about the fact that they may save the life of a person in trouble, even their own child. Don't be afraid to let someone be mad at you.

No law requires people to report what they see or hear, so creating a culture that encourages sharing concerns is essential. This is true whether we're talking about your library, school, business, hospital, religious institution, neighborhood, or even your family unit.

In 2017, a teacher off work from the International High School in New Orleans called immediately after receiving an email stating three armed individuals were going to take over the school. The school was safely evacuated.

In 2013, a witness in a grocery store parking lot reported seeing a student take a weapon from his car before heading toward the University of New Haven campus. The swift reporting allowed students to shelter in place until campus police successfully found the student who was carrying two loaded semiautomatic pistols.

A report-because-you-care culture takes time to develop and must be pushed from the top down in any organization, whether from the CEO, board members, pastor, or head of household. Fostering this culture has to go beyond posting a phone number on a lunchroom bulletin board.

In an office setting, coworkers and management can see changes in the person sitting at the next desk. In school, students are much more dialed in to what's going on with other students than the faculty could ever be.

Encouraging timely reporting includes teaching others to appreciate the role to be played not only in preventing potential violence but also in preventing self-harm, such as suicides. Social scientists call this being an **upstander** instead of a *bystander*. It's a twenty-year-old term whose popularity is credited, in part, to Pulitzer Prize winner and former US Ambassador to the United Nations Samantha Power. Training materials on how to be an *upstander* are plentiful on the internet and often found in the context of anti-bullying campaigns.[1]

Being an upstander also speaks to the broader social contract we should all have to be supportive and caring members of society. Upstanders pass the burden they bear onto other professionals to resolve. We saw a chilling example of a failure of this when calls made by a close family friend didn't stop the killing of seventeen people at Marjory Stoneman Douglas High School in 2018.

"I just want someone to know about this so they can look into it," the friend reported to county sheriff's offices in Broward and Palm Beach, Florida, as well as to someone on the FBI tipline. "If they think it's something worth going into, fine. If not, um, I just know I have a clear conscience if he takes off and, and, starts shooting places up."

When these tips weren't investigated, law enforcement acknowledged the failures after the shooting, fired people and made changes. But I mention it here as a good example of the burden this caller was carrying, a load likely lessened by those calls.

Scores of successful interventions rarely make the news because they aren't reported publicly. One that did occurred in 2013.

McIntosh County Academy High School in Darien, Georgia, was closed for the day after a person in the Caribbean discovered and reported that a seventeen-year-old student, who had been expelled, had posted a photo holding a weapon with the caption, "Today is the last day of high school." More disturbing, that day a school resource officer seized a shotgun from a car parked on school grounds that was registered to the seventeen-year-old's best friend.[2]

Where to Report

Another major hurdle to success can occur when someone wants to report but doesn't know where to report.

Surely every one of us can recall something we've heard directly or through another—things that make us pause. Perhaps it was overheard in a lunchroom or told to you directly by someone during a coffee break. Maybe your child mentioned concerns about another child, asking you to promise not to tell. As a parent, and a retired agent, I say, say something anyway.

Chat with a criminal investigator, and it is also likely that they have heard, "I thought something was up, but I didn't know who to call."

Where would you report at work or school if you heard something? Is there a human resources person or school counselor, a place to text, or a nearby mental health facility? What would it take for you to call your local police department?

Local police and 911 dispatchers take calls from concerned citizens daily. We rely on the police to handle whatever problem is called in, sort of a one-stop shop.

Experience, however, has taught us that, by the time the police get a call, it may be too late; and police may not be the best ones to intercede when a law-abiding citizen is struggling with relationship issues, emotional problems, or work challenges.

A supervisor struggling with an employee who is missing shifts and arguing with coworkers needs to have at their fingertips a way to pass along this concern to a team whose job it is to help people in distress. Just a call to the police won't do. When the supervisor is going it alone and misconduct rises to the level of a firing, it's only a short-lived fix if the employee returns with a gun.

Research has shown that sometimes people report what they hear but only to another friend or even to the very person who has displayed the behaviors of concern in the first place. This can be a fatal error when information is passed no further.

Reticent tweens and teenagers who worry about snitching are among the least likely to share unless there is a method that works for them. Where to report must include formal and less casual reporting mechanisms, anonymous reporting systems, and reporting that takes advantage of every social media platform and Information Age opportunity out there.

This variety of reporting mechanisms creates avenues—or pipelines—for the person who may not want to go to a pastor or rabbi, who fears risking their job, or who may be afraid of police. People who have had their own legal skirmishes may never approach the police or any authority figure.

This doesn't mean abandoning 911 calls in an emergency. Rather, it means taking a close look at how you can set up layers of options, identifying areas for improvement.

Officials in Germany sought a solution when they found that their country was one of the world leaders in school violence, dwarfed only by the United States. Germany had experienced a dozen incidents in eleven years that resulted in the deaths of twenty teachers and sixteen students. Similar to US offenders, all but one was male; but unlike in the United States, their offenders used guns, knives, axes, and other lethal tools.[3]

Frightened and frustrated, officials turned to the idea of a structured reporting system. Educational leaders initiated a pilot program that asked classmates and faculty to report potentially dangerous signs of leakage by students. In the first seven months of the program, at least nineteen high-risk cases were identified; those students were offered help, and violence was likely prevented.

Organizational leaders, managers, and educators charged with developing reporting systems should tap a variety of resources to see if you have both enough—and the right kind—of reporting systems in place. This includes policies, procedures, training, and ways to encourage reporting.

Take into consideration the different types of information you want to collect. This should include leakage, as was focused on in the German system, but also ways to report concerning behaviors that are observed and could indicate planning and preparation for violence.

Gone are the days when a cardboard box with a slit on the lid was the only way to gather anonymous information and suggestions at the office. Options now include the ability to report from smartphone apps, online sites, email, phone, text messaging, and face-to-face conversations. These options create a pool of people and places for reporting, and it's important that several employees at all levels be identified as having a willingness to take face-to-face information in a confidential manner. Kendra might report to a coach but never a principal. Maurice might report to a human resources person but never his boss.

Unlike ten or twenty years ago, there are now great anonymous and attributable reporting systems to mimic that have been set up and are operating both in cities and at the national level. Law enforcement, already operating with 24-hours-a-day 911 systems, is an integral part of any reporting labyrinth and most critically can cover times of day when call-takers may be unavailable at other reporting platforms.

Sophisticated commercial reporting software is available to track reporting but is not always necessary; if it's already being used at your location, the data collection on safety concerns can become part of that.

Some tracking method is necessary. If you have a system to report bullying at your school or employee theft at your business, you may already be 90 percent there. How about tinkering with software to expand the ways and types of information that can be reported? Make sure each system has a notification mode built in so the information can be reviewed immediately.

If you don't have a reporting system, you can call a nearby school district to see what they use, send out a request for assistance to your business leadership contacts, or ask at the next chamber of commerce coffee.

I've used both Facebook Workplace and LinkedIn to share and ask for assistance in my work in private industry. Connect with leaders running existing systems, or duplicate them in your own environment.

Your faith organization or school may have a calling tree already in place. Maybe you can modify this system and train call-takers to listen for concerning behavior, take note of and pass on information about concerns in a confidential manner.

Employees and students who have access to a text messaging system already can use that system to reach out.

Don't forget that that cardboard box on a desk in the lunchroom can still be part of the equation as long as someone is checking it daily.

Those are all places to start.

Marketing the various ways to report is as important as having the reporting systems in place. Encourage reporting as a way to keep your community safe. I know some innovative businesses use the first sixty seconds of every single business meeting to discuss prepared issues related to health, wellness, and security, including reporting mechanisms and mental health service availability. Proactive approaches catch problems before they escalate.

Market everywhere. This includes posting information where individuals can access it, such as in bathrooms, via text message, or by means of a monthly email campaign. These places allow people to absorb information on how to report on their own time and in private.

Evaluating information gained through these reporting systems also may improve business processes by shedding light on systemic problems with daily operations. For example, employees frustrated over the way vacation is granted, breaks are doled out, or complaints are addressed may speak out to others, and reporting will shed light on those troubles.

Anonymous Reporting Systems

Adding a way for people to report anonymously is essential to a thorough reporting system. Many schools recognize this need, but other organizations still lag behind, including big companies, mom-and-pop shops, and religious and social organizations.

Developing an anonymous reporting system, or ARS, may seem like an ominous task, but you may be able to tap into systems already in place. Most public companies have a system in place to address workplace violence or worker misconduct. And, remember, law enforcement takes information anonymously all the time.

Those stung by tragedies involving schoolchildren were among the first to recognize this need for ways to anonymously report. Not long after the Columbine High School shooting, Safe2Tell Colorado developed an ARS that started with a hotline and now includes an entire program of training, a smart app, and expanded services. The system, run by the Attorney General in Colorado, is supported by legislation that guarantees anonymity to those reporting.

Safe2Tell became the training ground for many school-based ARSs. Companion marketing should focus on caring instead of snitching.

After the 2012 Sandy Hook shooting in Connecticut, another powerhouse in the ARS business emerged—Say Something, formally known as the Say Something Anonymous Reporting System (SS-ARS).

Say Something quickly grew to be one of the most expansive nationally. Adopted by many school districts throughout the United States, its app has been downloaded nearly two million times. Sandy Hook Promise funds training and program support.

Kenji Okuma, the Say Something Crisis Center's director, has seen firsthand how using an ARS can prevent not only targeted violence but also potential suicides and other concerns that might otherwise go unreported. Above all else, he noted, those running reporting systems have to appreciate that students fear snitching, betraying someone, or being considered weak.

Successful ARSs have several common components, Okuma notes. Foremost, they must be available 365 days a year, 24 hours a day. Reporting from school-age children spikes between 3:00 p.m. and 11:00 p.m., when students are out of school and online and may be posting or talking about a breakup, trouble at home, or self harm.

A response team has to be in place to deal with urgent matters like a potential suicide, he said, and it's okay to have the police be that solution late at night and when imminent violence might occur.

In addition, Okuma said, the tipster must be notified within a minute or two that the information has been heard and will be addressed. This gives the program credibility.

In 2018, the North Carolina education system became one more state to utilize the Say Something platform. They now offer training, including a free

"Know the Signs" session for students, teachers, and administrators to share information about how to recognize warning signs and signals from people who may be a threat to themselves or others. They even train students to pass along screen captures of things they might see on social media.

Don't forget, too, that nearly all law enforcement offices have anonymous tiplines to share. The FBI takes calls in its fifty-six field offices around the country, online at tips.fbi.gov, and by phone at 1-800-CALLFBI (225-5324). Word coming in of a potentially violent person in St. Louis but reported in Boston can be relayed back to St. Louis in nearly real time to both federal and local law enforcement.

To market an ARS, find champions to support the system publicly—such as key supervisors, teachers, student body members, or prominent members of the community. When reporting systems are discussed publicly, reporting increases.

"It really is a numbers game, where the more information you receive, the more effective you can be," Okuma told me. "Out of sight, out of mind."

There is no formula for how many tips are enough, but everyone working in this area agrees that no tips or almost no tips means your system isn't working. Nationally only 2 to 5 percent of anonymous tips are consistently found to be non-credible. Those are often made by young people testing the system.

Studies have proven the success of ARSs in the medical field and other areas, but research on education-based ARSs is still in the early stages of validation. One of the first validating these systems is a team from the University of Michigan that includes Justin E. Heinze, Marc A. Zimmerman, Hsing-Fang Hsieh, and Elizabeth Messman (North).

Researchers are seeking to evaluate the effectiveness of the Say Something reporting system, focusing on a large, urban US school district. They are considering whether the system helps to improve the recognition of mental duress, violent antecedents, and other risk behaviors in school communities—and whether violent, criminal, and other risk behaviors among youth are prevented.

Their initial research proved encouraging. An examination of 140 tips collected during the 2019–2020 school year at that school district indicated that students use the ARS to report threats of violence, concerns about the mental health of themselves and peers, and instances of peers engaging in illegal or dangerous behavior (such as alcohol or drug use). A companion study, not yet released, will examine the nature of the tips through several years and the follow-up actions taken.[4]

Once the reporting systems are in place, we reach the third step of the toolbox: assessing and managing threatening behavior.

STEP THREE: ASSESSING
AND MANAGING THREATENING BEHAVIOR

The final step in a good prevention toolbox includes the inseparable pair: threat assessment and threat management. A few definitions:

- *Threat assessment* is a fact-based method of assessment or investigation that focuses on an individual's patterns of thinking and behavior to determine whether, and to what extent, they are moving toward an attack on an identified target.
- *Threat management* is managing a person's behavior through interventions and strategies designed to disrupt or prevent an act of targeted violence.
- *Threat management team* is a cross-functional, multidisciplinary team approach to assess threats and develop threat management strategies.

Threat assessment traces back to work done by the US Secret Service whose analysts were looking for ways to evaluate threatening behavior toward the public figures they protect. They collected and analyzed all potential types of circumstances around a threat.

For example, a threat report might indicate a person in Montana is saying he wants to kill the president. Secret Service investigators must assess the likelihood that this threat could be carried out. Perhaps if the individual is a homeless man, without a car, money, or even shoes, he is not likely to make it to Washington, DC, to harm the president. But if the individual owns several weapons, has the means to get to the nation's capital, and then purchases a plane ticket, his behaviors would put the Secret Service on high alert.

The threat analysis system was developed because the Secret Service knew checklists and profiling were of little value. Even today I am asked about a shortcut or checklist, but, in reality, they are not particularly useful and can, in fact, be harmful to any analysis.

Research on schools around this time by the Secret Service and the Department of Education was a watershed. They found that those intending to commit targeted violence often leaked their intentions to do so to classmates and others around them—and not just a little. In nearly 80 percent of the cases, school shooters shared their plans with at least one person.[5]

The Safe School Initiative, as it came to be known, was the influential work of Robert Fein, Bryan Vossekuil, Marisa Reddy, Randy Borum, William Modzeleski, and William Pollack. Called *Threat Assessment in Schools: A Guide to Managing Threatening Situations and to Creating Safe School Climates*, the final version was released in 2002, changing how threats were analyzed.[6] The companion report, "Implications for the Prevention of School Attacks in the United States,"[7] breathed life into the belief that prevention strategies could be replicated in any school setting. Bolstered by the findings, behavioral experts began recommending that schools adopt a similar method for systematically evaluating threatening behavior.

In the 1990s, a number of analysts and researchers began in earnest to apply threat assessment as a way to avert school shootings. Teams analyzing information on persons of concern came to be known as *threat assessment teams*, or TATs for short. Businesses and the military also began using the term *threat management teams*, or TMTs. I'll just call them TATs here.

These multidisciplinary teams bring together people with various skills. In businesses and organizations, team members may include leadership, human resources personnel, a general counsel, mental health professionals, risk managers, faith leaders, and security experts. In schools, team members may include the dean of students, law enforcement safety officers, school counselors, mental health professionals, coaches, and others.

TATs are one-stop shops designed to bring disparate information together and prevent critical information about a person's behavior from going into an unattended email or voice mail, or from just being shared between two complaining supervisors. Instead, a TAT provides a consistent and reliable place for friends, family, and coworkers to share confidential and sometimes anonymous information about the Joes of the world.

These teams are inherently more agile than law enforcement. With no crime identified, police may not be able to do anything about tips when they are told a person is acting odd or different or strange. In addition, many people are hesitant to call police about a hunch but may be willing to call an ARS.

These teams are essential in evaluating threats of violence, though they are more likely to navigate tips about potential suicides, bullying, domestic abuse, drug addition, alcohol troubles, and other situations where the persons involved may need help and not even know it.

The goal in this chapter is only to introduce you to the makeup and role of a threat assessment team, to explain threat management, and to get you started down the road to evaluate where you and your organization may be in the process of developing a team. Even if you are not part of a threat assessment team, everybody should know that such teams exist and how to interact with them.

A cadre of industry, academic, and health professionals have produced an abundance of books, research, and guidance to set up and run teams. If you are charged with developing a new system for your organization or business, I'd encourage you to look beyond this book to other references, as well. Virtually everything you need to know to set up and run TATs is available and detailed, on the internet, and free. I've referenced some resources here.

Look to the leaders, including the FBI's Behavioral Threat Assessment Center and the US Secret Service's National Threat Assessment Center. In addition, scores of experts offer materials for free via their websites, and most have published books often used in university courses and for reference. Some of the leading minds in this area include Robert Fein, Bryan Vossekuil, Mario Scalora, Frederick S. Calhoun, Stephen W. Weston, Kirk Heilbrun, J. Reid Meloy, Gene Deisinger, Marisa Randazzo, Molly Amman, Karie A. Gibson, Ron Schouten, and Andre B. Simons.

Among the academic leaders in this area is University of Virginia educator Dewey G. Cornell. Cornell, a thoughtful and talented forensic clinical psychologist and professor of education, has worked almost exclusively for two decades on the area of school safety. In 2001, Cornell and his team at UVA released the first evidence-based threat assessment model for schools. By 2013, Virginia became the first state to mandate TATs in all schools. The 156-page manual is for sale for $50 on Cornell's website[8] and through Amazon, but Cornell is so invested in sharing what he knows that the forms to actually do a threat assessment are available for free on his website.[9]

During a 2018 Capitol Hill briefing to discuss seventeen killed at a Florida high school, Cornell explained to Congress why school administrators should shift away from endless spending for building security and focus on prevention:

> Let me suggest to you that if we put a policeman in every single school we may stop one shooting in one building. . . . But if we put another counselor in that school we have the potential to help young people long before they go down the pathway to violence and to prevent shootings all across our community.
>
> Even if we spent the billions of dollars that businesspeople tell us it would take to make our schools absolutely impregnable, that would stop only less than one tenth of one percent of the shootings that take place.

Cornell and his extensive team continue to champion the value of TATs, offering comprehensive and free guides on creating teams as well as a threat assessment decision tree to help TATs, shared in the next chapter.

As a Virginia resident, I've had an up-close look at their efforts, as educators plod through stops and starts to make these teams work. It's a bit of a messy process. Elementary through high school programs in many Colorado schools stand out, too. Nonetheless, nowhere else have university educators worked so diligently on threat assessment and threat management as they have in Virginia.

Other state legislatures followed Virginia with varying determination: Florida, Kentucky,[10] Maryland, Texas, and Washington. Some states have found ways to voluntarily set up TATs.[11]

No states I have found require TATs in a business environment, the place where half of active shootings occur.

Even in the educational setting, however, effective and working teams are not a certain proposition. In the 2015–2016 school year, 42 percent of districts reporting told the Department of Education that they were using a threat assessment team. A majority indicated their teams only met "on occasion" rather than once a month or more frequently. This raises questions about implementation.[12] More recent numbers give encouragement. In 2017–2018, 80 percent of the K–12 schools reporting conducted at least one threat assessment that year.[13]

Privacy Laws and Sharing

An additional, and seemingly formidable, challenge to breaking the sharing barrier is a systemic misunderstanding of what can legally be shared and by whom. This Trojan horse is primarily seen in the worlds of human resources, education, the medical community, and occasionally law enforcement.

Office human resources personnel or school counselors may be in the best position to hear the most valuable tidbits. It may be the coworker who confides that the guy next to him has upped his complaint game and started talking about "solving" the problem. It might be a school counselor or teacher who hears from another student about a student's obsession with school shootings, anger at the principal, or talk of suicide.

But at the same time, too few people in the know are willing to share because they worry they might be sued for privacy violations. Some professionals might not know better; they just know someone told them "laws" prevent them from disclosing anything. I think others hide behind legal barriers because they don't want to get involved. Company human resources staff can be notorious information vaults—all deposits, no withdrawals.

Two federal privacy laws are the most often-mentioned barriers to information sharing, though each state also has privacy laws to hurdle. The first federal law you likely know from signing that paper you never read in the doctor's or dentist's office—the "HIPAA" form. Shorthand for the Health Insurance Portability and Accountability Act of 1996, HIPAA was passed to develop privacy protections in an ever-increasing digital age. The law itself is fantastic, unless your college student asks you to call his doctor and has forgotten to put you on the release list.

Only health care providers, health plans, and health care clearinghouses are covered entities bound by HIPAA, protecting the unauthorized release of Personal Health Information, or PHI. Generally, entities not subject to the

HIPAA privacy rule are plentiful, including employers, religious organizations, most law enforcement, many state agencies, and most people working inside schools and school district buildings.

The second is the Family Educational Rights and Privacy Act, or FERPA, a federal statute that seeks to control the gathering, maintenance, and release of personal information from educational settings: data called Personally Identifying Information, or PII. PII may include names, addresses, date of birth, participation in activities, phone numbers, disciplinary and academic records, and medical status.

When a tip is reported about little or adult Jimmy's growing antagonism toward his teacher or boss, this is often where stewards of information mistakenly believe they cannot identify to anyone else Jimmy's name and other relevant information. Some of that other relevant information could include details about past rule infractions, stressors, mental health challenges, and former run-ins with the law or other employees.

Keepers of the information oftentimes believe they cannot share, but they are wrong.

Both federal laws have detailed exceptions that allow anyone with PII or PHI to disclose that information to assist in resolving issues concerning a person who may be a threat to themselves or others. This might include someone who may be in a more brittle mental state momentarily and where suicide is feared. It could be someone with agonizing family circumstances or stressors or even a person having trouble adjusting to new medications. It could be someone who is involved in conflicts with coworkers, faculty, or classmates.

I am sad for the number of times I've heard school counselors, principals, and others in education parrot what some health care professionals say—that privacy laws and their professional standards prohibit them from sharing information. Every aspect of FERPA or HIPAA limitations has exceptions that allow for disclosure. Federal health care laws and scores of other state privacy laws and professional licensing rules and regulations allow you to set aside those concerns when you believe someone is in danger, and not always just imminent danger.

If your first go-to is that you can't share legally, reconsider your hesitation. It may be closer to the truth to say you don't understand the law or don't want to get involved to resolve a concern. If nothing else, call your general counsel and ask.

The Department Health and Human Services joined the FBI to release written guidance clarifying when it is appropriate and allowable to release PHI *without* that person's authorization:[14]

- To law enforcement officials reasonably able to prevent or lessen a serious and imminent threat to the health or safety of an individual or the public.

- When a covered entity in good faith believes there is evidence of a crime that occurred on the premises.
- When responding to an off-site medical emergency, as necessary to alert law enforcement to criminal activity.

The Department of Education and the FBI jointly released similar guidance for FERPA, noting that FERPA specifically allows for disclosure on matters involving "health and safety."[15] FERPA limits exclude School Resource Officer and "law enforcement unit" records and all personal observations. FERPA governs only educational facilities taking US Department of Education funds and specifically notes that PII can be disclosed to law enforcement without the consent of the named party. Joint ED/FBI guidance notes,

> **Schools may nonconsensually disclose PII from educational records in connection with a health or safety matter.** . . . When an articulable and significant threat exists—anything from an active shooter to a hazardous weather event to a chemical spill—school officials are permitted to disclose PII from educational records to appropriate parties, such as law enforcement, or other individuals [emphasis added].

Given that direction, reporting to law enforcement is likely the safest thing you can do to protect yourself and or your school from a privacy violation lawsuit.

Thoughts about Urgency

Lastly, I cannot stress enough how important it is for each individual to take responsibility for timely reporting what they know and for each business, school, or organization to establish a process to collect and analyze information promptly.

Some behaviors are dire in nature and considered to be behaviors that may signal imminent violence. Consider these signs among the most urgent:

- Fixating or having a preoccupation with a person or cause
- Buying guns or other components for an attack
- Acquiring skills that may be used for an attack
- Testing out ways to breach security
- Halting of prescription medications
- Planning for end-of-life matters, including giving away items
- Preparing a prerecorded audio or written statement and posting items of finality online

There are opportunities to intercede if a person is on the verge of violence, but the window of time may be very small. Having a multitude of ways to collect information and a team to receive and analyze the material swiftly allows for timely and more effective responses. Without a team in place, crisis response may be impossible.

Chapter Six

A Peek Inside
Threat Assessment Teams

Even if all those who see something say something, you may be wondering what happens to all that information going to threat assessment teams, or TATs.

In truth, not too many people know the specifics, and it is that way by design. The personal details of someone's life brought to a TAT can include embarrassing information and may reflect a time in one's life when they are struggling with work, family, school, financial troubles, friends, or physical challenges. Privacy and discretion must be at the forefront of a TAT's work, breaking confidentiality only to those who can help a person who is on a bad trajectory. In addition, laws limit what can be shared, just as law enforcement is limited on what it can share with the public.

Despite that, a brief explanation of the makeup of TATs and the operation of a TAT can assist in understanding how shared information isn't left in an in-basket that no one sees.

TEAMS DOING THREAT
ASSESSMENT AND THREAT MANAGEMENT

If you don't have a threat assessment team and are charged with developing one, there are many resources available to help get you started.[1] In 2018, the US Secret Service released "Enhancing School Safety Using a Threat Assessment Model," which offers these tips for establishing a team:[2]

- A team should have some written parameters that indicate membership desires, the process for taking in and analyzing information, and how it will meet and assess information of concern.

- The makeup is as varied as the needs of the community, and teams should include law enforcement and non–law enforcement. Remember that a good TAT has a great relationship with local law enforcement.
- Pick a set time to meet, which could be once a week, once a month, or just when called. Frequency depends on the volume of information the TAT needs to assess. Start with once every two weeks, for example, and set a time to reassess the workflow.
- The team should keep good records of information received and actions taken.

Here are some basic team operational considerations:

- How strong is the team? Is it a team that exists on paper alone and is not really functioning? Maybe there is a school counselor or principal or a human resources person or clerk working alone to consider random information coming in.
- Sometimes organizations don't have the right mix of people to look at the information as a whole and intercede. One person—particularly the person already responsible for so many other things—is apt to fail to connect the dots and is likely not able to devote the time to properly assess and manage a threat.
- Assess the membership and the members themselves. Look through the matters they have considered, and do a compliance check on your methods. Ask the group whether issues could have been handled better or if there are any changes that might need to be made.
- Do TAT members understand exceptions to privacy laws that allow them to share responsibilities?
- Though the team should include law enforcement support, are these team members aware that arrest isn't the first or preferred goal?
- Is the TAT operating to develop a reputation that information gathered will be evaluated promptly, discreetly, and thoroughly, making the community stronger and more likely to report concerns immediately?

Threat Assessment Operations

Once established, TATs have three primary functions: collect information, assess its value, and design a strategy to help the identified person who may be struggling. A TAT's function complements that of law enforcement, school disciplinarians, and human resources department personnel, since TATs are able to assess and resolve nonemergency matters and situations that do not warrant a call to 911.

Effective TATs meet on a regular schedule to assess information collected from various sources. Perhaps information comes into the team that high school student "Sally" has said she is so mad that she wants to kill someone. For the assessment, one TAT member is assigned to lead an evaluation of the information on Sally. Having one responsible person helps to maintain accountability and prevents any leads from falling through the cracks, particularly if people leave or retire from a school or company.

Maybe the school counselor is assigned this lead, and her initial checks show that Sally was heard making this comment at basketball practice. For a business, the human resources TAT member may be assigned the file, and he may learn that employee Sally made the comment at a union meeting. Whether the assessment is in a high school or a business environment, the TAT's task will be to use their collective skills and knowledge to resolve the concern. This is why the makeup of the team is important. It should reflect the diversity of the needs of the community served and include people who have the ability to make decisions, recommend changes, or act.

Therefore, a school TAT might have principals, counselors, teachers, coaches, a school nurse, in-house school security, and school resource officers. A business TAT might include many of those but also a representative from human resources, managers or executives, or an on-staff industrial psychologist. A religious organization may have clerics and laypersons, including teen group leaders, and congregation members. No matter the team makeup, each should have the ability to get immediate input on the assessment from law enforcement, as well as mental health and social service experts. Assessing the value of the information is a team effort.

For the team to assess Sally's "kill someone" comment, interviews may be required, and the team will need to review electronic and paper records to search out any previous incidents at work, at school, or in the criminal justice system. These could include criminal and mental health records, employee files, disciplinary records, and academic records.

This allows the TAT to look not just at what the last reported item is about Sally but also any history of violence, her exposure as a victim of violence, her mental and behavioral health history, any prior concerns raised, her social support structure, and other stressors in her life.

This may be trickier if Sally is a student who may move from one school to another or who has risen from high school to university. It may be even more challenging if Sally is new to the company or has brought her troubles with her from another city. The latter situation is where law enforcement may be able to help, since officers can quickly contact peers in another city and share concerning behavior without violating privacy concerns.

Cornell's team at the University of Virginia offers a free 23-page, editable document to guide TAT assessments.[3] Though Cornell's work was designed for schools, I know he is a sought-after consultant and his materials are easily adaptable for businesses. Many other threat assessment and threat management resources are widely available, but I reference the work from Cornell's team here because much of what they use, including interview forms and assessment checklists, is available for free in a Word format that is downloadable and alterable. I particularly like the forms for interviewing people because they already have some key assessment questions on the documents. This ensures that the interviewer doesn't miss important items. The guide walks teams methodically through an assessment using a decision tree.

I see two benefits to using a systematic way of evaluating. First, every person on the TAT understands the process and is more likely to apply it without bias. And, second, a consistent assessment method allows TAT members to work more efficiently and faster, preventing wasted time and burnout.

Cornell notes that about 90 percent of threats are resolved quickly, leaving more resources to focus on the remaining 10 percent that comprise the more substantive and serious threats.[4] He recommends using his threat assessment and response protocols decision tree, detailed in figure 6.1.

Analysis begins by assessing whether the threatening material is **substantive** or what Cornell has termed *transient.* **Transient** by definition means something that only lasts momentarily—like the anger you feel when you drop that bag of groceries or hit your hand on a door jamb as you walk by. The anger level is often disproportionate to the actual incident or injury, and the feeling is *transient.* Substantive threats are more of a concern.

Step one in a TAT evaluation is to look at the threat itself by doing interviews and considering circumstances. If Sally's communication or behavior demonstrates an intent to harm someone, then you move to step two. If not, the information is filed away in case another incident raises concerns about Sally.

In Sally's case, wanting to "kill someone" clearly gets her past step one.

In the second step, the TAT considers whether Sally's threat might be an expression of humor, rhetoric, anger, or frustration that can easily be resolved. Maybe Sally retracted the threat; maybe she apologized or had a good explanation. This is when the TAT would determine the threat was *transient* and there was no real intent to cause physical harm.

Initial research into threats at 339 Virginia public schools in the 2014–2015 school year found that 78 percent, or 652 of 841 threats, were categorized as transient threats.[5]

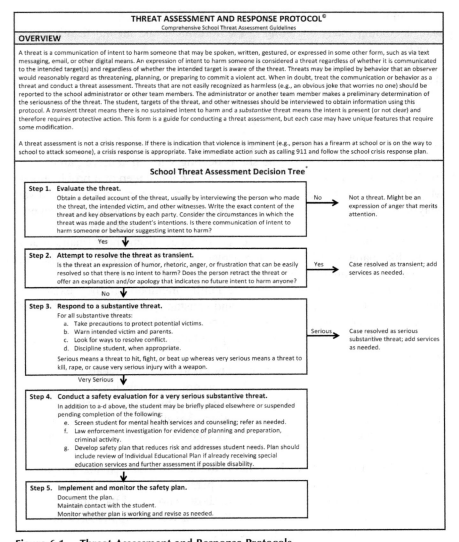

Figure 6.1. Threat Assessment and Response Protocols
Cornell, D. (2018). *Comprehensive School Threat Assessment Guidelines.* Charlottesville, VA: School Threat Assessment Consultants LLC.

If Sally's threat is deemed to be substantive, the TAT shifts into high gear. Their actions may include warning intended victims, parents, and employers to take precautions to protect them. A school-based TAT will look for ways to resolve the conflict, including disciplinary efforts. For businesses, this may be a dismissal, which can be a shortsighted solution if handled messily and Sally returns to take revenge.

The more serious the TAT finds Sally's threat, the more steps the TAT will take, including likely engaging law enforcement and mental health professionals.

Unless the matter merits that 911 call, the TAT's job is to then manage the threat.

Threat Management Operations

A threat management plan should help Sally turn the corner on whatever is going wrong in her life. Maybe she is dealing with an abusive parent or an ill child. Maybe she is dealing with an out-of-control teen or a problem boss. Maybe a relationship or job has ended. Maybe a friend has moved away. Maybe she is under mental health care but not taking her medication properly. Maybe she is hanging with the wrong crowd. Maybe she simply doesn't want to feel so alone. Maybe she feels she cannot get out from under financial debt.

Just like parents, TATs develop a plan to set boundaries, care take, and move a person from concerning behavior to stability.

Team members engage supportive family members, if they exist, help Sally set positive and realistic goals and constantly gauge her receptiveness to assistance. They learn how to help a person of concern develop a healthy social network and develop positive coping mechanisms for real or perceived problems.

Threat management can be a one-day effort or extend years. Often these actions fly under the radar of nearly everyone, so, though you may not see something happening, that does not make it so. This is particularly true where a younger Sally has displayed concerns and a watchful TAT helps guide her through those challenging teenage years where her brain is developing from child to adult.

An endless list of options is available to make this happen and mitigate the situation. If Sally makes the threat to a person at work or school, the TAT could recommend that she apologize to those who heard the threat and help her carry out the apology. This may allay their fears, help her save face, and get her back into her old social structure.

If Sally is a student, a parent conference might be part of a plan if her family can show how they can support her. They could help her build a social network by encouraging her to join school activates, clubs, or sports groups. If Sally has money troubles, financial counseling resources might help, or maybe she can find comfort if encouraged to seek support through a religious organization of choice. Maybe Sally is asked to stop by the school counselor or company industrial psychologist once a week to touch base.

County mental health departments and company employee assistance programs can be a resource for mental health counseling and added support. Sally could be invited to engage with a volunteer group or be asked to mentor or tutor someone to help her gain confidence in her own skills and value. Still, serious threats could result in days off work or school suspensions to give Sally time to cool off. Law enforcement engagement that results in an arrest can be part of a plan too, but most TATs see little information actually rising to that level of concern.

Every situation is unique, so it's impossible to say what is a typical scenario for TAT members as they work through threat assessment and threat management, but their essential duties involve identifying a person of concern and finding ways to help them.

TATs Under Scrutiny

The TAT way of managing threats is not without critics. Many have voiced concerns about TATs unnecessarily tracking, documenting, and elevating what traditionally would have been considered someone's random braggadocio or momentary frustration.

Pennsylvania is one of several states mandating the TAT system in schools, though criticisms occur. In 2019, officers from a police department in Pennsylvania spent time interviewing parents of a six-year-old with Down syndrome who pointed a finger at a school administrator and declared, "I shoot you."[6] When news of the police involvement went public, the parents were frustrated to find the information on their daughter would remain in TAT files, a permanent digital stain on her reputation.

"This is a real setback," Harold Jordan, senior policy advocate at the American Civil Liberties Union of Pennsylvania, told the *Pennsylvania Gazette*. He worried that excessive involvement of police in schools could make students less likely to report concerns to adults. "This is not a process that's going to catch the next school shooter," he said.

And compare that to a recent situation in Los Angeles where a parent of a seven-year-old second grader insisted her daughter be moved from a classroom where a child had written a "kill list" on a piece of construction paper.[7] The classmate was not removed from his classroom because the TAT found the threat to be transient, what with the boy's not even having access to weapons. But the girl's mother felt the school was "brushing it aside," she told the *Los Angeles Times*.

When deciding whether to support a TAT for your business, school, or religious organization, consider this: In June of 2020, Pew Research Center polled 4,708 adults in the United States, asking them how they felt about the "way things are going in this country today." Eighty-seven percent said they were dissatisfied.[8]

Pew researchers also asked those surveyed, "In thinking about the state of the country these days, They feel _____." Americans responded: 71 percent felt angry, and 66 percent felt fearful.

With more states mandating TATs and the social and political climate of the past few years leaving the country angrier as a whole,[9] it seems sensible to encourage more ways to not only detect brittle individuals going down the wrong path but also give them the tools to reverse course.

Right now, I vote yes on TATs.

Chapter Seven

School Building Challenges

On my daily sojourn to keep healthy, I walk past my youngest daughter's old junior high school. The one-story brick building has bird-like wings of classrooms and tinted windows to filter away the baking southern sun. In the spring, I enjoy the flowering cherry and dogwood trees surrounding a front patio filled with pre-fab pink and blue plastic tables and chairs where students meet friends before class. Buses and cars mold around the circular drive and stop within steps of the eight glass doors that welcome students daily. The driveway is about 200 feet long, the length of my driveway. It's a pretty common configuration for suburban and rural school settings.

When my daughter attended this school, the horrendous Columbine shooting had already occurred. Yet, even as a law enforcement officer, I didn't obsess about her safety at school. I freely walked through the unlocked door of the band room off the back parking lot, seeking out my musical wizard. Sometimes I found her there, sometimes in the library, and other times in the gym.

How often have we all thought, *What are the odds of a shooting happening at my child's school? Not likely.* I probably thought that way, too. I rejected the image of terrified kids running from school with their hands up, an image that is now a fixture in our minds.

As a parent you can picture nothing more horrific. As a teacher you fear nothing more. As an administrator you carry no heavier burden.

Yet most parents don't ask and don't know about school safety plans or even what their child has been told to do in an emergency.

Most teachers are struggling just to meet their obligations and focus on student learning, though no one stands more in the line of fire than teachers.

Teachers drill annually on tornadoes and earthquakes and even power outages, but in speaking with many, I have found they fear a shooting more than anything. Ask them if you don't believe me. They try not to visualize what they know they would do to protect their kids. Knowledge reduces stress.

Teacher ethos is what likely gave seventy-six-year-old engineering and science professor Liviu Librescu the strength to hold tight his unlocked door and keep the Virginia Tech shooter from entering his classroom until all but one student had jumped to safety out the second-story windows. Tragically, the Romanian-born survivor of the Holocaust was killed—a life traded to protect his students.

School and district administrators, likewise, carry the burden of responsibility. What did they do—or what have they not done—to prevent violence and prepare the school to respond and recover? What is the responsibility of the school district administration?

Higher education campuses generally have complex security challenges requiring the most targeted and individual security consulting. Most have 24-hour operations in multiple buildings, sometimes scattered around a city, requiring sophisticated security plans that match the most challenging plans for large businesses. Police department and full-time security are on duty daily. And federal and local laws in place provide guidance and more stringent security requirements at the university and college level.

Though much of what I write about applies to higher education, this chapter focuses on the kindergarten-to-twelfth-grade buildings, often stand-alone features. Generally, American schoolchildren are safer than they have ever been. They've been taught how to evacuate a school in a fire, and teachers know how to hustle students and visitors into bathrooms and other concrete structures or to lower levels when a tornado threatens.

Scattered data collected by the federal government supports that school violence and victimization of students in schools is on the decline and students are feeling safer. For example, a Department of Education survey shows that between 2001 and 2017, the percentage of students age 12–18 who reported being afraid of an attack or harm decreased from 6 percent to 4 percent.[1]

The percentage of students in grades 9–12 who reported carrying a weapon on school property during the previous thirty days decreased from 6 percent in 2001 to 4 percent in 2017.[2] The percentage of twelve- to eighteen-year-olds reporting access to a loaded gun without adult permission decreased from 7 percent in 1993 to 4 percent in 2013.

Plowing through this awkwardly collected data from the Department of Education, I found that between 1995 and 2013 students and teachers reported feeling less threatened and saw a decrease in violent acts against them. Some 50 million children attend about 140,000 schools in the United States annually. What are the odds that on any given day a shooter will choose my kid's school from among the 25,000 middle schools? After all, in the past 20 years, the FBI has counted only 62 active shooters in schools.

But then, I'm not a gambler. I don't want to play the odds.

SAFETY PREPAREDNESS

My daughter is now a middle school teacher herself. I know that, with her five-foot-nothing frame, she will do whatever she must to protect her students. I want her to have the best chance at survival, not just pretty good odds.

Before she was "allowed" to start teaching at her first post, we strolled through her newly built school, walking the hallways, looking for exit doors, identifying escape routes and vulnerabilities—perhaps the one advantage of having a mom so focused on security.

Safety isn't about the odds of whether it will happen; safety is about being prepared if it does happen. And, though this chapter focuses on schools, these materials are easily adaptable for your library, government building, place of worship, private company, or organization.

We diligently lock our doors to prevent a burglary every night though only 0.01 percent of the 140 million homes in the United States are burglarized annually.[3] Rarely do we need the spare tire in a car, yet there it is. The ice and snow scraper stay under that front seat even when the sky is clear.

School shootings, though, are so frightening that we tend to look away and not do what we can to be ready. It's easy to believe safety and security are someone else's job. But they aren't, of course, and everyone really wants safe schools. The best news is that school administrators have available to them more free research, training, and analysis materials than ever before.

For example, in 2019 I joined with other criminal justice, education, social work, and public health experts in school safety research and practice to establish the National Center for School Safety (NC2S).[4] NC2S is a clearinghouse for all aspects of school safety, coordinated by a dedicated team at the University of Michigan and funded by the US Department of Justice's Bureau of Justice Assistance, Office of Justice Programs.

The mission of NC2S is to promote school safety and violence prevention through expert-led training and technical assistance—bringing together research and academics with operations and practice.

Safety preparedness has two elements—policies and physical security.

The first—policies—includes rules requiring classroom doors to be locked during school days, prohibiting the propping open of doors, and requiring controlled points of access before, during, and after school hours. It also includes giving guidance on the responsibilities of security personnel and school resource officers, some version of Run. Hide. Fight.® training, and other policies designed to control risk.

Remember too that a policy is only as good as the application learned through procedures and training. Many schools have front doors with buzzers, but who has pushed a buzzer only to hear in reply the familiar click of a lock being released? Do they know who I am? Is that person on the admittance buzzer not trained to inquire, or perhaps they are too far away or too busy to check? That buzzer could be a single point-of-access failure if anyone can come by and push the button just because they hear the bell.

The second part of safety preparedness—physical security—involves assessing vulnerability and finding ways to reduce risk. I'm going to focus on that aspect here, to show how anyone can make their school environment safer, whether they're a parent, administrator, or teacher.

These are the most substantial potential weaknesses in building security:

- Doors and locks
- Vehicle and bus access points
- Windows
- Loading docks, delivery areas, kitchen entrances
- Security patrol areas, including parking lots
- Perimeter fencing
- Proximity and configuration of building and parking spaces
- Alarms and closed-circuit cameras to see who is at entry doors

This list may seem daunting, but attack it the way you would eat an elephant—one bite at a time.

Whether you are a parent, religious leader, or administrator, you can help harden your target. *Hardening your target* means making your location less appealing to troublemakers and criminals. A harder target may discourage a bad actor altogether or delay a person's action, giving potential victims more time to react and police more time to arrive.

One word of caution, though, as you embark on this effort: maintain control of your security plan, and only make the changes that are thoughtfully evaluated. School security is a big business, and there are plenty of companies that will review and assess your building and grounds and provide a long list of recommended changes costing tens or hundreds of thousands of dollars.

A security evaluator could suggest impact-resistant doors, surveillance equipment, and crash-rating tests on walls, and discuss an array of window and wall configurations, supplementing that with bulletproof- or shotgun-resistant glass; don't be overwhelmed. They may even suggest reconfiguring the driveway entrances, putting up roadblocks, using metal detectors, and hiring guards.

Countless products are sold to harden the building from outsiders, and just as many for inside. You can install window coverings in classrooms and buy school desks and whiteboards that are bullet resistant. You can even hand out bullet-resistant backpacks to students.

Some companies offer expensive key fobs and panic alarms, kind of like "Life Alert" for your dad, that come with monthly fees for monitoring. Others offer biometric data systems limiting access to guns and bulletproof vests to turn teachers into first responders.

No criticisms here on spending money to hire a consultant or products to make any building more secure, but I recommend you do some research and get the best bang for your buck. Don't let someone scare you into constructing a fortress by telling you how you must do all kinds of work to protect yourself from future legal action. That's not true. Adequate security is not all-or-nothing or based on must-haves.

SECURITY ASSESSMENT, ONE STEP AT A TIME

Security is an ongoing process, so determine what has already been addressed, and develop an understanding of present security strengths and weakness. Before you spend your limited school funds on an expensive plan you can't afford to implement, do your own assessment of what is needed, and consider what can be done in-house or with in-kind assistance from the community.

For example, every big city property owner knows that well-placed cement-filled flowerpots can stop a car careening down a sidewalk toward a door. This solution works anywhere. Stop by for a selfie in front of my old office at FBI Headquarters on Pennsylvania Avenue in downtown Washington, DC, and see their own rock-filled planters.

Any security assessment is best started at the perimeter of the property to find ways to deter troublemakers or detect problems early. Some troubles have started by someone jumping a low back fence.

Paid security and law enforcement evaluate cars coming to Columbine High School well before cars get to the school entrance doors. The same is true at Los Angeles International Airport—the scene of three shootings— where analytics assist in identifying areas hourly for evaluation of vehicles approaching the airport.

Pedestrian and vehicle traffic at schools makes them very porous, creating an open feeling. But closing gaps to reduce risk is possible. Look where buses load and unload during the morning and evening hours. How often do you see a person standing in the driveway, waving drivers away or waving buses into a parking spot? Maybe someone places orange traffic cones out to discourage people from using certain driveways. People and orange traffic cones are not vehicle deterrents.

With no place to put huge flowerpots in the middle of a street, it might be practical to park employees' cars as well as buses in strategic positions or in a serpentine pattern. This makes it impossible for someone to speed up in a vehicle, whether the intent is to begin shooting, to ram the building, or to strike students at the beginning or end of the day.

It's likely your school has already evaluated the walkways for students, making sure there are clear paths and bright lighting for when it gets dark. If so, you can add to that how to route children walking from vehicles.

State and local laws require safety features in all buildings, and an assessment may show some existing policies and equipment that are not up to speed. A walk around also can show some simple fixes that can be changed by policy, such as locking interior doors between some floors to protect those on upper floors.

Maybe there are proposed changes that were set aside last time, or maybe it is time for a fundraiser for a particular improvement still unmet. Whether you are a parent, a teacher, or an administrator, find out what work has already been done.

If there is no plan and you are starting from scratch, that's okay. If you are reading this because you have safety concerns about your business or organization or maybe about your home or favorite local restaurant, just begin with one item. If you can, recruit a few others for a team to support the effort, whether those are friends, parents, employees, or concerned businesspeople; so be it.

Read, read, read, and check the source for what you are reading to make sure it isn't just someone trying to sell something you might not need. Consider your particular buildings. Modern marvels in educational construction reside in the same districts with sixty-year-old structures whose building codes have long been eclipsed. Modifications to older buildings might trigger a requirement that the building be brought up to existing codes.

Begin with the many free checklists available through the Federal Emergency Management Agency and other school safety resources.[5] If you are a business or a religious organization with or without a school, you can do the same. This may seem like a slow method, but it is important to be realistic. Whatever deficiencies exist now, you can improve your situation with every step you take.

Take a walk around your building, inside and out. If you are working security as an extra task, ask someone from the police or fire department to walk the building with you on a school day. Parents and other advisors might see what you may not. An hour or two on a Saturday could do the trick; however, assessing during operations is even more valuable.

Start with one item on your list above. Maybe you start on one a week or one a month or one a quarter. As you consider your initial assessments, accept that the answers rarely are all simple, quick, or inexpensive. After a Transportation Security Administration worker was shot in 2013 at Los Angeles

International Airport, executives developed a 100-item checklist of improvements and changes, many of which took years to implement. It's okay to be aspirational.

Doors and Locks

After you've taken an initial assessment, I suggest you begin with doors and locks. Some of you might be giving a slight shrug of your shoulders while silently saying, "A door is a door, a lock is a lock." Not really. Doors are the most critical physical aspect of security in any building.

In hundreds of shootings I've worked and researched, open and unlocked doors made the difference between life and death. These include unlocked doors and doors teachers weren't able to lock in time, allowing a murderer to enter. Professor Librescu was compelled to try to hold his unlocked classroom door shut against the shooter at Virginia Tech. A teacher at Sandy Hook Elementary School was shot when she stepped out into the hallway to lock her door.

Doors don't just keep shooters out; we know they also let survivors escape. More and more schools recognize that classrooms should have an escape route besides the main door into the hallway. Nine first graders were able to flee from their Sandy Hook classroom thanks to an available alternate door and the bravery of their teacher, Victoria Leigh Soto, who died in the shooting.

Assess exterior doors individually; how they open, when they are locked, and who has access to them. Then do the same for interior doors, many of which have no locking mechanism at all and may need a jamming mechanism to keep the door shut in an emergency.

Front doors are the most common point of entry for trouble, but not always. The Columbine shooters entered in the back, where the cafeteria was located. Often schools leave doors unlocked by the cafeteria to allow students to enjoy the outdoors.

School shootings can occur at any time of the day, but research shows the early morning and the end of the school day are the most frequent times, validating the criticality and risk associated with open and unguarded doors, even outside of class times.

Violence also can begin before a shooter gets to the door. In FBI research, 14 percent of school shootings began outside of a building, and the vast majority happened outside the classroom. The most frequent starting location for these attacks inside was in the hallways of the buildings (28 percent), followed by classrooms (22 percent), administrative offices (17 percent), and cafeterias (11 percent).

Some classrooms may have back doors. This is particularly true for music rooms and gym areas or in newer buildings. Large doors are located in the back or on the sides of schools where loading docks and doors exist for deliveries. Every kitchen likely has a door or two for deliveries, sometimes propped open. Are there doors less obvious to the casual observer? What about that always-open door students and faculty use as a shortcut?

You may consider how you could add or change the configuration of the doors in the school, whether by adding new exterior doors or putting in doors between rooms. That may seem ineffectual, but I do know that schools have added strategically placed, additional doors in the backs of classrooms to give students and faculty better escape routes, Columbine among them.

Every school is built differently, and the way a door swings open, how it is locked, and how it can be blocked is generally governed also by local fire and municipal codes. Don't choose a one-size-fits-all plan for your building that will only work on certain doors.

As you assess how you can improve the entry and exit areas around buildings, engage the local fire inspector, village engineer, or city planner for advice. Doorstops and other products can hold doors closed in an emergency, but check first with those offices to see what's within code. Don't waste money on gadgets you find on the internet or via email advertisements that you can't ultimately use because they don't meet code.

Door locks can be complicated too. Assess whether your school has key locks, push-button locks, or push-bar locks and mechanisms that prop doors open.

The estimated $48 million in repairs and improvements made after the Virginia Tech shooting, paid for by Virginia taxpayers, included $2 million to retrofit more than 1,000 door locks in 150 buildings.[6] The change came after investigators learned the shooter chained together push-bar doors to prevent entry, delaying responding officers. Another factor to note—no classroom doors were locked during that attack, allowing the shooter to enter several rooms to shoot students, including entering one room three times.

Locks on doors and key access is a practical need in schools to control mischief or worse. The Columbine shooting illuminated the vulnerable moment when a teacher has to step into a hallway to lock a door. Some schools began installing new locks, commonly referred to as Columbine locks, which allow doors to be locked from both the inside or outside while still meeting fire safety codes. These also allow students and teachers to exit the locked classroom door.

In 2008, just a week after a shooter killed five people and injured twenty-one others at Northern Illinois University, the San Mateo, California, school district authorized spending $263,000 to buy and install 581 Columbine locks for its schools.

And don't assume the newer buildings have the best safety measures. My daughter teaches in a school building constructed in 2018 with classroom doors that must be key locked from the hallway.

A few years ago, Columbine High School Principal Frank DeAngelis walked me around his school as he discussed the heroics and tragedies of that day in 1999. The school doesn't look like a fortress of bulletproof glass and metal detectors. It remains a warm and inviting place to learn. They made changes thoughtfully.

When evaluating policies, write tight and enforceable policies on when and who has authority to lock and unlock doors. As school starts and ends, consider having a school resource officer or another security person on guard to watch for safety concerns instead of adding this burden to the principal, who is there to greet students. Trained officers scan the parking lot, approaching cars, and the surrounding area as a matter of habit. If possible, require all students and faculty to enter the school through a few doors or areas where watchful eyes can take note of potential trouble.

Determine who is responsible to ensure each door remains closed and locked during the school day. This is one of the common security breaches I hear about. Someone has propped a door open to take a smoke break or let in a friend. Maybe the air circulation in the gym begs for propped-open exterior doors. Find the reason why the doors are left open, and fix the genesis of the problem. High school kids prop doors open all the time so mom can come by with the homework and textbook they forgot, dad can bring a Starbucks coffee, or a friend can sneak in.

Deliveries during school hours also expose those inside to risk. Loading dock doors should remain closed and locked. Is there a policy on when deliveries can be made and how they are handled? Most deliveries can be anticipated and scheduled, allowing for someone to accept the delivery and also open a locked door.

Don't minimize the benefit of minor changes. Researching hundreds of shooters, only one or two have ever taken the time to breach a locked door. Secured doors make it harder for a shooter to enter, and shatterproof or bulletproof film on glass doors or windows provides even more opportunities to prevent or reduce casualties.

One more thought on doors: Consider what is right inside those doors and who is the most vulnerable. Ask yourself, *If someone enters with a weapon or smashes through the front with a vehicle, even by accident, who is more at risk? What simple steps can be taken that might make the people inside safer? Can desks be moved away from the windows and doors? Is there a way to move back the queues for students waiting to board buses?*

With this much analysis on the first item on the list—doors and locks—you can see why I suggest you take one item at a time if that works best. The other security improvements might not be as daunting. But Rome wasn't built in a day, and neither is good security.

Don't Forget the Small Stuff

While I have filled your head with thoughts of expensive projects like installing new doors, remember, some of the simplest and most overlooked things you can do today can help keep people safe in your building.

For example, provide easy-to-affix window coverings to classroom windows—don't just talk about doing it. A parent group or a scout looking for an Eagle Scout project could undertake this charge. I live near the Manassas National Battlefield, where my Eagle Scout organized the clearing of the main hiking path. Scouts are always looking for projects they can plan and manage.

Another important task for schools—take "active shooter" off the taboo-to-talk-about list. Talk openly with your staff about the rare but real possibility of an active shooter at your school. Ask them what they fear, what they would like changed, and how the school could be better prepared. They know their school.

One of my personal missions is to have every building, school or otherwise, affix emergency information inside each room, perhaps by the light switch or telephone handsets, or both. Just like the exit signs over doors that can send us to safety, affixing accurate emergency numbers, the building address, and the room location can save lives.

Anyone who has stayed at a hotel has seen the maps on the back of the door that tell you where you are in the building, the escape routes, and the name and address of the hotel. This came about as hotel use grew and emergency calls left dispatchers and hotel guests struggling to identify where to send first responders.

In the same way, every building owner should be required to place a plaque or sticker by every light switch or on every door to identify the building address and room numbers, printing them in glow-in-the-dark materials. A panicked student calling 911 or a stressed visitor or teacher can turn to the signs by every interior door to retrieve this critical information.

Buildings with addresses posted on the front and address signs near the curb help dispatchers and first responders too. Few can be as coolheaded as the manager in Aurora, Colorado, who described to me how, in 2012, she stepped into her office to call for help while a shooter was killing twelve and wounding seventy in the theater with a semiautomatic rifle just 20 feet away from her. In the 911 dispatch audio playback, you hear her calmly identify herself, indicate a suspected shooting in Theater 9, and relay the address—14300 East Alameda Avenue—all in one sentence. This at the same time dispatchers were receiving calls like, "Help! I'm at the Century 16 theater. Please help. Oh my god, there are bodies everywhere. Please help."

The School Resource Officer Debate

Ask five people, and you'll get six opinions about whether school resource officers (SROs) are a welcome addition to the kindergarten-through-twelfth-grade school security plan.

As school shootings have increased in the last twenty years, many schools have embraced the addition of SROs, though many have struggled in recent years with the legacy left behind from confusion over the role of SROs in discipline, including those sometimes employing heavy-handed tactics.

The killing of George Floyd on a street in Minneapolis in the spring of 2020 ignited a new level of debate about SROs.[7] Districts in Minneapolis, Seattle, Chicago, Los Angeles, Portland, Oregon, and others quickly announced plans to remove SROs altogether or had citizens or teachers' unions insist they do so. Anecdotes in support evidenced children pepper-sprayed, on-camera body slams, arrests, and officers using other intimidation techniques against students.

Poorly structured use of SROs can be part of the problem. Well-intentioned zero-tolerance programs have had documented negative effects in juvenile dropout rates, juvenile court rates, and the school-to-prison pipeline. These programs can isolate and exclude students at a time when they need support the most, prompting some to question their effectiveness or value.

In a Congressional briefing in 2018, UVA's Dewey Cornell warned lawmakers that the $5 billion spent on school security around the country after the Sandy Hook shooting took money away from more important prevention programs, such as counseling and anti-bullying programs.[8]

And yet a massive student and faculty climate survey of Virginia schools conducted by Cornell's team in 2019 found 73 percent of students and 85 percent of staff agreed or strongly agreed that having an SRO in the school made them feel safer.[9] The survey illuminated the racial disparity in those feelings, with 32.5 percent of Black students disagreeing or strongly disagreeing that SROs make them feel safe. This compares to roughly 25 percent of students identified as "White" who feel that way.

Equally instructive is the relatively limited contact students have with SROs. The survey asked students how often they've spoken with the SRO during the previous school year and found a range from weekly or every day (6 percent) to once or twice a semester (23 percent) to never (71 percent). This is the most expansive survey every done looking at attitudes toward

SROs. It included approximately 106,000 students and 15,000 staff from 299 schools. The schools were located in rural and suburban areas, in densely and lightly populated areas, and were comprised of students from all socioeconomic levels.

Poor training or no training for SROs is partly to blame. SROs assigned twenty years ago were often the officer who couldn't hack it on the street, the guy too overweight to chase suspects, someone ready to "retire" to a slower job, or a person under disciplinary action who was being punished with the assignment. There were just as many and maybe more through the years who became welcome fixtures in schools, supporting students and enhancing the relationship between law enforcement and even the most jaded student.

Training and SRO programs have come a long way since then, and some states require SRO-specific training before an officer can be assigned to a school. In the 2021–2022 school year, my company created six digital shorts with the National Center for School Safety to train SROs. These free resources are a great place to start if you want to better understand their role and how SROs can have a positive impact.[10]

Templates are available for well-crafted memorandums of understanding (MOUs) based on best practices. They guide SROs on how to avoid arresting or disciplining students.[11] Strong SRO programs give students confidence in law enforcement, although many barriers to trust remain.

Shootings often end before police have a chance to arrive, so having a trained law enforcement officer in the house may make a difference—this despite those celebrated disasters where an SRO fails to act. Guns in schools are addressed in another chapter, but having an SRO in your school is way, way more about having another good role model in the school who is there to help. This is consistent with a number of research efforts that have focused on how students perform better when they have a positive perception about school safety.[12]

John McDonald is Executive Director of the Department of School Safety for Jeffco Public Schools, home to Columbine High School. The job is challenging, he told me, as the area has suffered from nine separate school shootings within a few miles of each other in recent history.

McDonald's team of 157 people includes thirty-three armed officers working with eight surrounding law enforcement agencies. His $6.1 million budget for the 2019–2020 school year was in addition to the $4.5 million local law enforcement budget, covering the cost of forty SROs.

The same year, McDonald's team responded to 4,200 incidents in a district with 86,000 students in 157 schools. Many, he explained, dealt with people who wanted to feel and experience Columbine. The district's threat assessment team identified fifty-two threats that rose to the level of active threats, and twenty-seven guns were taken off of students.

McDonald's advice? Have the conversation in your community, and own your security. He doesn't mean hire security; he means make the decision that is best for your district.

One size does not fit all. One of my consulting clients is a large hospital system that has some hospitals with armed guards and others without. I discourage you from listening to others who say you must do this or must do that. It has to work for your district and even for each school. Remember to weigh available budget funding, response time for law enforcement, threats facing the community, crime rates, and other factors. Either way, I think all would agree with Cornell when he says, "Our decisions about school safety have to be based on a careful analysis of the facts and not just be driven by fears and emotions, however important they are."

BALANCING SAFETY WITH CREATING A HEALTHY SCHOOL CLIMATE

When the Virginia Tech shooting occurred, I did not know I would become friends with one of the most seriously injured survivors, Kristina Anderson. She has dedicated her life to supporting other survivors and engaging everyone around her in the topic of campus safety. Her own words are saved for a later chapter.

Kristina and I travel in the same circles and are often invited to speak at the same conferences. She shares her unique life story and asks people to focus on what they can do to open their eyes to the vulnerabilities in front of them.

"People don't take as much agency about safety until it's personal, so I try to make them understand that the tools they need are often already at their disposal," Anderson told a group gathered on the tenth anniversary of the Virginia Tech shooting.

Balance is key to maintaining a good climate while improving safety. When students feel they are taking classes in a correctional facility, their stress levels go up, and the school environment suffers. Creating a good school climate is as important as securing the building. Remember, FBI research found that five of six middle school shooters and twelve of fourteen high school shooters were students at their own schools.

So how can improvements be made to appear less intrusive when you are trying to block front doors from vehicle attacks? Swing by a Target store and notice the huge red balls in front—vehicle assault deterrents.

An entertainment company I worked for faced the same dilemma when our security team set about evaluating how they were protecting entrances to their dozens of outdoor amphitheaters, a move made while hoping to obscure the harsh reality of added security. The amphitheater closest to my home has a very savvy general manager who learned the business from his father and knows how to spend his pennies wisely. To protect the front, he used a forklift to move huge boulders from around his property into strategic places like sidewalk entrances and in front of the box office. He created vehicle assault deterrents.

You may not have boulders sitting around your school property, but look around for them, stop at a rock quarry, or maybe ask a building company to keep an eye out for something they need to get rid of on a construction site. I assure you, these boulders can become focal points for school pride. Virginia construction often involves blasting caps, and the large rocks left behind are painted by students to celebrate graduation, memorials, or monthly causes.

Another overlooked but often-used free item that can protect front doors are vehicles themselves. Faculty cars, the many buses, and police cars are already on-site. A line of buses or cars at a curb will make a vehicle attack on the front doors nearly impossible.

IDEAS TO SUSTAIN SECURITY EFFORTS

Sustaining your focus on security is essential, too. Lots of security preparation happens with a single plan, and then everybody seems to forget about it. Consider these added ways to improve security long term:

- If you have a parent-teacher group, ask them to send an email to parents seeking volunteers to join a security advisory council. It's a bonus if any have experience in emergency management, security, law enforcement, engineering, and more. They are there; just ask.
- Volunteers can draft some policies, take notes, and meet with city administrators to lighten the load and review plans annually. Though safety is a continuing concern, that first safety evaluation is the most difficult.
- If your school district is large and has resources or a facilities director tasked with security, consider enlisting a consultant for limited hours to review policies and do a walk-through to see what you may not see. It may only cost the district or school the price of the consultant's afternoon.
- Or use a small team of employees who can look at these exterior items in a comprehensive way every few years. They can weigh priorities based on risk and recommend what to ask for that year in funding and personnel assistance.

- A district with multiple buildings should consider the risk to students in each of the buildings equally. Though the number of school shootings varies by grades, the numbers are small and not statistically significant. Therefore, don't consider the students in a particular age or grade to be more or less at risk.

And don't be myopic. Are you talking to the neighbors around your building? Do the neighboring businesses and residents know what is going on at your school and where to call if they have a concern? They may not be inclined to call police if they see someone walking out the front door of the school on a Sunday or rummaging around the front bushes before class. Maybe you would want them to call you or a designated person.

Positive Impact

Right now, a majority of US teens ages 13 to 17 (or 57 percent) fear a shooting could happen at their school, and most parents of teens share their concern.[13] Those numbers should not discourage you but instead encourage you. Every single step you take to improve awareness about safety will count toward allaying their fears. Remember, most violent incidents end in five minutes or less, and half of those in two minutes or less. Lives have been saved by a locked door—ten seconds to flee or warn others by intercom, and a few more seconds to call 911.

Layers of security delay a potential shooter, and every step taken can impact the effectiveness of a shooter's plan. Done right, students will react positively to the changes.

Progress and Perspective

Hardening your school from targeted violence is incredibly important but must be done in conjunction with other efforts to improve school climate. Remember that middle school and high school shooters often attend the school they attack.

Now that I have another teacher in the family, I have joined the legions of those who are connected to schools directly. I worry more because I know my daughter is at the mercy of her district's budget and she is on the front line of helping maturing students find their way in this challenging world.

And nowadays, my daughter's old junior high building is still on my exercise route. It has remained nearly the same in the dozen or so years since I needed to run missing lunch money over to her. But what my eyes see now is vastly different.

Huge numbers are over the doors to help first responders. Those tinted windows prevent someone outside from easily looking in. I am happy to see a buzzer at the front door and a police car at the school that was not there when my daughter attended.

But improvements must be ongoing. That expanse of welcoming front doors and windows likely creates a sense of false security, as a fast-approaching car could kill anyone queued on the inside. The police car? It's still parked over on a side access road.

And on my daily walk, as I turn the corner and pass by, I often whisper to myself, *Please move that police car up by the front doors.* They've made progress, but, like in every school, security changes come one move at a time.

Chapter Eight

Workplaces and Houses of Worship

"If someone runs past me shooting an AR-15, should I stay at the gate and direct people out?"

I gave him a minute to consider what he had asked. "No, run!" I said emphatically to our employee. He gave me a smirk, knowing he already knew the right answer. *Of course* he needed to run.

But at the same time, the question reminded me that this $10-an-hour employee, training in the hot summer sun of Austin, Texas, was mistakenly more worried about losing his job at Stubb's Bar-B-Q than getting shot.

His question speaks to the complexities of emergency planning, not only for billion-dollar corporations, such as the one for which I was working at the time, but for smaller public and private environments that include an estimated 350,000 religious congregations,[1] a million-plus restaurants,[2] and some 30 million other small businesses in the United States.[3]

Some locations may be held together by volunteers, part-time workers, and revolving personnel. Training money is a rare commodity. The same person who is interviewing people to hire may be working behind a counter and sweeping the floors at night. In houses of worship, the spiritual needs of the congregation take priority, and limited funds are more likely designated for benevolent efforts than security.

Businesses are the most common target for active shooters, and those open to the public are twice as likely to fall victim to such a shooting.[4] These facilities are often designed to encourage visitors and, as a result, are most vulnerable to unexpected violence. Less frequently targeted, houses of worship are often victims to planned and targeted attacks by those seeking to commit hate crimes. Their open schedules of public events add to their vulnerability.

At times, leadership fails to prepare because they believe prevention efforts are too expensive and difficult, they are afraid, or they simply don't believe they will ever be targeted.[5] It's easy to be a bit shortsighted when you're just trying to keep the light bill paid.

But after a disaster, communities need their houses of worship and businesses open to facilitate healing.

If you read the school chapter, you already know the basics about building security. If you skipped it, go back and read it. Educational facilities, like hospitals, are more often mandated to have emergency-operations plans and therefore have plenty of free and up-to-date online resources.

Any way to make your facility a less desirable target is the way to start. The shooter at the Pulse nightclub in Orlando, Florida, drove around for hours looking for a desired target and, investigators believe, was within feet of the House of Blues on the Disney Boardwalk before the presence of law enforcement officers appeared to have scared him away, along with his cache of weapons hidden in a baby carriage. He wanted to bring death to someplace, but his choice was just random.

The lesson here is that, with judicious use of time now, small steps matter in preventing disaster later.

In February of 2014, the Shelby County Sheriff's Office teamed up with the FBI to provide active shooter training to the vendors at Oak Court Mall in Memphis, Tennessee. A few weeks later, shoppers were running from a shooter to save their lives.

Word came back to me at FBI headquarters that the mall had been shut down in "less than a minute" and that store employees knew to "pull people into their stores and pull down their gates." Store clerks, consistent with the one-hour training they had received, shepherded the shoppers who were packed into the mall into back rooms to safeguard them.

In this chapter, I'll address some best practices and must-haves that are specific to houses of worship and businesses, many of which apply to both.

WHERE DOES WORKPLACE VIOLENCE FIT IN?

It's likely the term *workplace violence* is more familiar to most than *targeted violence*. The terms aren't interchangeable, but they do overlap.

Workplace violence is defined as any act or threat of physical violence, harassment, intimidation, or other threatening and disruptive behavior at a work site.[6] Generally, workplace violence includes a large swath of incidents that might occur at a particular location, often perpetrated by employees, resulting in the disruption of operations.

In 2011, the Occupational Safety and Health Administration (OSHA) reported approximately two million Americans were victims of workplace violence each year, costing businesses up to $120 billion annually.[7] Every day, on average, two people are killed and eighty-seven are injured as a result of workplace violence.[8]

Targeted violence can be the result of workplace violence, but it also can include violence that spills over to a location simply because of the ability of a shooter to access that particular house of worship or business location. An estimated 15 percent of women and 6 percent of men are stalked at some point in their lifetimes, with some of that violence spilling over into the workplace.[9]

An estranged husband was the shooter in a 2012 incident at a day spa in Brookfield, Wisconsin, that left three killed and four injured. This workplace violence incident also was categorized as an active shooting because of the ongoing risk to the innocent victims at the time. And then, consider that workplace violence was ruled out as a cause two months later when a twenty-two-year-old active shooter killed two adults and injured a fifteen-year-old girl when he fired on people as he walked around a mall in Oregon.

The different terms are literally just academic. Researchers parse out a variety of terms as a way to explain their methodology in choosing to look at some incidents and not others. Preventing violence and preparing people to react to it involve the same actions, whether researchers categorize what happens as workplace violence, active shootings, targeted violence, domestic violence, mass killings, or anything else.

It's more important that you prepare and less important what terms are used. Many workplace violence programs exist, some even mandated by state laws, and generally involve training of some sort. So, if you have a prevention effort in place, that's a great place to start, and enhance from there.

In my consulting business, I sometimes see unnecessary stovepiping where one person owns security, one owns workplace violence, and others own efforts to improve the office climate and support inclusion. They are all struggling to have their message heard when they might be better able to address these issues if they worked in concert.

HOUSES OF WORSHIP

Active shooter and *house of worship* aren't words that anyone wants to hear together, but we do. Each time something happens, victims and survivors struggle with the question of why it happened. But shooting motivations can vary from terrorism to robbery to hate crimes to domestic acts and random violence.

Hesitation to train seems, however, to stem from faith leaders' oftentimes-unfaltering belief in the goodness of humankind. Their hope is that if they can be more attentive, more caring, more aware, then these things just won't happen. But they do. To note some from the last decade:

- Tree of Life, L'Simcha Congregation, Pittsburgh, Pennsylvania—eleven killed, six injured.
- Living Church of God, Brookfield, Wisconsin—seven killed, four wounded.
- Jewish Federation of Greater Seattle, Seattle, Washington—one killed, five wounded.
- Youth With A Mission Training and New Life Church in Arvada, Colorado—four killed, five wounded.
- Tennessee Valley Unitarian Universalist Church in Knoxville, Tennessee—two killed, seven wounded.
- Sikh Temple of Wisconsin, Oak Creek, Wisconsin—six killed, four wounded.
- First Baptist Church of Sutherland Springs, Texas—twenty-six killed, twenty wounded.
- Burnette Chapel Church of Christ in Nashville, Tennessee—one killed, six wounded.
- al-Furqan Masjid, Queens borough, New York, New York—two killed.
- Emanuel African Methodist Episcopal Church in Charleston, South Carolina—nine dead.

Some faith leaders want to believe it won't happen to them, but, as with hurricanes and tornadoes, faith can't stand in place of preparedness. No one discounts the need for fire extinguishers in a building even if people are praying to protect the building from fire.

In 2012, who could have predicted a homeless man who had been turned away at the church food bank for coming too often would come back to kill a priest, a church secretary, and himself at St. Peter's Episcopal Church in Ellicott City, Maryland? But it happened.

Faith leaders are intertwined with their community, and the idea that anyone in their flock might perpetrate violence is often another reason why preparing for disaster is put on the back burner. So, the first step in preparedness is changing the mindset in the faith community to believe that such inexplicable violence can happen.

I recall being on a conference call at the US Department of Justice with hundreds of faith leaders and one of them saying he had too much trouble with the "fight" part of Run. Hide. Fight.® training. He said he would likely to try to reason with a shooter or even pray with them instead of attacking them. It's not in faith leaders' nature to respond violently even to a violent person, he said.

I appreciate that, I told him, but these shooters have already killed or decided to kill, and confronting them with words may be fatal. And faith leaders are often the target of the violence themselves. Besides, I encouraged them, putting an effective team together is less of a challenge in the faith-based community as long as leadership is amenable to letting others help. Sometimes stubbornness about being the leader of the flock prevents this, so if that's you, please reconsider.

Faith organizations have deep ties into the homes and families of a community, and trained staff and congregants are more likely to see and identify suspicious behavior early. With this deep bench, faith communities too can build a strong threat assessment team by tapping into their membership, which may already include mental health professionals, law enforcement, schoolteachers and district officials, and human resources experts.

To protect their charges, I urge faith leaders to lead by planning and providing training so that every community member has a chance to think about what they might do if confronted by a shooter, whether at home or during services.

The Department of Homeland Security (DHS) and the Federal Emergency Management Agency (FEMA) provide a great assessment checklist for faith-based organizations.[10] The list will ensure you are assessing not only the physical security of buildings but also whether you have developed an adequate emergency operations plan and threat assessment team and established training on See Something, Say Something and Run. Hide. Fight.®

Spending time to take a general physical accounting of your building and grounds is a great first step. For houses of worship, begin by downloading a copy of the "Guide to Developing High Quality Emergency Operations Plans for Houses of Worship."[11] The guide was released in 2013 by our White House–led team and offers a specific section on incorporating active shooter considerations into emergency operations plans.

"Understandably, this is a sensitive topic," the guide's authors note. "As appropriate for the house of worship's congregation, it may be valuable to schedule a time for an open conversation regarding this topic. Though some congregants or staff may find the conversation uncomfortable, they may also find it reassuring to know that as a whole their house of worship is thinking about how best to deal with this situation."[12]

FEMA also has put together free webinars, including one that guides viewers through the development of an emergency operation plan for houses of worship, and other webinars focus on keeping offices and community centers safe.[13] If your house of worship already has an emergency operations guide, reevaluate whether it has adequate planning for situations that involve active shooters and other targeted violence.

In 2019, the DHS released a ten-minute film filled with interviews from individuals from different faith communities.[14] Standing in their sanctuaries, they provide their own tips, encouraging faith communities to work together, to get to know first responders, and to seek out their advice on security matters.

FEMA resources are comprehensive, so make sure you look at the links I provided in the notes section at the back of the book, and search for the particular advice on active shooter preparedness, because you'll find it in the same place as their hurricane and tornado preparedness materials.

If you are a team of one, you might consider putting together a less-complicated plan initially. Near my home in Virginia, the City of Fairfax offers a very nice and simple how-to guide for houses of worship that includes the following recommendations on incorporating plans for active shooters:[15]

- Describe the policies and procedures for the response to an intruder/active shooter situation, including alerting staff and visitors to the threat and notifying them of the all-clear signal.
- List the roles and responsibilities of staff/lay personnel during intruder/active shooter incidents, those such as schoolteachers, ushers, and greeters.
- Describe the facility lockdown process so entry and exit to all parts of the facility can be controlled. List when and how this process was tested.
- Describe the process to minimize and control points of access and exit in buildings and areas without use of lockdown procedures.[16]

Also, don't overlook the free support you can get by asking local first responders.

SECURITY IS A COST CENTER

In all aspects, security is generally considered a budget *cost center*, meaning it provides no revenue to the company's coffers. Year-to-year, this means that security-minded managers are competing with the corporate budgets for operations, research and development, and equipment and supplies as they seek money for training and equipment.

In this section, I'll highlight a handful of must-haves for businesses, including a check on company culture, threat assessment teams, crisis communications planning, and crisis response teams.

Once you start the conversation at the office, you may be surprised where it goes. At one meeting with business leaders a few years ago, security directors spent the day dissecting the challenges of the ever-increasing active shooter situation and focused all morning on why they couldn't afford to put more money into security.

No added revenue, no return on investment, and low probability of occurrence, I heard. Others mentioned competing mandatory and priority training on privacy, workplace violence, civil rights matters, cyber security, worker's compensation, and more. Still others feared training for active shooters would just scare people.

As the day progressed, more voices with experience took to the floor, and a better appreciation of the devastation that comes with a shooting and the choking cost of recovery emerged. We have all learned during the COVID-19 pandemic that closing a business, even temporarily, is expensive. In fact, lost revenue is one of the largest residual costs identified when calculating losses after an active shooter incident or any violent or human-made situation that closes down a business.

When the Los Angeles city schools closed for a day in 2015 because of identified threats, district officials estimated the costs to be at least $29 million.[17] After the 2017 shooting at Fort Lauderdale–Hollywood International Airport, officials spent $832,000 to reunite travelers with their luggage and to replace carpet and tiles. Another $314,000 was paid just to evaluate an assessment of the airport's crisis response.[18] Shutting down an entire terminal for a day and stopping all domestic and international travel was just one of the costs incurred in 2013 after a shooting at Los Angeles International Airport.

Lawsuits follow all shootings and go on for years. Out-of-court settlements for lawsuits arising out of workplace violence average $500,000 per person, with jury verdicts averaging about $3 million. In all, it is estimated that American businesses lose approximately $36 billion per year as a result of workplace violence, with much of that resulting from shootings. This figure includes monetary costs from lost productivity, legal fees, settlement costs, and jury verdicts.[19]

MGM, owner of the Mandalay Bay hotel, agreed to pay shooting victims a total of up to $800 million after the active shooter attack at Live Nation's country music festival in Las Vegas, $49 million over the company's insurance limit.[20] As a promoter of the event, Live Nation was sued in a class action by ticketholders seeking refunds, as well as by those injured.[21]

Millions are spent on rebuilding efforts. The Sandy Hook rebuild cost about $50 million. The same goes for unanticipated costs to train new employees. One source I recall estimated that as many as half of affected employees choose to leave a business after an act of violence at their workplace.

Employees sue, alleging that the employer failed to provide a safe workplace, pursuant to Section 5(a)(1) of OSHA's General Duty Clause, which mandates that employers provide employees "employment and a place of employment which are free from recognized hazards that are causing or are likely to cause death or serious physical harm to his employees."

Shootings may seem unpredictable and therefore outside the scope of the clause, but the courts and OSHA distinguish between unpredictable and a recognized hazard. An OSHA opinion letter indicates a violation may occur when a company "does not take reasonable steps to prevent or abate the hazard."[22]

In 2002, OSHA reported that workplace violence has emerged as an important safety and health issue in today's workplace. The most extreme form, homicide, is the third leading cause of fatal occupational injury in the United States.[23] In addition to those murdered, about 18,000 workers per week are victims of nonfatal workplace violence.[24]

Legal actions will focus on whether a company could have predicted the hazard of an active shooter and what reasonable steps were taken to prevent or minimize the hazard. Now uncertainty has given way to certainty. It's clear that ignoring the potential risks of violence is not a good business practice. OSHA has an extensive resource page for businesses, including a whole area devoted to advising on the need to provide active shooter training to employees.[25]

Proactive measures can potentially help lower insurance too. In 2016, Forest Lake, Minnesota, spent $130,000 on security enhancements, including a new key-card access system, panic buttons, and bullet-resistant protection where the public approaches personnel[26]—worth a discussion with your insurer.

COMPANY CULTURE

Brittle people may be less likely to act out violently when the culture or climate at their workplace is more compassionate. I recall many witness interviews and much investigative work indicating some people or places had been spared because of acts of kindness.

A warning though: changing the business culture to be more compassionate is a slow process that must be regularly nurtured. Culture change isn't putting a poster up near the wall-mounted iPad used to sign in shifts. It requires consistent daily and weekly efforts that demonstrate genuine care for employees and their families. And the messaging must come from the top.

If you are big enough to have separate people working in human resources or a legal department, have them look at policies and procedures, or develop some programs that can be leveraged to support inclusion, boost morale, and improve overall company culture. Communications departments, too, can develop campaigns to create a culture of inclusion.

It's essential that all employees have a means to air grievances without retribution, including through regular but small management and leadership meetings. Try to ensure consistent and fair discipline with no disparate impact. Consider how external pressure could lead to internal violence. This might be employees with marital problems or those managing the stress of special needs children or dealing with illness for themselves or family members.

Company programs focusing on suicide prevention and workplace violence can be retooled to layer over the broader concern of preventing all violence, whether self-inflicted or directed at others. Compassionate managers and well-used Employee Assistance Program resources can make the difference when trying to spot and help a grievance collector or brittle person who is struggling. They can also be leveraged to provide compassionate methods for employees leaving the company, even those who are fired.

FBI researchers looking at active shooter situations found that current or former employees were almost always the shooters in businesses closed to the general public, and many of those shooters were acting out on the day they were fired. Sometimes employee failures are the result of external stressors, such as financial challenges or domestic problems. An underperforming employee may have to be fired, but giving that employee a way to save face when they leave, a chance to retire, an extra paycheck, a chance to air grievances, or even an opportunity to talk to managers may be a small price to pay in the long run.

I cannot overstress the benefits of demonstrating compassion at these times. In addition to being humane and the right way to treat people, it demonstrates to employees who remain on staff that the company isn't just about rules and making money but truly cares about its employees. As people who know me hear me say all the time, kindness is free.

DO YOU NEED A THREAT ASSESSMENT TEAM?

If you're any bigger than a mom-and-pop store, take the plunge and develop a threat assessment team that can evaluate risk and set a course for intervention when you receive information about observable warning signs of violence. Piecing together those signs is essential to uncovering concerns. Violent behavior may come with no warning. Consider that an FBI study of active shooters noted "the absence of a violent criminal history in an overwhelming majority of adult active shooters."[27]

Just a small and informal team can be the beginning. Two or three people can evaluate what kind of team is needed, who should be on the team, and how often they should meet. Threat assessment teams can overlap with all types of threats to the organization and its employees.

"Businesses today face an ever-growing array of threats to the security of their critical data and IT assets," Tony Miller wrote in a SecurityMagazine. com article on how to build an effective threat assessment team to evaluate potential IT breaches. "A threat assessment team can assist business leaders in sifting through this information and prioritizing security initiatives that will help ensure the business does not become the next security breach headline."[28]

Getting a budget to support a team's additional work, overtime, or added expenses can be challenging. But remember that business locations make up half of the active shooter incidents in the United States, so your risk is higher. Businesses following the workplace violence program model used by the Secret Service may already have the framework in place for a threat assessment team.[29]

CRISIS RESPONSE TEAMS

Every business or organization also should have a team ready to respond to tragedy. This team can pre-stage a tremendous number of things to help the company during a crisis, as well assist first responders.

The first task, *pre-staging*, means having methods in place to communicate and account for personnel during an emergency, keeping the company's emergency operations plan up-to-date, supporting training, and ensuring that first responders have what they will need before they arrive, such as site maps and the access keys or the location of those keys. This team also can consider the aftermath, preparing how to reopen a business or finding an alternate location, and what to do about inventory, incoming shipments, customer needs, and employee needs.

The second task requires identifying who will meet first responders during an emergency. First responders often need access to water shutoffs, other utilities, closed-circuit camera systems, and access controls—whether via keys or swipe badges—to external and internal doors. Delays in access can mean lives lost.

Imagine if a sprinkler system is going off in your building, tripped by the smoke from an automatic weapon, not a fire. How quickly would you want that water source cut off to save damage?

Officers responding to the Navy Yard shooting in Washington, DC, in 2013 met with many locked internal doors but took a door swipe card from a security guard who was killed to give them quick access. Another challenge at that particular shooting was that emergency operations plans mandated that exterior gates be shut and locked immediately during any incident, which only served to delay first responders' ability to get into the building.

Also frustrating to learn was that there was an extensive closed-circuit camera system hidden behind a locked door and never accessed while law enforcement officers hunted for a shooter for more than an hour. The man with the key locked the door and then left when the fire alarm was pulled, per his protocols. With everyone in a panic, no one thought to tell first responders they could have had eyes into the building.

CRISIS COMMUNICATIONS

Since I've worked both as a member of the news media and as an FBI *public information officer*, or PIO, I have so many stories I could write a book about how businesses could better control messaging during disasters. Skeptics may say, *Who cares about the media during a disaster?* But savvy business communications and media executives understand how brand protection includes aggressive news media management. For example, management can tell the world if employees are accounted for and safe during a disaster, relay specific actions leadership is taking to care for survivors and families, and participate in press conferences run by first responders.

Once while providing consultation to a Fortune 500 company media team, I was surprised to learn they had no crisis communications plans and no member of the team with experience to prepare on-the-spot talking points or speeches, something that we took for granted when I worked as a PIO. Corporate communication teams have a methodical process for statements, and they often involve a number of people weighing in and signing off. But there is no time for that when the police chief says the press conference is in fifteen minutes.

Communications teams also might mistakenly believe they will plan and host press conferences from a corporate office—where leadership is located—even if a shooting occurred miles or states away. Realistically, the media will send its limited resources to the location of the disaster, not to a brick building in the suburbs. Don't waste time doing that.

Communications teams may want to host a press conference or release information but should not do so without coordinating other messaging coming from first responders and government officials. Those groups will likely control media messaging in those first disastrous hours and days. The exception to this is the Twitter, text, or other immediate statement of remorse, sadness, support for the community, and assurance about the safety of employees.

A company person with law enforcement and the fire department in unified command can pass along pre-crafted details on the company so the media doesn't characterize, or mischaracterize, the company in the heat of the moment. Most companies have fancy "About" pages on their company website. But what the media needs is a just a few sentences to describe who you actually are; prepare something simple in advance instead of hoping news organizations will find it as they are scrolling a complex and colorful website.

I can tell you as a former journalist, these are the essentials to have handy, and in electronic form: a good point of contact for the company; the company's proper name and location; its corporate affiliate, if any; how many employees it has; what the company produces or otherwise does; and then information more specific to the incident.

You don't have to release all this information as you gather it, but make sure you are tracking how many were likely on site at the time of the shooting; issue an acknowledgment of casualties, as appropriate, and in coordination with unified command. Other information, such as if company doors are shuttered at that location or other locations, what the company is doing for employees, and any plan to get back to business, can come the next day.

Having a succinct description of the company and adding the last few facts, when the time is right, eliminates the preapproval process and stress of press conferences and press releases. This same message can be posted on your website for news media use, emailed to those inquiring, posted on social media sites, and reinforced at press conferences and in news releases. Consistent messaging is essential, because, once it's out there, you can't get it back.

If you want a handy checklist on how to preplan and host press conferences, download a copy of the FBI's "Crisis Communications Quick Reference Guide."[30] A fellow PIO, Andrew Ames, and I put this guide together to give law enforcement officials a road map of what they should do and not do, say and not say, during a press conference. It includes essential, sometimes forgotten ideas, such as asking for additional media assistance, coordinating releasable information with other agencies, and properly identifying all involved agencies and speakers.

EMPOWERING EMPLOYEES THROUGH TRAINING

I've done a lot of training in emergency response, so I sympathized with that young employee who'd asked me whether he should be helping business patrons and manning his post at that Stubb's Bar-B-Q.

Employees, particularly younger or less-experienced ones, do not really know what they have the authority to decide. They are more inclined to uncertainty and lingering thoughts about consequences. Employees have been known to worry about punching out or getting fired because they left without permission.

I was training a security person at a front desk once, and I asked him what he would do if he saw a man coming toward the building with a shotgun in his hand. He told me with all seriousness that he would have to call his supervisor offsite before he could leave his post. I asked, "Even if you saw a guy with a shotgun?" Yes, he replied. No one had ever told him otherwise, and he didn't want to lose his job.

Executives and managers have earned their positions by learning to make decisions, even under the most stressful situations. But it's easy for managers to forget that employees may not yet have learned those lessons.

Quality training can empower employees. I had a chance, for example, to watch Aric Mutchnick perform dozens of live emergency drills with his unique training that allows operations to continue without customers knowing that training is underway. Mutchnick's team has trained professional sports organizations, corporations, and organizations worldwide in practical drills. Live training during operations virtually eliminates all other training costs.

His risk management team, Experior Group, does security assessments under the brand name Red Ball Drills®. On site, Aric can be seen standing in a hallway or at someone's desk, working employees through their emergency plan—magic when they recognize they are gaining confidence and changing the plan. He's conducted these drills while a professional baseball game is underway or while the manufacturing plan is in operation, showing how to make critical decisions in an emergency.[31] His trainings are worth every penny.

I have counseled many managers who want to write details into their emergency plans, believing there will be time to make leadership decisions, make announcements, and control where people go and what they do. Trust me when I say you will not—particularly with an active shooter in the area. Given that, the most important leadership message you can provide to employees or congregants—more than security cameras, extra guards, or expensive gadgetry to predict from where gunshots are emanating—is arming them with the tools and confidence to decide how best to save their own lives.

In 2020 the FBI released four short films, two filmed in bars and two in a house of worship, to encourage people to be in charge of their own fate. They run from thirty seconds to just over four minutes, providing lots of flexibility to get the message out.[32] They are a good starting point, free to use, and can be posted anywhere.

EMERGENCY OPERATION PLANS

Sometimes when I ask a client if they have a plan for handling active shootings, they'll say they have training in Run. Hide. Fight.® or another program. Training is a good start, but you need more.

Emergency operations planning requires an understanding of prevention, response, and recovery efforts. People working in this area say those three words swiftly because they really know what happens before, during, and after any human-made or natural disaster.

Historically, emergency planning meant creating a one-size-fits-all response to many incidents—power outages, lightning, tornadoes, and floods. The road map in the guide identified who was responsible for what and how to open a business back up.

Plans often identify when to leave the building or stay inside and specify contingencies to repair damaged property. If you have a plan but haven't seen it lately, I'd encourage you to dust it off and make sure it has accurate names, contact information, and roles and responsibilities listed.

Then, see if the plan lists an active shooter as one of your potential threats. If it doesn't, you need to add it. Active shooter situations require dramatically different planning in all three areas: prevention, response, and recovery. Like a tornado, an active shooter may be on a scene for minutes. While a tornado is clearly a duck-and-cover situation, the volatility of an active shooter requires training that is more nuanced for the best chance of survival. Security safety is often not a priority unless businesses chose to make it a priority.

For a time, I worked a few yards away from one of the rooms where people would go if the United States faced a nuclear threat. It is probably not surprising to learn that emergency phone lines, numbers, names, computer systems, and more were checked at least on a weekly basis—I mean a pick-up-the-phone-and-call-the-Pentagon kind of check. This is what you do to assure systems won't fail us in our most dire circumstances. Most reading this likely don't need to call the Pentagon, but every emergency operations plan must be kept up-to-date to eliminate unnecessary decision-making under duress.

If a shooting were to occur at your location, is there a plan to continue worship at another location, an alternate location for business operations to continue, or a system for diverting or canceling incoming inventory? Would you know where to call to get help for victims, survivors, and their families? Would you know whom to call from your corporate office or faith organization leadership team? Would you have prewritten statements to give the press with accurate information about what your organization does?

These are some items to address in an emergency operations plan. The plan doesn't have to be overly complicated or long. If you have a corporate-issued generic plan because you are a franchise or chain location, start there, and then make it specific to your location.

To keep everyone on track, a two-page planning process checklist can be found at the back of the FBI's "Developing Emergency Operations Plans: A Guide for Business."[33] The checklist is a handy way to divide duties and make sure that nothing has been left out. The list is from FEMA, the center of the universe for federal government emergency planning. The FBI's 42-page guide is fashioned after similar guides released by other federal agencies in 2013. Depending on the size the organization, the steps may prove quickly accomplished. Each step is filled with questions that should prompt a more thorough planning effort.

Highly respected business organizations, such as ASIS International, are on board to encourage members to share information on protecting employees and preventing damage to the business.[34] ASIS is a global leader for security practitioners, each of whom has a role in the protection of people, property, and information. It offers members educational programs, pulls interesting articles specific to active shooters in various industries, and releases strategy publications.[35]

Of note, in 2020, ASIS released a revised "Workplace Violence and Active Assailant—Prevention, Intervention, and Response Standard" workbook.[36] The book walks through threat prevention efforts, building and policy assessments, prevention models, and response protocols for businesses. It's free online to members or available to nonmembers for a pretty reasonable $35.

I mentioned OSHA above. Another reliable resource is the Centers for Disease Control and Prevention's National Institute for Occupational Safety and Health or NIOSH. NIOSH's "Emergency Preparedness and Response Program" takes a variety of threats into consideration, including chemical, biological, radiological, and natural incidents and events.[37] The program integrates occupational safety and health measures to protect responding and recovery workers. This is done with the help of partners from industry, labor, trade associations, professional organizations, and academia, as well as other federal agencies.

The Security Executive Council, another established and strong private organization, offers a practical and easy-to-understand flowchart useful in developing a strategic master plan for security, which includes *key performance indicators*, or KPIs.[38]

Though only mentioned briefly here, it is essential that your plan considers those with special needs. This may include taking care of the very young, even babies, the very old, and those who cannot move or can only move slowly. Guidance from the Department of Health and Human Services provides particularly helpful information for addressing these concerns.[39]

Chapter Nine

Three Training Essentials

My first apartment in Chicago was in a cockroach-infested third-floor walkup I accessed down an alley and up a rickety wooden stairway. Work often kept me away until 2:00 a.m., and by then there was no street parking for blocks.

When I did finally find a parking spot, my ritual was to lock the car and then run—high heels, briefcase and all, and no matter how many blocks— passing city streetlamps until plunging into the unlit alley to scramble up those deteriorating stairs.

I was terrified each time.

Fast-forward many years, and I recall climbing a stairway in a dingy building in downtown Milwaukee with a team of agents in the pursuit of a drug dealer. My handgun pointed forward, my eyes fixed on my assigned door, I was praying no one would emerge with a gun. I could be in a shootout in an instant.

I was not terrified; I was trained. Training is the key to reducing our fear and teaching us to change our circumstances to protect our safety.

From a young age we are bombarded with safety rules: look both ways when crossing the street, hold the handrail going down the stairs, stay on the sidewalk when riding a bike. My folks and five older siblings in Michigan kept me from touching a hot burner, falling out of a highchair as I tried to stand, or killing myself when riding the toboggan too fast down the icy hill at Cascades Park. I watched Dick Van Dyke demonstrate how to stop, drop, and roll on television.

At school, I joined students everywhere learning what to do when the fire alarm rang or a nuclear bomb was incoming (for the unenlightened: go to the lower level, and hide in the hallway or under a desk).

I developed the habit of buckling my seatbelt before starting the car. I learned to not stand in a field during a thunderstorm and to go down to the basement or climb into a bathtub when a tornado siren wailed. The protective wall of safety we place around ourselves as adults was built experience-by-experience, rule-by-rule. Scary experiences beyond the lessons of childhood are training grounds for the decision-making process required in life.

As adults, we are routinely challenged to discover not only our own set point for what makes us "feel" safe but also how to move beyond fear to control our own safety when facing possible threats.

Safety training for adults—we'll get to children—should reinforce that decision-making process by putting adults into hypothetical situations they may encounter. And each training opportunity must be in a safe environment.

Repeated and consistent training has two benefits. First, it teaches us to trust our instincts—for example, that the sound heard is gunshots, not firecrackers or a car backfiring. And second, training gives us the confidence to push past fear into action.

In all situations, you are a first responder. In 2015, North Dakota health officials reported that 76 percent of emergency personnel were volunteers. Minnesota reported the same, about 60 percent statewide, for ambulance services. This is true across our country. It takes time for first responders to arrive.

This chapter pulls together proven concepts for delivering quality active shooter and targeted violence training. In a companion chapter that follows, I'll briefly address challenges and best practices I've seen while teaching Run. Hide. Fight.®, as well as provide practical ideas for training children and the best resources for that. Whether modifying existing training or developing new training, these materials should provide a good foundation to assess where you are in your current training needs.

Here are three essential topics for every targeted violence training that can be applied to train family in the home, employees in a business, kids at school, or those in your religious or benevolent organization. Consider these, and then look at the notes that follow to evaluate your current training plan.

TARGETED VIOLENCE ESSENTIAL TRAINING TOPICS

Active shooter training is a term often first heard in the context of training schoolkids or perhaps meeting some growing checkbox of required training at work. If you have mandatory training, chances are it's squeezed between requirements like fire drills, understanding new computer privacy laws, and sensitivity training to shed light on implicit bias.

Active shooter training developed years ago may be good, but chances are it could use some dusting off and updating. New research gives us so much more to work with these days.

The foundation of training in this area should include three key components: how to report suspicious activity, how to respond if you are caught in a violent situation, and how to help someone seriously injured.[1] These comprise the best chance to prevent or respond, whether the violence you face is brought on by an active shooter, a domestic dispute, or workplace violence.

Strong, federally supported, and well-researched free training is available in all three areas: "If You See Something, Say Something,"[2] Run. Hide. Fight.®,[3] and STOP THE BLEED®.[4] All three include training program materials on a number of government and organization websites that allow you to tailor your training to your audience. They were created by local, state, and federal entities—meaning they are free, they are compliant with the Americans with Disabilities Act (ADA), and they offer a variety of items in multiple languages.

Materials can be shared in team and organizational meetings, put in online training, posted, emailed, re-shared, and/or handed out to strengthen and bolster self-learning. STOP THE BLEED®,[5] discussed below, is the program with some limitations because, though free, the hands-on portion should be taught in person. In all, each of these three programs allows you to tailor training, particularly when sometimes-expensive classroom training is not an option.

Don't take this to mean you shouldn't use a qualified instructor who knows these materials and can bring them to life for your audience, if you are fortunate enough to have that option. Live training by a skilled instructor is by far the most effective type of training, as instructors take the original materials and tailor them to the needs of the audience.

Live training can be particularly helpful, especially the first time around, to give the audience nuance and lead a constructive conversation about a difficult topic. Even federal government experts working exclusively in this area struggle to find the right tone when teaching Run. Hide. Fight.® concepts.

"I think it's important for everyone to go through some kind of training in that level of *run, hide, fight* before an active shooter situation actually happens," Virginia Tech survivor Kristina Anderson told me while reflecting on her own situation. "When it actually happens, unfortunately, if you haven't thought about it beforehand, our instinct is to kind of go into our fear places and to lock down and probably not to act or do anything. And that is the worst-case scenario."

She continued, "To take any course of action is better than nothing. I think what Run. Hide. Fight.® does is it gives people the prewarning of, *Here is something you can do.* Whatever it is, here's one way of looking at it, and it opens it up to this whole conversation they never would have even had because it's too scary to go down that path by yourself. It's letting a very important model at least open up that conversation."

Some adults may not have access to training because they live alone or their business, school, or organization doesn't or refuses to support training. That's okay. The value of most of this training is to develop for yourself a personal plan on how you will move to safety in an emergency.

As you read, consider how you can implement the options on your own or with those around you. Practice like you would for a fire drill. When you go someplace, take a minute to observe where emergency exits are and where they lead. Take different routes if you can. Weigh the options for yourself.

Fearing a shooter around every corner isn't the goal—in fact, it's just the opposite of what's helpful. Normalize some of your fear by seeing what is already in front of you. What is outside that doorway in the back? How can I get out a different way than I came in? No one wants to run outside only to find a six-foot fence facing them. I've seen it happen.

OBJECTIVES AND HISTORY

A look at the objectives for these three training topics and a bit of history aids in understanding how they came about and where they fit into essential training.

See Something, Say Something

This training is comprised of talking points and a conversation developed based on who is being trained (age, experience, rank) and where they are located (business, school, bar, library, church). The objective of See Something, Say Something training was originally to raise the public's awareness of the indicators of terrorism and terrorism-related crime, as well as the importance of reporting suspicious activity to state and local law enforcement. Over time, this training was expanded to guide citizens in identifying and reporting any type of suspicious behaviors, whether terrorist-related or not.

Since September 11, 2001, we have ingrained into our culture the New York City Metropolitan Transportation Authority (MTA) mantra, *If You See Something, Say Something*, often shortened to *See Something, Say Something.* This call to arms tells citizens to join the police and MTA employees as watchful partners, helping to ensure security within the transportation system. They are urged to look for unattended packages, suspicious behavior, people in bulky or inappropriate clothing, exposed wiring or other irregularities on vehicles and packages, and anyone tampering with surveillance cameras or entering unauthorized areas.

Much of this teaching involves topics detailed in earlier chapters on how to identify leakage and individual behaviors of concern. Additional training can teach people to look not only for behaviors of concern and leakage but suspicious activities and packages as well.

Though savvy MTA marketers dreamed it up and the Department of Homeland Security (DHS) requested permission to use the slogan nationwide in 2010, it is the commitment by citizens that's become its legacy. In essence, by embracing See Something, Say Something, we have chosen to deputize even our youngest citizens with superhero powers: the power to save lives.

The Time between See Something and Say Something: Run. Hide. Fight.®

The objective of Run. Hide. Fight.® training is to teach individuals to react immediately to a potential threat of violence and gauge available options to protect themselves.

Adding this training to the national messaging was not without its challenges, but it was necessary. Creating national active shooter messaging began simply when I asked the Biden team I was working with to watch a six-minute film called *Run. Hide. Fight.*® that depicted people in an office setting who were faced with the decision of what to do when they saw a gun or heard gunshots.

The Sandy Hook shooting had clearly shaken the nation, and as we watched one young child's funeral after another, we needed answers. We had discussed creating a best practices public service film to help teach people what to do if they were in an active shooter situation. The FBI volunteered its film studio and its experienced professionals, but we knew that would take time.

We had agreed we wanted a catchy *stop, drop, and roll*–type phrase. Several private companies had developed training they were selling, primarily to school districts and some businesses, but their mantras were not as easy to follow nor as memorable, and in some cases they were actually more cumbersome. On top of that, few were free or helpful to someone who might have limited English-language skills or for organizations with limited funds.

Looking for solutions, I had come across the six-month-old *Run. Hide. Fight.*® video on YouTube and the companion materials developed along with the film. A team at the City of Houston gets credit for the now-universal phrase that is part of a continuing and aggressive effort to develop regional disaster preparedness planning in Texas. It had been packaged together through funding with DHS, the Urban Areas Security Initiative grant, and the Regional Catastrophic Preparedness Grant Program initiative.

My crisis communications background instincts kicked in. These three verbs are how people respond in a shooting. I wanted to push Run. Hide. Fight.® out as the national federal message.

DHS and FEMA already had messaging but were willing to consider changing their course. The Department of Education (ED) team expressed concerns about steering away from the terms *lockdown* and *lockout* used by many schools. People in the film are seen hiding, but the narrator rightly urges, "First and foremost, if you can get out, do."

ED leadership opposed the word *fight*, which they viewed as too violent. They worried children fleeing might be harmed. ED finally agreed that the *hide* part of the messaging is consistent, not contrary, to *lockdown* and *lockout*. But they weren't buying the FBI research underway that was telling us most shootings at schools and businesses took place outside classrooms or offices, so *lockdown* was simply insufficient.

With or without the film, I wanted us to agree to adopt the three-word catchphrase as the federal standard. We were looking for national messaging for 300 million people, not just 50 million schoolchildren. I have seen about a dozen similar films since this one came out, and unlike most, this film has no simulated blood or scenes of injured people. The only weapon is displayed for about 10 seconds, with a few gunshot rounds heard in the beginning.

As we debated this, we all knew those children at Sandy Hook had gone through active shooter lockdown drills just a few months before the shooting. Students, teachers, and administrators practiced hiding in bathrooms, gathering beside interior walls, scattering to corners of the rooms, and locking classroom doors. They did exactly as they were told—and their reward was twenty students and six adults killed. As a nation, we had failed them.

We had discovered a gaping hole in training because we never told people what to do if they *saw something* and had no time to *say something*. Like Einstein's black hole, the hole was always there, but until Sandy Hook, we didn't see it.

I saw the *run, hide, fight* as filling that hole. It was simple and compelling and part of a comprehensive preparedness package. The general mantra was a perfect starting point. The Houston mayor's office granted permission for free use by federal agencies, noting they had been supporting cross-country requests since posting the popular video and training materials five months before the Sandy Hook shooting.[6]

The director of the Houston Mayor's Office of Public Safety and Homeland Security at the time, Dennis Storemski, explained to Yahoo! News, that they sought to create a common-sense reaction that would be easy to remember.

Run, hide, fight is not complex. Most children understand the words readily. So too do people with limited knowledge of English. And the materials are available in six languages; Spanish, Vietnamese, Chinese, Arabic, and French.[7]

We agreed the film could be used as part of broader training and that those who can do so safely should run—to prevent being shot or used as hostages. We agreed that hiding must be done strategically and that training would be needed to teach people to evaluate their proximity to the threat and the best methods of concealment and cover. We agreed that fighting is a very personal decision and can be done with words, by outwitting an opponent, with fists, and by using the most aggressive means possible.

Within weeks, the agencies, even ED, signed off and placed their department seals on federal emergency planning documents that advocated for the use of Run. Hide. Fight.®[8]

Since then, ED has backtracked a little, dropping the active shooter information from most of their available materials. But the national messaging train has left the station. The adoption of Run. Hide. Fight.® has drawn a common starting line and moved the conversation from catchphrases and challenging acronyms to an impressive effort to teach everyone how to save lives. No matter who does the training, the essence is the same:

Run means

- Your best course of action is to try to leave the area.
- Leave all belongings behind.
- Don't hesitate or waste time discussing whether to flee with others.
- Try to take others with you, but do not let yourself get held back by those unwilling to leave.
- When exiting, try to keep others from entering.
- Even before you see law enforcement, keep your hands up and visible, fingers spread.
- Move to a safe area as far away as possible.
- Call 9-1-1, and provide dispatchers with the location of the emergency, and try to answer their questions to the best of your ability.

Hide means

- If you are unable to escape, conceal, hide, or lock yourself someplace safe such as a room, closet, or ceiling space, anywhere where you believe the shooter cannot see you.
- Lock the door, turn off the lights, pull the blinds, and cover the windows if there is time.
- Barricade the door with heavy objects.

- Turn off electronic devices like cell phones; even vibrate mode makes noise that can give away a location.
- Wait for help to arrive; don't group up; spread out, and don't open the door or answer people calling out unless you believe you are truly speaking with police and they can provide proper proof of identification.
- Remember, lying or crouching on the floor or climbing under a table or desk out in the open is not a hiding place; running or fighting is a better option

Fight means

- If you are faced with confronting a shooter and have no other option, do your best to defend yourself and others.
- You may need to improvise weapons with items that are around you, such as fire extinguishers, chairs, books, or anything that may in some way be useful.
- Use the element of surprise to your advantage; hiding to the side of a door or behind a large object may help if the wall you are beside will protect you.
- Recruit others to join you; there is strength in numbers.
- Throwing items and multiple attackers can surprise, confuse, distract, and even disarm a shooter.
- Act with purpose and aggressively to make your actions count.
- Fight like your life depends on it, because it does.

Some places, most particularly schools, still focus on the *hide* part of training. Schools should spend most of their time on the hide portion, whether called *lockdown*, *lockout*, or something else altogether. But schools that fail to include discussion about running or fighting, where age appropriate, are doing their students a disservice.

Today, nearly every high-quality training underway discusses these three options, but none makes such a clear and unmistakable directive immediately understandable, whether the audience is schoolchildren, churchgoers, or employees at a local law office or meat packing facility.

STOP THE BLEED®[9]

The objective of STOP THE BLEED® is to train every citizen to be a first responder by teaching basic techniques to control severe bleeding, whether that bleeding is caused by gunshot wounds or any other unexpected trauma.

Unlike other training, the essence of STOP THE BLEED® training must be practiced in person. This free training is available using instruction materials specially developed to teach bleed control techniques that demonstrate how to pack a bleeding wound and how to properly apply a tourniquet, the basics of which you can learn from the companion website.

Before you reject this as unnecessary training for your organization, consider that extensive bleeding can result not just from a gunshot wound but also a car accident, a severely broken bone, or an in-home accident. And, ideally, this training is an extension of other training such as first aid, cardiopulmonary resuscitation (CPR), and automated external defibrillator (AED) training.

In 2014, the FBI and other police agencies routinely began issuing tourniquets in standard first aid kits, and immediately reports came of officers and agents saving the lives of citizens and even other law enforcement officers.

The well-organized materials for STOP THE BLEED® are packaged by the American College of Surgeons (ACS) and include downloadable free posters and instructional materials for review.[10] (Make sure you check the permissions.) STOP THE BLEED® has trained more than one million people with a goal to train 20 million. You can register for the two-hour class offered around the country.[11] A few classes charge in order to pay for the training space, but almost all are free for the asking. Instructors also have been sent to single locations on request.

This is another good result borne from the terrible Sandy Hook tragedy. Developed in parallel to our active shooter efforts, it was stewarded by battle-tested Dr. Richard Hunt of the White House National Security Council (NSC) staff and the US Department of Defense (DOD). The Obama administration had tapped Hunt for the NSC staff after his eight years of focused injury control efforts while at the Centers for Disease Control and Prevention.

He knew DOD medical experts had been evaluating whether soldier mortality rates would decline if wound care were provided before a person was transported from the battlefield. Initial DOD researchers had found the number one cause of preventable deaths in the Vietnam War was extreme hemorrhaging.

This prompted the development of new regulations for battlefield trauma. Tactical Combat Casualty Care (TCCC) requires all personnel to be trained to help slow or stop bleeding.[12] Evaluating the value of TCCC during the wars in Iraq and Afghanistan, analysts found an estimated 1,000 to 2,000 soldier lives saved by incorporating TCCC tourniquet use into battlefield medical care.[13]

Hunt's team knew the medical community was struggling with a similar question about whether civilian lives could be saved during an active shooter incident or in any situation where enhanced medical care in the field could reduce death from traumatic injury. Traditional best practices dictated limited intervention in order to get a bleeding person to the hospital faster.

After the Sandy Hook shooting, Hunt elevated the public posture of work done by the ACS and its Joint Committee to Create a National Policy to Enhance Survivability from Mass Casualty Shooting Events. Sitting as chair was Dr. Lenworth M. Jacobs from Hartford Hospital, who is a member of the ACS Board of Regents.

In 2015, the group released recommendations that came to be known as the "Hartford Consensus."[14] Nearly ignored by mainstream media, the collective recommendations and training have resulted in a ripple effect nationally that will eventually result in waves of lives saved, or even a tsunami if we can get more people trained.

The Hartford Consensus recommended, for the first time nationally, that civilians be trained in how to apply tourniquets and how to pack a wound to slow or stop bleeding, something far beyond the typical first aid learned at a scout meeting or online through a Red Cross class. "The overarching principle of the Hartford Consensus is that in intentional mass-casualty and active shooter events, no one should die from uncontrolled bleeding," Lenworth and his team wrote. "The Hartford Consensus calls for a seamless, integrated response system that includes the public, law enforcement, EMS/fire/rescue, and definitive care to employ the THREAT response in a comprehensive and expeditious manner."[15]

In committee, ACS and DOD experts were joined by an impressive list of experts attached to the federal government and private industry. My counterpart from the FBI was Dr. William P. Fabbri, our director of operational medicine. Among the private industry partners were Massachusetts General Hospital, Tulane University, Parkland Memorial Hospital, Eastern Virginia Medical School, University of Arizona, University of Maryland School of Medicine, Harvard University School of Public Health, and the Mayo Clinic. On the federal side, there was input from the US Surgeon General and chief medical officers in the FBI, DHS, and FEMA.

The Hartford Consensus created two new terms. First, they coined a new name for civilians who provide this care, calling such medical interveners **immediate responders**. These individuals render aid until professional responders and trauma experts are able to respond. And second, to summarize all the steps necessary to save a life, an acronym was created—**THREAT**—incorporating *Threat* suppression, *Hemorrhage* control, *Rapid Extrication* to safety, *Assessment* by medical providers, and *Transport* to definitive care.[16]

I'm thrilled to have taken the training because it has made me feel that I could help save a life in an emergency. I learned quite a bit, including how most people misapply or tie tourniquets too loosely out of fear of hurting someone or because they don't know how to get the leverage they need to tighten it enough.

Since STOP THE BLEED® was released, initial research on civilian tourniquet use has emerged in support. This is very important, as it counters the view of generations of people raised to believe civilians should never apply tourniquets.

First reported in the *Journal of the American College of Surgeons* in 2018, researchers identified as the Texas Tourniquet Study Group evaluated 1,026 patients with vascular injuries admitted to trauma centers in Texas from 2011 to 2016. Their efforts focused on how tourniquets and amputations affected mortality rates.[17]

Overall, 9.6 percent of the study patients had amputations, but more than one-third of them—35.7 percent—had received a tourniquet. Those with amputations who received a tourniquet had significantly lower mortality rates than those who did not—2.9 percent versus 7.9 percent, and the non-tourniquet group had almost six times greater odds of death.

"This is the first time that we were actually able to prove the survival benefit of using the tourniquet in the civilian population," said lead study author and trauma surgeon Dr. Pedro G. R. Teixeira of the Dell Medical School at the University of Texas at Austin.[18]

Great news. Next step: we need to add bleed control kits in public spaces just as AEDs have been added near first aid kits and fire extinguishers in airports, malls, schools, and businesses.

INCORPORATING ACTIVE SHOOTER AND SECURITY TRAINING INTO YOUR PLANS

Security planning should address four critical topics in trauma and violence training, which I'll outline below. Just as everybody knows about computer security training, fire drills, and privacy training, it is wise to plan emergency training, remembering that preparedness is more about messaging, consistency, and frequency.

I've consulted and built training plans for both the government and the private sector. If you are starting from scratch, answer these questions below to get started. Take into consideration the budget available, the changing landscape of employees, and delivery methods as you plan.

First, whom are you trying to train? Adults? Children? What about senior citizens and those with mobility difficulties? Are you training employees who will be paid while taking the training, and what do you do when new employees are hired or people miss the training? Should you add specialized and more detailed training for executives and management because that team will work with first responders during a disaster?

Second, where are the people you are training going to be located? Will the people you are training be out in public, in cubicles, at a loading dock, in classrooms, or in front reception areas? Is it a large, open space?

Third, how will the training be delivered? Will it be ten minutes before a shift begins, a couple of times a year? Can it be delivered in an hour, once a year? Does the training need to be live, in different languages, available online, offered remotely, or all three? Is it possible to run exercises where participants move from their desks, classrooms, or job sites to safety?

Fourth, and finally, who will deliver the training? Are you a parent talking to your children? Are you looking for a specialist to train your executive team, provide train-the-trainer sessions, or create snappy digital shorts that can be used worldwide on a continuing basis without interfering with day-to-day operations? Are you a teacher, an imam, a scout leader?

As you start, double-check to make sure what you put together will dovetail with what might be out there already and what you already offer. Schools, colleges, universities, airports, and health care facilities are among the many entities that have policies or even laws mandating that they maintain emergency operations plans. This training should be part of that larger plan.

Some plans may exist on paper but only management has seen them. If a plan exists, when was the last time someone looked at it? I say this because, despite laws requiring emergency plans, some places may fail to tailor them to their own site, their employees, and their needs, choosing instead to document something only to meet legal requirements and check a box. I saw that a lot in private industry, and this type of carelessness is hard to defend in court.

If you are developing or modifying an existing curriculum and have limited funds, maybe consider asking others if you can sit through or borrow their training to adapt. The essence of training plans is the same, so if funds are tight, I suggest that you look for free materials first to get an idea of what the training should look like or pay for a few hours of a consultant's time to send you in the right direction.

Training costs can escalate quickly, so a plan is important. Some catchphrases have trademark symbols on them, and you must pay to use posters, handouts, and place training materials on websites. Bringing in someone to instruct one time without considering whether to also develop a train-the-trainer program or companion training for online learning may increase costs. Companies that market training are selling you their instructor, not the materials, since the content is very similar. That's okay, as long as you are getting a good quality instructor. Local law enforcement too may be able to provide training if they have time.

TRAINING IN EDUCATION ENVIRONMENTS

Training kindergarten through twelfth grade is possible and important, but this subset is quite different, and therefore the training must be quite different. In the next chapter, you'll find a number of resources to help talk to kids about school safety, including potentially violent situations.

Foremost, schools are no place for aggressive training designed to simulate the stress of an active shooter; aggressive training should never be used in schools—or anywhere, for that matter. Surprise drills and activities that involve paint balls or pellets shot at teachers, requiring people to play dead, or instructing them to throw things in their own defense should be off the table. People teaching these methods may be well-intentioned, but they are misguided.

Instead, training in school should be designed based on the age of the students, relying on the knowledge of their teachers to use age-appropriate language and actions, introducing the aspects of safety without adding to the fear. Though perhaps millions of schoolchildren have participated in active shooter drills over the past two decades, no evidence suggests that training, when aggressive, is effective; and new research shows it may leave lasting scars.[19] This, despite the estimated $2.7 billion spent in the school safety industry, which includes active shooter drills.[20]

A report that evaluated social media posts after some types of training suggested that overly aggressive training may, in fact, cause trauma. The report, released in 2020, examined nearly 28 million social media posts tied to 114 schools and found higher rates of depression and stress following active shooter drills.[21] A first of its kind, the report was funded by Everytown for Gun Safety and conducted by Georgia Institute of Technology (Georgia Tech).[22]

"The results were sobering," Everytown concluded. "Active shooter drills in schools are associated with increases in depression (39 percent), stress and anxiety (43 percent), and physiological health problems (23 percent) overall, including children from as young as five years old up to high schoolers, their parents, and teachers," they wrote. "Concerns over death increased by 22 percent, with words like blood, pain, clinics, and pills becoming a consistent feature of social media posts in school communities in the 90 days after a school drill."[23]

The study identified social media posts from teachers, students, and others, displaying the uneasiness with being locked in closets, afraid of the unknown, and a residual impact. "I felt more traumatized than trained," one teacher told *Education Weekly*.[24]

Accounts of examples of aggressive training as well as legal actions have been in the news for years. Lawsuits and complaints abound for stress and injuries caused in this training and other aggressive training efforts.[25] In 2020, teachers from Meadowlawn Elementary school in Monticello, Indiana, sued after training by White County Sheriff's deputies. During the training teachers were ordered to kneel and face the wall by deputies who informed them they were about to be killed. The teachers were then shot in the back with airsoft pellets. Traumatized, two of the plaintiffs quit teaching afterward; the training was condemned by the Indiana State Teachers Association.[26]

The training used had been created after the 1999 Columbine shooting. Two police officers developed active shooter training they call ALICE, a shortcut for *alert, lockdown, inform, counter, evacuate*—though every time I hear it, I need to look up what it stands for. According to their website, ALICE-certified trainers have trained tens of thousands across the country. Though the program was created with the best of intentions, research now shows its potential negative impact—something they're re-evaluating.

In addition, ALICE training can cost school districts thousands of dollars—$32,000 in one school district in California,[27] $106,000 in Alaska.[28] The training is charged per person, and company officials can "certify" each person and "certify" trainers for a cost. Certifications purportedly lasting a year or two push districts to believe they must recertify annually for fear of being sued if a shooting happens. But one investigative report found the company inflated the success of its training, taking credit after school officials effectively responded during actual incidents even when the responses were in opposition to the ALICE training they'd received.[29]

Although some state statutes direct schools to participate in active shooter or intruder response training with local police annually, no federal or state certifications or specific requirements exist.

Instead of an expensive quick fix, step back and see how active shooter and violence prevention training may already exist in some form in your organization. Local, state, and federal laws mandate many safety efforts, allowing for discussions about the need to have planning include both human-made and natural disasters.

Federal law supports organized planning efforts to train and communicate during an emergency. In 1990, Congress passed the Clery Act, which mandates that US institutions of higher education—what we all call colleges and universities—collect data on campus security procedures and crime statistics and, most importantly, compels these facilities to notify those who might be in danger *in a timely fashion.*

The level of compliance has varied, but changes have been successfully implemented in Illinois and Virginia, where five people were killed and sixteen injured at Northern Illinois University in 2008 and thirty-two were killed and seventeen injured at Virginia Tech in 2007.

The Clery Act was later modified to require "procedures to . . . *immediately notify the campus community upon the confirmation of a significant emergency or dangerous situation involving an immediate threat to the health or safety of students or staff.*"[30]

Currently, forty states require some safety drills for school-age students.[31] After the 1999 murders of twelve students and one teacher and the wounding of more than twenty at Columbine High School, the Jeffco school system aggressively began constructing a program to support students, district personnel, and others facing active shooters.[32]

Nearly all Colorado schools adopted the impressive, and free, I Love U Guys Foundation active shooter training for all school-age children. Their standard response protocol, which also has adaptations for businesses and other organizations, covers the same things covered in Run. Hide. Fight.® training but instead uses the watchwords *hold, secure, lockout, evacuate,* and *shelter.*[33] After each word is announced, the protocol is to provide additional specific directions.

The federal government's adoption of Run. Hide. Fight.® in 2014 isn't the only option; it's just a very good one, and it put all federal agencies on the same page—a very hard thing to do.

The American Federation of Teachers, the National Education Association, and Everytown for Gun Safety urge districts to follow six steps in developing and hosting training:[34]

- Notify parents in advance.
- Announce to students and educators in advance.
- Do not mimic or simulate actual incidents.
- Make training age and developmentally appropriate.
- Marry drills with trauma-informed approaches to focus on student well-being.
- Track data about the efficacy and effects of the drills.

Great training is out there, and you may want to pay for it. Just be cautious if someone is pressuring you to sign up for expensive training with a threat that you face legal jeopardy without it. I've seen this strong-arm tactic used, and it usually accompanies expensive but poorly designed per-person training that ultimately provides limited value to those attending.

Now that's something that *should* make you run.

Chapter Ten

Run. Hide. Fight.®
for Children and Adults

One of those unexpected things I discovered in my research is how people in the New York World Trade Center's Twin Towers reacted after their buildings were pierced by jetliners and turned into horrific infernos on September 11, 2001.

In a nearly ignored study of evacuation effectiveness of the buildings (WTC 1 and WTC 2), researchers found that people on floors directly impacted by the planes were the most likely to delay evacuating—and not by just a little. In WTC 1, for example, a median time of three minutes occurred before occupant-initiated evacuations from floors 76 and below.[1] But that time grew to five minutes for those on floors directly impacted, floors 77 to 91.[2]

Occupants in WTC 2 had more time available to process what was happening, since many knew something bad had happened in WTC 1, sixteen minutes before their tower was hit. Those occupants also had to decide for themselves whether to evacuate because conflicting loudspeaker announcements told them to both to evacuate and stay in their offices.

Researchers found that about 90 percent of those who survived from WTC 2 started to evacuate their building before the second plane hit it, and 41 percent made it out of the building before the impact. Delays occurred for several reasons, depending on the perceived risk, the surrounding physical conditions, and the time spent gathering information, collecting things, and "milling" around.[3]

Researchers concluded, however, that "those who delayed, for whatever reason, with few exceptions, did not survive." The 260-page report is devastating to read. It's filled with interviews of people who made split-second decisions, reflex reactions, and lived because of it.

I often mention the report when I teach Run. Hide. Fight.® to adults. I say, you can't necessarily get all the information you need to make an informed decision, but waiting to gather it can be fatal. Get out. Run away. You can't get hurt if you aren't there.

Teaching people to respond to an active shooter or any violent situation at work, in a sanctuary, or at school can be challenging. But good planning can help every instructor leave their audience more secure in their ability to control their fate while at the same time not having everyone leave the room a frightened mess.

To assist those who may teach Run. Hide. Fight.®, this chapter provides an overview of the framework I use. These are just suggestions, since, each time I teach or lecture, I tailor my discussion to the particular audience. But they should provide a leg up for anyone putting training together.

I also have included some practical ideas and resources for training even the youngest children, so please read these. They are ways to discuss disasters with your children and grandchildren, preschoolers, and school-age children.

RUN. HIDE. FIGHT.® TRAINING FOR ADULTS

The most successful training on Run. Hide. Fight.® is face-to-face, guided discussion. Training for adults can take place in an hour or two, including question time, depending on the audience and location.

The essence of the three options is simple to understand, and going through the practicalities of each gives the audience a chance to process what each word means in relationship to their own circumstances. I might note, for example, that many who ran from their offices in the Twin Towers stopped to turn off computers, gather belongings, and make phone calls, which affected how quickly they left.

I have three specific learning objectives for each class and one variable at the end. These include explaining the purpose of the Run. Hide. Fight.® model in responding to an active shooter, identifying best practices for each element, understanding how to apply the model by watching the film, and understanding specific objectives tied to your location, whether a home, business, religious facility, or school.

Run. Hide. Fight.® training is primarily a visceral experience, and the training should be completed in a safe environment so each person can explore what they might do in a shooting situation. No one has to say what they would do. No single answer is correct, and nobody in the audience should be allowed to challenge what another would do. It's a chance to discuss how running may not seem like a good choice at first but then circumstances may change, or how a person may choose to move from a hiding place to run to safety.

No one wants to ponder the possibility of hearing gunshots close by or, worse, seeing a gun pointed at them. Our natural thoughts go to the police who can help. But, practically speaking, focusing on police intervention doesn't address the minutes between the first shot and law enforcement's arrival. I note that our FBI research on active shooters found that 69 percent of shootings ended in five minutes or less, and half of those ended in two minutes or less.

We are the first responders, as I noted earlier. In my trainings, I always discuss an encouraging and surprising result from the same study, explaining how unarmed, selfless civilians stopped 13 percent of the active shooter incidents—citizen soldiers saving lives.

A discussion about shootings can be frightening, so don't let anyone convince you that training should include surprises or be designed to catch people off guard. Training should not include pointing starter pistols, cap guns, or paint ball or inert guns at unsuspecting audiences. These types of trainings have caused unnecessary trauma or, worse, serious medical problems, such as heart attacks. They are simply wrong.

"This does not have to involve scary scenarios but should include them doing something they will remember, like walking out exits near them they might have never paid attention to, finding a location where they could safely hide and barricade themselves," the FBI's Steven Bennett told me. He trains extensively in Run. Hide. Fight.®.

And one added concern: Before any training, provide a face-saving way to let potential attendees opt out of all or part of the training if there is a concern about re-traumatizing. No one should be ashamed to protect themselves from additional or unnecessary trauma. This may apply to those who have previously been in a shooting, family members, or former members of the military or law enforcement, or those who have been traumatized in other ways.

CURRICULUM FRAMEWORK

I break my training into three segments: an opening and a viewing of the six-minute *Run. Hide. Fight.®* film,[4] prepared talking points to address some of the questions I know will come, and then a question-and-answer period. The first segment should only take about fifteen minutes. Leave the bulk of your time for sections two and three.

In the first segment, introduce the speaker, and be sure the audience is aware of the content of the six-minute film. Here is my cheat sheet of essential talking points when introducing the City of Houston's short film, *Run. Hide. Fight.*®

- Explain that the training is to help people confronting the unlikely but possible active shooter or targeted violence situation—awareness they can use at work, at home, and while out with family and friends.
- Always stress that we will discuss matters sensitively, that we won't talk about shooters, and that they will see no gory video footage.
- Explain that the goal is to help them feel empowered and less afraid, not to tell them what to do in any situation.
- Tell them they are free to get up, walk around, or even leave at any point if they desire—no judgment and no explanation needed.

I add this about the film:

- Describe the short film as an opportunity to learn a bit more about what is meant by each word—*run, hide, fight*—and explain that the film's value is to help discuss options.
- Assure them there are many other good films that have been produced—particularly for universities. This film depicts a situation in an office building, and I use it because it has no blood or injured people and the shooter in the film is seen only briefly.
- Explain that the movie has no dramatic or loud movie music that would tend to glamorize the whole thing, but warn the participants that they will see a person with a shotgun who appears to shoot a few people who then fall backward, and they will hear the sound of five gunshot rounds being delivered all in one spot early on.
- Explain that the *Run. Hide. Fight.*® training film was developed by the City of Houston using a grant from DHS. The free film is on YouTube and the City of Houston's website and has been seen by millions. Anyone is welcome to rewatch the film or show it to others. Free supporting training materials are available for the asking from the City of Houston, available in six languages.
- Invite anyone to step out briefly if they are concerned, but encourage them to return. Reemphasize that the film was designed to focus on what to do, not on a shooting.

I always watch the audience for reactions during the film to gauge the room.

When the film is finished, I note that the reasons why the federal government as a whole decided to adopt this film were many, but convincing me was my review of hundreds of shooting incidents while at the FBI and the endless evidence that in nearly every one, someone was running, hiding, and at times fighting, or a combination of those actions. Every person involved in a shooting had to make a decision to do two, or even three, of these options.

In the second segment of the class, I briefly break down aspects of Run. Hide. Fight.®—see my talking points below—and make sure to fill in where I can anticipate questions. I use the room and building as I explain where to run and how to hide.

With so many variables, I don't develop rigid training and discourage decision-making by checklist. I focus on empowerment.

Besides the Run. Hide. Fight.® talking points, I emphasize that

- No one needs to ask for permission to act.
- Afraid people freeze; empowered people act.

If the audience is management, administrators, or anyone in charge, I stress that they must grant their charges the confidence to explore and choose their own options in an emergency. I say they must assure people that their own personal safety is foremost.

I take the time to explain to employees, in particular, that they don't need to get permission to leave, don't need to lock doors if they can't, and don't need to worry they will get fired for taking life-saving action.

One question I get all the time to which there is no good answer is whether or not to pull a fire alarm. Truthfully, no research exists on whether this is a good idea, only anecdotal information. People teaching in schools almost always say no, for fear of flooding the hallways with potential victims. There is anecdotal evidence only on the pros and cons, though we know it happens sometimes. Mistaken reports said the shooter at Marjory Stoneman Douglas High School pulled the fire alarm, but the school superintendent said it was likely tripped by the smoke from the automatic weapons fire.[5]

Those in businesses and organizations being trained almost always say, yes, pull the fire alarm. The fire alarm was pulled by someone during the Navy Yard shooting in Washington, DC, in 2013, sending hundreds into the streets and into nearby buildings for safety. The shooter spent the next 45 minutes roaming the building looking for people to kill. Not being there was a blessing.

I say there is likely never going to be a good answer, but in a big facility, a fire alarm gives everyone in the building immediate notice, and the notice also is accompanied by a well-trained response we know when confronted with fire—RUN!

One challenge I bring into the fire alarm issues is that it generally takes fire officials, or someone else with the know-how, to turn off the alarm. This deafening confusion often prevents first responders from communicating by radio or hearing where a shooter might be. I think the latter reasons are why you'll hear first responders say not to do it.

In the third segment, I let people ask questions and engage them in discussion. This is perhaps the most critical segment, so don't give it just ten minutes at the end. If you are training a group, big or small, you will find most people want to be able to discuss and ask questions about their own particular circumstances.

Because of the touchiness of the subject, it may take a while for the audience to open up. And, inevitably, I am always asked about the shooters' motivations and also about prevention efforts. This may be the first time many have ever discussed active shooter situations. Don't let the training go too far away from the stated objectives, but if you know your subject, you should find this a good opportunity to cover other questions.

No matter how silly or minor you think a question might be, or how long it takes someone to get out their point, talk through the idea with the group, and assure the questioner that there are no bad questions or wrong answers. Make it clear you don't have all the answers.

I would suggest taking notes on the questions asked. They will be asked again and again and become the basis for your "Frequently Asked Questions" section on a company web page or in a church bulletin.

Some people won't ask a question in a group but are thrilled to read written answers or talk to you after the lecture. This helps you, too, to see what you still need to answer and what people are most worried about.

TALKING POINTS FOR RUN. HIDE. FIGHT.® TRAINING

Nearly everyone understands and has training on *hide* or *lockdown*, whether that is from lockdown drills at school or work or experience living through a tornado warning. Most audiences struggle more with *run* and *fight*, so focus your time on answering questions that cover these more challenging aspects of the training. I can't stress enough, however, that training needs to include all options, not just the most preferred.

It helps to explain that this is really safety training that can be applied to daily activities, no matter the disaster they may face: a natural gas explosion in a home, a terrible fire at an office building, and even violence that may erupt at a restaurant, ballgame, or park. Thinking through the idea ahead of time is what makes a person act instead of freezing.

Run

Though not universally taught, **convincing people it is okay to run is actually the most important aspect of training for this type of emergency**. A few important points:

- Running taps into a person's most basic instinct for self-preservation, our fight-or-flight response. Running is our first natural reaction, so teaching people to hide first goes against that.
- Though loud noises tend to make us all duck briefly, little benefit can come from dropping to the ground. A bullet fired across pavement or a hall floor skips along the ground until it finds something to hit. You are allowed that first flinch, but then get those feet moving.
- No fact-based research supports the claim that running provides more targets for a shooter. Nearly every shooting is over in minutes, in some cases in seconds. With research on twenty years of shootings, the FBI still advocates escape or *run* as the first option.
- Running down a hall, out through a door, across a field, or behind a car may and has proved to be the difference between life and death. School executives are particularly concerned about accounting for their children, which is understandable. But they need to get past that. In real instances where children have fled a school shooting, neighbors and businesses have quickly taken fleeing students in and helped keep them safe.
- That parking lot or empty 180-acre field behind your building provides very good protection. The farther away you are from a potential shooter, the harder it is for an adrenaline-filled, likely confused or angry person to fire handgun or rifle rounds in your direction and hit you, let alone at a scattering group of people moving away. Even trained police struggle with hitting a target at longer distances.
- Running isn't possible for everyone, such as infants or the physically impaired. In a hospital training session, emergency lockdown plans will already be in place. Discuss options for the most vulnerable—emergency room personnel and patients—in addition to those in patient rooms, lounge areas, and operating rooms. When training school and day-care operators, allow employees to safely explore the challenges and options of moving more babies than staff can carry.
- Emphasize fleeing beyond the property line rather than to a predesignated rally point, which allows for secondary targeting. And advise that they not just go sit in a car in a nearby parking lot.
- Tell them to call 911, their boss, and family, in that order, to let them know they are safe but not to call until they have cleared away from a danger zone.

- Most people are creatures of habit, and that includes which door they use to enter their house, their office, or their school. Encourage people to not only see where other exits are in a building but also actually use some of those different doors on a regular basis.

Repeat the bullet points on *run* listed in the training film, which include warning others, leaving belongings behind, keeping hands empty, and leaving even if others won't.

Hide

Hide is the most familiar, least controversial, and easiest option to explain to anyone who might fear being caught in a gunfight.

Sometimes I hear people say, "We do lockdown training that conflicts with Run. Hide. Fight.®." I explain that these policies do not conflict. *Hide* is *lockdown, lockout,* and all those other words used to mean secreting yourself away.

This training expands to explore the full range of responses that actually happen at shooting scenes. What protection is there for people in a school cafeteria, a parking lot, a grocery store, or a mall? *Lockdown* training is nice but never enough. A few important points:

- If you are trapped or hiding, try to hide behind something that gives you both cover and concealment.
- *Concealment* gets you out of the sight of a shooter, preventing you from being seen. This may be a wall made of wallboard, a wooden door, or an office partition. **Concealment** means to prevent something from being known.
- **Cover**, however, gives you a protective layer between you and the shooter, such as a brick wall, a car engine block, or a large tree trunk. If you are in a cinderblock building, huddling by those sturdy walls may prevent a shooter from seeing you and will also give you good cover.
- Consider hiding behind a cinderblock wall by a door to try to fight if a shooter should enter, but remember that you may be concealed but not covered if there is only a piece of wallboard between the two of you.
- Also look for ways to run if the opportunity arises or is necessary.
- If you are faced with hiding under a desk or crouching down on the ground providing neither *concealment* nor *cover*, your better option might be to run even if you must run toward and past the shooter.
- Discuss how to secure a door or make it harder for someone to enter, and maybe highlight that ten people in one classroom at Virginia Tech survived

when they were able to successfully prevent the shooter from entering by barricading a door.

Repeat the additional steps mentioned in the film, including turning off lights and phones, locking doors, and blocking doors and windows. Rooms that have no windows prevent a shooter from looking in and seeing potential victims. More than 100 people found refuge in a small choir closet during the Columbine shooting, including some who climbed into the ceiling space of the room.

Fight

Sometimes bosses, administrators, pastors, or board members don't want to participate in the *fight* portion of this training at all—because they are afraid. I urge them to push past the fear and not see it as an all-or-nothing proposition. A legal or ethical quagmire, too, may cause hesitation. This is particularly true for religious organizations dedicated to nonviolence. Even if your school won't teach your kids or your boss won't teach you these lessons, learn them yourself. Wouldn't you fight for life if you were confronted on the street in a carjacking attempt? Why is this different?

If you are teaching *fight*, a few important points:

- Note, finding yourself in a situation where you have to fight is rare and unusual, but preparing for it will make you less afraid to act.
- Shooters are often very focused, so any confusion, any confrontation, can stop them in their tracks. I've seen it many times. If you have time, consider showing the 45-second video of the student who stopped a shooter at Seattle Pacific University in 2014 when he sprayed him with pepper spray and stepped up beside him and grabbed his weapon. The video is available on YouTube.[6]
- Don't get bogged down on how to fight or what to fight with at a given moment. Anything can become a weapon. A bunch of people waving arms, tossing couch cushions, or rushing the shooter can be distracting. I'm sitting in my small home office right now and can see a half-dozen things offhand: a portable printer, my chair, a table lamp, a small flat-screen television, this laptop, and my mom's 1930s Royal manual typewriter that guards over me on the shelf. Look around, and ask the audience to do the same.
- People have died trying to talk the shooter into stopping, so get that idea out of your head. Yes, there are a few success stories where a shooter was talked into putting a gun down, but there are far more that resulted in more deaths.

- Commit to fighting for your life. Ordinary people do extraordinary things to survive so they can see their children and their families again.

RESOURCES FOR TEACHING PRESCHOOLERS
AND THE YOUNGEST SCHOOL-AGE KIDS

My most animated conversations occur with people wrangling over whether and how to train children. Hear me: Schools are doing it. It can be done, but the training they get is not perhaps what you think. Remember that children have been taught all their lives to be wary of strangers and danger.

I participated in active shooter training with third, fourth, and fifth graders in Colorado not too long ago and noticed how the kids took it in stride. The school executives noted that they start the trainings when the students are young, relying on their teachers to use age-appropriate words. They treat it like other safety training for fires, snow emergencies, and power outages. The parents I spoke to in the back of the room were very supportive, though some were surprised at how well the students had been trained and about how casually it was discussed.

Understandably, training the *fight* part of Run. Hide. Fight.® prompts the most discussion and has to be done thoughtfully. Seeking to engage young students in this third part of this training, one Alabama school began having students bring in canned goods to be used against an intruder and donated to the food pantry at the end of the school year. A Pennsylvania school put buckets of river rocks in the classrooms.[7] I'm not sure those options will work. But I'm not sure they won't. And, if they give students a sense of calm, all the better.

Preschoolers

For preschoolers, you can't beat a series of award-winning books written by Heather Beal and illustrated by Jubayda Sagor. The books help to teach safety concepts to even the youngest kids. I've purchased many, many copies for kids of family and friends.[8] You should ask your library to order a few sets for yourself, your school, your day-care center, or your religious organization's nursery.

This book series is the brainchild of Beal, a Navy vet with a PhD in public policy and administration. She specializes in emergency management, but it was her inability to find good books for her own preschoolers that prompted her to start writing. I met Beal while I was in the FBI, when she was still in her early days of finding non-scary ways to train children.

She established Train 4 Safety Press, a Service-Disabled Veteran-Owned Small Business (SDVOSB), to help parents, childcare providers, and caregivers talk to young children about disasters and other disturbing topics in a way that is empowering and does not frighten them. I asked why she was creating her own publishing company, and she told me the issue was too important and she didn't have time to wait for another publisher to agree.

The books explore emergency preparedness themes—though not active shooters—and are designed to allow very young children to explore the concepts of emergencies, how to react, and on whom they can rely. Her current books that should be on every preschooler's shelf are *Elephant Wind: A Tornado Safety Book for Children*, *Tummy Rumble Quake: An Earthquake Safety Book for Children*, and *Lions, Leopards and Storm, Oh My! A Thunderstorm Safety Book.*

Another one of my other favorites is an often overlooked and hard-to-find book that helps teach even the youngest how to be quiet when faced with danger. The out-of-print book *Epossumondas Plays Possum* was published in 2009 and can still be found on the resale market. The cute illustrations alone are enough to draw you in.

This delightful book was written by acclaimed, now-deceased storyteller Colleen Salley, a distinguished children's literature professor at the University of New Orleans. This is one of many books Salley wrote about a beloved and mischievous possum and other characters. The book, illustrated by Janet Stevens, tells the tale of a little possum who gets himself out of some scary situations in the swamp when he remembers his mama taught him that "playing possum" can keep him safe if he can just remember to be quiet and still.

Often kids don't need to know the why as much as they need to know what to do. There is no need to over explain and scare anyone. But you can teach a child what to do. Parents and teachers who I have seen use this book give their kids a chance to curl up into a ball, secret themselves away, and learn to be very, very quiet. Buy this book before you can't find a copy of it, or perhaps convince a publisher to reissue it and Salley's other amazing works.

Parents of preschoolers also can count on the creativity and credibility of Scholastic Books, which offers Saxton Freymann's *How Are You Peeling?* and other books designed to help teach children to express their feelings. I first learned about this book from a therapist who helps children learn to express themselves if a sexual predator begins to pay attention to them prior to an assault. The book is a great way to begin discussing fear with children and matches that by helping them understand all the ways they can stay safe and all the people out there who will help them do so.

Sesame Street and the City of Houston developed two other noteworthy and tested resources, both available for free via the internet:

- Sesame Street has developed extensive materials to help walk children through disaster preparedness and deal with potentially traumatic experiences. Elmo talks about feeling safe in his safe space; printable materials include "H Is for Hope" and "A Guide for Grown-Ups Helping Children Through the Toughest Times," a "Feeling Safe" workshop, and a video for adults called *A Child's Perspective of a Traumatic Experience*. Just search "Sesame Street Feeling Safe" for a slew of child-friendly materials.[9]

- "Ready Heroes" can help youngsters sort through their fears and thoughts, compliments of the City of Houston. Guidance helps children deal with the fear and the realities of preparing for and dealing with disasters. The City even provides a prepared curriculum for K–fifth grade and middle school students, available in six languages. The federally supported program allows schools and families who might be homeschooling to download lesson plans and to order take-home booklets and classroom posters. If you live in the Houston area, you can request a live performance from the Ready Super Heroes. If you don't, you can watch the Ready Super Hero performance online and download the "Are You Ready?" song.[10]

Elementary School Training

Thoughtful educators face hurdles deciding what to teach their students about active shooter safety. It might be discomfort over training *run* out of fear of losing track of the children, or it might be the challenge of teaching *fight* at the same time educators are trying to teach a climate of inclusion and kindness. A teacher may want the training, and a school board may not.

Scores of experts are at odds about what is the best method—if at all—to train and drill students. We can't come to a definitive conclusion here because there isn't enough data to support either position.

But if we are being honest with ourselves, turning eighteen doesn't suddenly make a child aware of school shootings. Don't take my word for it. Ask ten elementary school kids you know. What was once taboo is no longer, and, though many districts shy away from training younger students, districts are making progress, at least on paper.

Very few active shooters darken the doors of elementary schools. But with an estimated 300 to 500 million guns in the United States, active shooter training and gun safety should be part of all school safety training. In addition to the City of Houston's work mentioned above, some good guidance exists nationally. This is important in those situations where school administrators and district officials have left teachers without training beyond the basic close-the-doors and turn-off the-lights. Hopefully these free or inexpensive resources can help them as well as stay-at-home dads and moms, day-care workers, homeschool parents, and others on their own.

In April 2019, the Denver-based *5280 Magazine* reported National Center for Education statistics that indicated "[t]oday, 94.6 percent of American public schools conduct lockdown drills and 92.4 percent have written plans for active shooter scenarios. . . . For the so-called Columbine Generation, practicing how not to get shot during homeroom is nearly as commonplace as standardized testing." A kindergarten teacher told the magazine that the drills they run are stressful, sad, and scary, but she still supported them.

For elementary school kids, I'd urge school libraries to pick up not only the Train 4 Safety books by Beal but also two other great books targeted to elementary school kids. Released in 2019, *The Elephant in the Room: A Lockdown Story* is offered in both English and Spanish. This pre-kindergarten to second grade–level book, written by Alicia Stenard and illustrated by Greg Matusic, tells the story of students who must lock down in the school to protect their peanut butter and jelly sandwiches after a circus train accident leaves animals roaming about looking for food. The book focuses on teaching children to follow instructions and not panic instead of on the negative circumstances leading to the lockdown.

Another, *The Ant Hill Disaster*, was written by Julia Cook and illustrated by Michelle Hazelwood. This pre-K through kindergarten book explores how a little boy and his community come together after his anthill school is destroyed and discusses his fear about returning to school once a new school is built.

Schools that train the youngest students tend to have curricula that blend safety considerations for a multitude of dangers. In Colorado, they may tell kids that a bear or mountain lion might get into a school, so they need to be prepared to hide safely away.

Today we train kids about all kinds of things we wish we didn't have to teach them. We're stacking cybersecurity for a five-year-old's iPad on top of their stranger-danger training and don't-eat-your-Halloween-candy-until-you-get-home warnings.

Find a way before a disaster strikes.

TO TRAIN OR NOT TO TRAIN

All training is good, so if there is no money for separate classes on Run. Hide. Fight.® where you are, maybe your office can spend ten minutes at the beginning of a workday to discuss this as one of the types of emergencies they may face. If your office won't offer the training, share the information with those around you.

If it's too sensitive for your faith leader to take on, offer to take it on for them. Offer to discuss this after services in the sanctuary or at an open meeting for the organization to which you belong. Maybe engage local first responders to come discuss these procedures.

For yourself, consider taking the many free, individualized general courses available through DHS or accessing FEMA's downloadable, free active shooter workshop resources, whether you take a class or not.

Training can save lives. When reviewing survivors' statements from that study about September 11, 2001, I was most moved by the following comment, which encourages me to remember that good training saves lives.

"I opened the doorway to the staircase," one survivor told the researchers. "There was a lot of smoke, and there was no one in it. I quickly closed the door to not bring smoke into the floor. The group of people that was with me started running back to the office."

The survivor continued, "I began running after my coworkers and yelling at them to come back to find a different staircase. I was trying to do the right thing, and they were doing the wrong thing, based on the fire drill training we had. The coworkers weren't listening, so I let them go their own way, and I went by myself back out to the hallway to find a different staircase."[11] He survived. Many of his co-workers did not.

Chapter Eleven

Guns

In 2020, as I was exploring the nuances of the Second Amendment with my class at DePaul University College of Law, the country was reeling with uncertainties from a nation-engulfing pandemic and election season.

Record gun sales reflected the fragility accompanying the pandemic as buyers said they needed to defend themselves during uncertain times. Relegated to the back of our minds were not-so-distant memories of seventeen murdered and seventeen injured at Marjory Stoneman Douglas High School and scores of shootings that had followed.

Gun debates aren't just about whether we should have guns or not, I told the class as I level set the first day. To be good lawyers, you have to understand not just why you do or don't want people to have guns, you have to understand the history and laws surrounding the Second Amendment, cultural and political opinions, and how to bring someone over to your side of the issue.

Gun violence debates bring with them unchecked emotions. That's probably the only thing about guns about which everyone can agree. At the same time, I was writing this book, fraught with concern that writing about guns would send readers scurrying to their respective corners.

It was my law students who unwittingly convinced me that it was possible to provide something of value. The class makeup swung like a pendulum, from students believing every gun should be confiscated to those insisting the government has no authority to regulate gun ownership at all. Added to the mix was one very bright student from Canada who seemed gobsmacked at the American gun obsession.

I had told them, to better understand the influence culture has had on today's gun debate, our path must take us through the various influences, including movies and television, rural and urban interests, the National Rifle

Association (NRA), the complexities of quantifying *any* real numbers, and the US Supreme Court's cautious guidance to future legislative efforts.

As our class progressed through the summer, students defended positions oftentimes brilliantly and without vitriol. They represented imaginary client interests when I made them argue positions with which I knew they did not agree. Many said they had started the class with a limited understanding of issues about which they had already formed opinions, such as an assault rifle ban.

We talked about the unlikelihood of ever lifting all restrictions on gun ownership and debated the slew of laws under consideration in various states, including mandatory registration, restrictions on gun sales and on the types of guns sold, as well as laws that would make it easier to take guns out of the hands of people dealing with mental health issues.

As the class ended and I thought about the book I was writing, I recognized readers here would not turn their opinion on an 8,000-word chapter. But my students had taught me that if I guided with a neutral hand, we could all be better grounded in facts.

With that in mind, I designed this chapter to equip readers with information on the history of the Second Amendment, US Supreme Court guidance, gun-related laws currently under debate, and cultural influences, such as race.

FAR APART

How divergent are opinions in the United States?

Andrew Betts, who produces a news program for the website AR15.com, told me individuals should be able to carry any gun that a government person can carry, in order to keep the government in check. "Any weapon that is too dangerous to entrust to the people is far too dangerous to entrust to the government," he said, not explaining how an expansion of weapons of war available to civilians would work.

Betts speaks for many when he identifies his top two priorities: lifting the ban on fully automatic weapons and granting the right to carry a concealed weapon without a permit. Well-educated and well-spoken, he speaks for many who are frustrated by current gun regulations, including high fees, purchase limits, and other inconveniences to gun owners—impositions compelled because of what he calls "other people's limits."

Equally troubling, he said, is the unwillingness of the Bureau of Alcohol, Tobacco, Firearms, and Explosives to prosecute straw purchasers or file criminal charges against felons attempting to buy guns.

The deaths and turmoil caused by mass killings are big issues to tackle, Betts agreed, but laws and rules won't guarantee an end to the violence and human suffering. Instead, he said, collective efforts should focus on mandatory gun safety training in schools, mental health support, and other ways to ferret out those in trouble.

Not everyone agrees with Betts.

Joshua Friedlein, who was caught up in the 2015 Umpqua Community College shooting that left nine dead and eight others wounded, was in class elsewhere on campus when the lockdown order came in. His now-wife was in a building near where the shooting occurred. It was three hours "waiting to die," he told me. "Personal rights stop when you infringe on another and cause harm."

Friedlein had been homeschooled, and his father, a professional forester, and his grandfather had taught him to shoot in the small timber town where he'd grown up. They lived in a "red area," he said, referring to the Republican strength in Roseburg, Oregon, where residents quickly stepped up to the cameras after the shooting to say they supported gun rights.

But the shooting changed Friedlein. He has joined the ranks as a Survivor Fellow with Everytown for Gun Safety and now supports universal background checks, red flag laws, and a ban on assault-style weapons.

Plenty of opportunities remain for choosing sides in the gun debate, whether the topic is ghost guns, 3-D printing, smart guns, gun buybacks, or maybe something no one has yet thought about. One thing is certain: no matter what side of the pendulum swing you're on, it's unlikely you are going to get exactly what you want. Increased mental health awareness is the common ground on the Venn diagram depicting changes needed by those for and against gun regulations. But more still divides than brings together those in the gun debate.

THE STATES DECIDE

Active shooter incidents and mass shootings involve an infinitesimal number of the guns that are involved in homicide deaths annually in the United States. In fact, six in ten gun deaths are the result of suicides according to the Centers for Disease Control and Prevention.[1]

Americans own hundreds of millions of guns. But researchers looking over 28 years of data found only 118 shootings in which four or more people had been killed, and only 228 weapons were used in those shootings. Of those weapons, 143, or nearly two-thirds, were handguns, 55 were rifles, and 30 were shotguns.[2] And yet it is precisely these incidents that produce the most vocal demands for changes to gun laws and regulations.

After the murders at Marjory Stoneman Douglas, several gun retailers, such as Walmart Inc., Kroger Co., and Dick's Sporting Goods Inc., announced they would no longer sell guns to anyone under twenty-one years of age.[3] Dick's has since discontinued gun and ammunition sales in more than half of its stores. Some gun and ammunition manufacturers, too, have repositioned themselves and sold off manufacturing companies, likely to avoid the legal quagmire resulting from many shootings.

On the legislative side, each new legislative session brings lobbyists looking for change. At the state level, they play at the high-stakes tables. Unlike federal challenges, state legislatures are more nimble, local concerns are more easily met, and laws more easily changed. That may not be important in some places, such as Montana. Montana doesn't require licensing, registration, or permits for shotguns and rifles and has limited permit requirements for handguns. But in other states, expansive change may be just over the horizon.

Virginia is perhaps the best recent example of this, a state where firearms use is the leading cause of death among children and teens.[4] Six months after the 2019 Virginia electors turned the legislature into a Democratic majority, Governor Ralph Northam, a pediatric neurologist, signed five new laws, and proposed amendments to two others, to further limit and control access to guns in Virginia.[5]

Virginia has had its share of infamous gun tragedies. Less than a year earlier, twelve people had been killed in a Virginia Beach mass killing. In 2017, six people were injured, including US House Republican Majority Whip Steve Scalise, while practicing on a ballfield in Alexandria. In 2015, a news reporter and a photojournalist in Roanoke were murdered by a fired employee during a live television broadcast. In 2010, two police officers were injured during a shootout at the busy train stop outside a security checkpoint at the Pentagon in Arlington County. In 2007, the Virginia Tech shooting killed thirty-two. And, less than a year before, two Fairfax County police officers were ambushed during a shift change just a mile from my house by an eighteen-year-old shooter who lived nearby. Virginians are tired of gun tragedies.

Northam, who was a medic in the US Army during Operation Desert Storm, said the 2019 legislative efforts stopped short of his desire to also enact some sort of assault weapons ban. "We don't need those weapons on the street," he told *Courthouse News*. "If anybody thinks they are needed, I'd ask them to go into a mass casualty tent to get a glimpse of what they do to human beings."[6]

The new law reflected concerns like those expressed by Vijay Katkuri, a software engineer, who told the *New York Times* after the election why he had voted Democratic in the 2018 midterm election. "Guns, that is the most pressing issue for me," he said. "There are lots of other issues, but you can only fix them if you are alive."[7]

When Joseph Biden was sworn in as President of the United States on January 20, 2021, his ambitious agenda included a federal ban on the sale of assault weapons, a voluntary firearms buyback program, and $900 million in funding for community-based gun violence prevention initiatives. Despite assurances to the contrary, Republicans and gun advocates warned of court-packing to ban guns, magazine size limitations, universal registration, and gun confiscations.

State efforts are faster. Once the capital of the Confederacy, and the current home of the NRA, Virginia long has had some of the country's most lax gun laws. The legislature's approach was sweeping. A portent of changes to come in some other states, the boutique package surgically closed disparate loopholes in laws involving not only gun sales but also gun safety for children and people in crisis. Signed into law in 2020 were the following:

- A law requiring gun owners to report their lost or stolen firearms to law enforcement within 48 hours or face a civil penalty.
- A law designed to prevent children from accessing firearms by increasing the penalty for recklessly leaving firearms in their presence.
- A law establishing an Extreme Risk Protective Order, also known as a red flag law, which creates a legal mechanism for law enforcement and the courts to temporarily separate a person from their firearms when they represent a danger to themselves or others.
- A law reinstating Virginia's one-handgun-a-month purchase rule to help curtail stockpiling of firearms as well as trafficking.
- A law requiring background checks on all firearm sales in Virginia, closing what is commonly referred to as the gun show loophole.

At the signing, Virginia became the nineteenth state to enact a red flag law, which some gun owners oppose. Some believe they have a better solution.

In 2020, Sarah Joy Albrecht and Genevieve Jones cofounded HoldMy-Guns.org after the suicide of a family friend. The mission of the not-for-profit organization is to provide gun owners facing mental illness or personal crisis with a national network of partner gun shops and federal firearms license holders who can legally hold the weapons on a temporary basis.

The nascent organization may provide a valuable option that encourages the temporary voluntary relinquishment of weapons, one that will not stigmatize someone in public records. The effort relies on the sensibilities of the gun owners—not necessarily helpful, for example, when a domestic abuser or a person intent on suicide is not inclined to give up their guns. And storing the guns costs money.

Northam also proposed amendments to two existing Virginia laws. The first would allow localities to regulate firearms in public buildings, parks, and recreation centers and during permitted events. The second would prohibit individuals subject to protective orders from possessing firearms, requiring them to turn over their firearms within 24 hours and certify to the court that they have turned over their weapons. The law would allow judges to hold people in contempt of court if they fail to comply.[8]

Efforts to prevent gun violence will continue to be the cause of many local candidates who have campaigned in recent years on a promise to tighten state laws, but the data they will rely on is hard to interpret. A 2017 Harvard study found one in five guns were sold privately, without a background check—those sales deemed as utilizing "gun show loopholes."[9] But a study on deaths related to weapons without background checks at gun shows in California and Texas found "no evidence that gun shows lead to substantial increases in either gun homicides or suicides, or reduce the number of firearms-related deaths."[10]

Not all states are moving in the direction of Virginia, although political candidates continue to receive the support and financial backing from advocate groups such as the Coalition to Stop Gun Violence, the Brady Campaign to Prevent Gun Violence, and Everytown for Gun Safety. The last includes both Moms Demand Action for Gun Sense in America as well as Mayors Against Illegal Guns, largely funded by former New York City Mayor Michael Bloomberg.

Some states are arming teachers. In recent years, Texas and Georgia have legalized the carrying of a concealed handgun at all institutions of higher education—with Georgia also allowing knives, knuckles, bats, clubs, and nunchucks. The law stands even though gun owners and non–gun owners in campus communities largely believe that allowing concealed carry on a campus will harm the academic atmosphere and diminish a feeling of safety in contentious situations.[11]

THOSE TWENTY-SEVEN WORDS: A BIT OF HISTORY

At a mere twenty-seven words, the Second Amendment is half the length of the important Fourth Amendment prohibition against unreasonable search and seizure.

> *A well regulated Militia, being necessary to the security of a free State, the right of the people to keep and bear Arms shall not be infringed.*[12]

Scores of scholars have opined about the collective minds of the founding fathers as they drafted, rejected, amended, and ultimately agreed upon our country's three foundational documents: the Declaration of Independence, signed July 4, 1776; the Constitution, ratified in 1788; and the Bill of Rights, ratified in 1791.

The Declaration did not mention gun rights when it was signed, but it's fun to point out in today's climate that after a public reading of it in Bowling Green, New York, on July 9, 1776, New Yorkers pulled down a statue of King George III.

Only the Constitution and the Bill of Rights discuss guns, and then only in relationship to military activities. At the time, the US military was primarily made up of the state militias that supplemented a minimal standing national army. These militia troops had fought for independence under the command of General George Washington.

Little discussion was recorded about standing armies or state militias during debates about the Declaration of Independence. But eleven years later, over four hot and muggy months in Philadelphia, the debates over the drafting of the US Constitution shed some light on the founders' thinking.

The draft constitution explicitly granted Congress the power to call up state militias. This power, stated in Article 1, Section 8, also gave Congress authorization to raise and support armies, as well as "provide for calling forth the Militia to execute the Laws of the Union, suppress Insurrections and repel Invasions."

The authority to appoint officers was designed to appease those in the states who feared losing control of the state militias. The debate was not theoretical. Having just wrestled independence from a country with a military ever-ready to protect the monarchy, many feared a centralized military could be used against the states in times of unrest, which is exactly what happened during the Civil War.

Trying to dissuade the framers from rejecting strong federal armies, Alexander Hamilton argued that a strong military would solve a future problem of underfunded state militias that might deploy with insufficient or various types of guns and ammunition. He had seen those challenges firsthand, working beside General Washington during the war. "If a well-regulated militia be the most natural defense of a free country, it ought certainly to be under the regulation and at the disposal of that body which is constituted the guardian of the national security," he wrote in Federalist No. 29.

George Mason led the opposition to support for the strong federal controls, refusing to sign the Constitution and discouraging states from ratifying it unless a bill of rights was adopted at the same time.

James Madison, in Federalist No. 46, noted that the number of state militias would always outweigh the number of federal regular troops, adding that Americans were better armed than the people of almost every other nation.

The end result was a 4,400-word Constitution signed in 1787 with little or no mention of individual rights, including the right of gun ownership.

But at the First Congress in 1789, Mason introduced a seventeen-point Bill of Rights, which included a version of the Second Amendment. Those opposed to the amendments noted that many state constitutions already had in place many of these rights, including protections for individuals to bear arms to defend their family and home—among them Pennsylvania and North Carolina. Besides, they said, the US Constitution only grants certain rights, and all others are left to the states.

The think-tank National Constitution Center described the Second Amendment this way: "The Second Amendment conceded nothing to the Anti-Federalists' desire to sharply curtail the military power of the federal government, which would have required substantial changes in the original Constitution. Yet the Amendment was easily accepted because of widespread agreement that the federal government should not have the power to infringe on the right of the people to keep and bear arms, any more than it should have the power to abridge the freedom of speech or prohibit the free exercise of religion."[13]

A more practical reason also existed. Representatives from slave states feared that federal control of state militias would pull resources from the militias' primary mission, slave patrols. These patrols were the early police forces in the South, maintaining slave discipline outside the courts, hunting down runaway slaves, and "providing a form of organized terror to deter slave revolts."[14]

After two years, with enough state representatives assured they would have control over their own militias, the required three-fourths of the states ratified ten of the amendments, what we now know as the Bill of Rights.

Many books on the Second Amendment are designed to direct you to one conclusion or another. If you are looking for excellent overviews, however, read Michael Waldman's *The Second Amendment: A Biography*, Adam Winkler's *Gunfight*, and Stephen P. Halbrook's *The Founders' Second Amendment: Origins of the Right to Bear Arms*.

So, whatever is debated today, recognize that the individual right to bear arms was never actually debated by our founders. People who could afford expensive and handmade guns had them, and in some states, militia duties were mandatory, as was having a gun to bring with you.[15]

And what of our founding fathers' fear of a large standing army that could turn on its citizens?

The country's Continental forces gave way to the formalized US Army, Navy, and Marine Corps, branches that fought in many wars in the succeeding years: the War of 1812, the Mexican-American War, the Civil War, the

Spanish-American War, and World War I. When each war ended, the majority of military personnel were decommissioned and sent home.

At the end of US involvement in World War II, 12 million men and women wore a US uniform. Two years later, 10 million of them had been sent home. By 2020, the number of active duty military had decreased to 1.4 million.[16]

With hundreds of millions of guns in the hands of civilians, the founders' fear of strong-armed federal forces should be a distant concern. But in reality, many still cling to Madison's notion that distrust in the government is their best position.

Today many thousands, if not millions, of militia members drill and equip themselves with a belief that they may be required to act to defend against tyranny or to be a force multiplier during an emergency, including providing security so law enforcement is free to do its job.

The challenge is that federal and state laws do not grant civilians this broad authority, leaving many legally able to carry a gun but potentially liable for murder or other crimes if they use the gun.

The assault by domestic terrorists on the US Capitol, the foiled kidnapping plots against Michigan and Virginia governors, and the coordinated attacks on Washington, DC, and state capitols in the months and weeks before President Biden's inauguration January 20, 2021, put those theories to the test nationwide.

TODAY'S CULTURE IS YESTERDAY'S CHILD'S TOY

A common refrain I hear when lecturing is that violent video games are to blame for mass shootings. Pointing fingers is a great deflecting technique, but if blame is to be placed on mass shootings in society, I say start by looking in the mirror.

Violence has been woven into the fabric of American lives for decades. Video games are just the latest iteration. Generations alive today fought in wars and then came home to children playing on the floor with green plastic army men. Baby boomers remember cowboys chasing Indians with every "good" kid carrying a toy rifle complete with gun belt and holster. They spent their days playing outside and their nights inside, watching justice served by the Lone Ranger or the Rifleman and by US Marshal Matt Dillon in Dodge City, Kansas, during twenty seasons of *Gunsmoke*.

Sunday night's *Wonderful World of Disney* glorified Daniel Boone and Davy Crockett as well as their prowess with guns. The popularity of cap guns and Daisy Red Ryder BB guns waned only as paintball and home video game consoles became popular in the 1970s. Captain Kirk, James Bond, and Luke

Skywalker replaced cowboys, and other gun-carrying heroes, taking America's gun culture both international and into space on the big and little screens.

Not much has changed. Today, gun violence is wrapped up nicely under the categories of action movies and video games. Netflix rates the best gun movies, including gunslinging Westerns and epic shootouts.[17] Modern warfare and urban violence both oblige.

Thirty years ago, dozens of psychologists gathering to look for answers to youth violence noted the reality of violence in our culture. They didn't say it exactly this way, but reading their notes, I think they concluded that the culture we say we want is not the culture we embrace.

"Our folk heroes and media images—from the cowboys of the old west, to John Wayne, Clint Eastwood, and Arnold Schwarzenegger—often glorify interpersonal violence on an individual and personal level," they wrote. "Violent films are widely attended. American news media present image after image reflecting the violence in society, and in some cases may exploit or contribute to it. Football, one of the most violent of team sports, is an American creation. A plethora of guns and war toys are marketed and coveted and possessed by small children."[18]

Hunting had been a sport of kings and a necessity for paupers for centuries, but violence-for-sport has become part of our modern culture. Therefore, it's too simple to point to video games as the problem when violence is everywhere around us. If you aren't watching it on your home screen or at the movie, you can head to Las Vegas and pay hundreds to have the "machine gun experience" of your life.

This violence culture has fostered a sense of power and invincibility too, leading to an NRA-created talking point that has spread across the country—Good Guy with a Gun.

GOOD GUY WITH A GUN

As school shootings and other mass killings began to increase dramatically, the NRA, politicians, and pundits—those opposing gun regulations—popularized the mantra, *The only thing stopping a bad guy with a gun is a good guy with a gun.* It's a nice sentiment, or at least a catchy phrase, but it is not founded in fact, particularly with regard to these types of shootings.

Responding to a shooting is stressful enough for law enforcement, causing many instances of accidental discharges and wayward bullets. Twenty years of data disproves the theory, if not the political debate, that putting guns in the hands of civilians will have a positive impact.

After evaluating 305 active shooter incidents between 2000 and 2019, the FBI found three instances where an armed civilian killed an active shooter and another six where gunfire was exchanged for some period of time but no bullets hit their mark. In one additional situation, an armed civilian who pursued a shooter into a store was shot and killed before he could fire his gun.[19]

In contrast, FBI research found thirty-three active shooter incidents where unarmed civilians successfully stopped a shooter. In one case, bus drivers Steve Potter and Jim O'Brien put their own safety aside to tackle a shooter with a rifle at Deer Creek Middle School in Littleton, Colorado, in 2010. Most of these situations involved one or more civilians tackling a shooter or talking them down, in some cases including students. You can find the summaries for each instance on the FBI website.[20]

Another half-dozen active shooter incidents involved armed security guards. These trained and armed guards experienced more success in these encounters, though some have been wounded or even killed. Increasing security at some locations may result in more exchanges like these, but with all the research being done, none yet suggests that more guns at a scene will improve the outcome of these fast-moving situations.

The inherent flaw to the "good guy with a gun" theory is an assumption that people carrying guys have the gun with them, have it loaded, and are particularly proficient in shooting. And they must be in the right place at the right time. Consider that one armed school resource officer or several security officers in an office park or hospital still have to see the shooter coming and find a way to intercede, no matter the size of the campus. The armed off-duty police officer working security at the Pulse nightclub in Orlando was in the parking lot dealing with an underage drinker when the shooting started there.

As a trained law enforcement officer, I cannot overstress that weapons proficiency is a continuing, lifelong effort and must carry with it an appreciation for the stress, discipline, and responsibility it involves. To make that point directly but in a light-hearted way, I'd suggest you take a look at comedian Jordan Klepper's two-part investigation for *The Daily Show*, available on YouTube, called "Jordan Klepper, Good Guy with a Gun."[21]

None of this is intended to criticize the legal carrying of firearms by well-trained individuals. It's just not realistic to pin hopes there. And discard the idea that some places are more dangerous because of political leanings. Per the FBI, the highest number of active shooter incidents have occurred in California, Florida, Texas, and Pennsylvania.

Fears about the increased vulnerability of gun-free zones also are not yet supported by any data, but, despite that, more schools are considering arming teachers. On my last check, 28 states have passed laws allowing armed teachers and staff in schools, and some are paying to train them and providing the guns. This includes Alabama, Arkansas, Colorado, Florida, Georgia, Hawaii, Idaho, Indiana, Iowa, Kansas, Massachusetts, Michigan, Minnesota, Mississippi, Missouri, Montana, New Hampshire, New Jersey, North Dakota, Ohio, Oklahoma,

Oregon, South Dakota, Tennessee, Texas, Utah, Washington, and Wyoming.[22] Given that state laws all likely allow armed security and police on school grounds, the reasoning for this is maybe just to make some people feel better.

In Idaho, a college chemistry professor accidentally shot himself in the foot during a class just months after lawmakers there passed a law allowing firearms on state campuses. At the time, a national survey of more than 900 college presidents found that 95 percent opposed permitting concealed weapons on campuses. National Education Association (NEA) members and other teacher and school administrator associations also released formal statements opposing arming teachers.

After then–US Education Secretary Betsy DeVos sought in 2018 to use federal Student Support and Academic Enrichment grants to allow the purchase of guns and to train teachers, immediate opposition was voiced by the NEA, the American Federation of Teachers, the National Association of School Psychologists, the National Association of Secondary School Principals, and the National Association of Elementary School Principals.

The American Bar Association released a statement in opposition to both more guns in schools and the use of federal funds for such a purpose. "There are many known, evidence-based means to address the complex issue of school shootings," the ABA statement noted. "Arming teachers is not one of them. Available data suggests that arming teachers will increase the risk of students being shot, not reduce it."[23]

I agree. Arming teachers is truly a local decision and may depend on the distance between the school and first responders. But schools that choose to arm teachers should do so in a thoughtful and comprehensive fashion, including adding gun safety to their kindergarten through grade 12 curriculum. This would prepare them for the inevitable situations where an exposed gun may be in reach of a child.

LEGISLATIVE CONTROL AND THE COURTS

After the Bill of Rights, including its Second Amendment, was ratified, federal gun rights remained primarily untouched in the United States until a handful of pivotal events over time set the wheels in motion for federal gun legislation, giving us the resulting Supreme Court decisions we primarily live by today:

- 1920s—The effects of the Volstead Act, the law enacting the Eighteenth Amendment, which ushered in the Prohibition era.
- 1960s—The time of civil rights and counterprotests, the rise of the Black Panther Party, and the assassinations of four prominent men, two Black

and two White—Martin Luther King Jr., Malcolm X, President John F. Kennedy, and Senator Robert F. Kennedy—bringing tremendous pressure to bear on legislators. This happened on the coattails of the Supreme Court decision *Brown v. Board of Education*, which found legislated racial segregation of public schools to be unconstitutional.

* 1980s—The assassination attempt on President Ronald Reagan in 1981, wounding him, his press secretary James Brady, Secret Service Agent Timothy McCarthy, and DC Metropolitan Police Officer Thomas Delahanty.
* 1990s to now—The aftermath of shootings from Columbine High School in 1999, Virginia Tech in 2007, Sandy Hook Elementary School in 2012, and Marjory Stoneman Douglas High School in 2018.

Those historical events prompted legislators to act. The 1920s produced two significant federal firearms laws at a time when a small and outgunned federal law enforcement cadre faced weapons-laden opponents willing to go to war with them, as well as other violent mobsters carving out territorial control of big cities.

The results:

The **National Firearms Act of 1934** was passed to confront organized crime violence during the Prohibition era. The law placed control over machine guns, short-barrel rifles and shotguns, and other weapons in the hands of what is now the Bureau of Alcohol, Tobacco, Firearms, and Explosives.

Quickly challenged, the statute was upheld by the US Supreme Court in *United States v. Miller*, with Justice James McReynolds writing "In the absence of any evidence tending to show that possession or use of a 'shotgun having a barrel of less than eighteen inches in length' at this time has some reasonable relationship to the preservation or efficiency of a well-regulated militia, we cannot say that the Second Amendment guarantees the right to keep and bear such an instrument. Certainly, it is not within judicial notice that this weapon is any part of the ordinary military equipment, or that its use could contribute to the common defense."[24]

The **Federal Firearms Act of 1938** (FFA) established licensing for firearms sellers and prohibited gun sales to convicted felons and other prohibited individuals. This Act was repealed when the **Gun Control Act of 1968** was passed and the provisions were incorporated into it, along with the FFA requirement in place today that requires sellers of firearms, called federal firearms licensees (FFLs), to be licensed.

The 1960s brought additional opportunities for those seeking to tighten gun control after the assassinations of four prominent figures.

The killer of President Kennedy in Dallas in 1963 had bought his gun after clipping a coupon from a classified ad in the back of the NRA's magazine,

American Rifleman. The rifle, scope-mounted, was shipped directly to a pawnshop in Texas where he produced a $21.45 money order and the gun was handed over to him.[25]

Malcolm X, a human rights activist and Black Muslim minister for the Nation of Islam, spoke candidly about the double standard applied to gun ownership and the use of guns by Blacks versus Whites. During the same time period, formative members of the Black Panther Party encouraged Blacks to use their legal right to openly carry guns to protect themselves and others, and they demonstrated their beliefs by patrolling the streets of Oakland, California, with shotguns and handguns.

Fifteen months after President Kennedy's assassination, Malcolm X too was assassinated. The civil rights cause carried on despite FBI Director J. Edgar Hoover's public characterization of the Black Panthers as the "greatest threat to the internal security of the country."[26]

Black Panther leaders marched to the California State Capitol in 1967 and read an open letter to then-Governor Ronald Reagan, stating, in part, "Black people have begged, prayed, petitioned, demonstrated, and everything else to get the racist power structure of America to right the wrongs which have historically been perpetuated against Black people. The time has come for Black people to arm themselves against this terror before it is too late."[27]

The march prompted the swift passage of California's Mulford Act, banning the carrying of weapons in the open. Reagan quickly signed the law, saying, "There's no reason why on the street today a citizen should be carrying loaded weapons."[28]

Any discussions of the limitations or rights of the Second Amendment simply didn't happen for much of the nation's first two hundred years. Until 1986, the Second Amendment was known as the "lost amendment" because it was so rarely litigated or discussed, and this provided little guidance for lawyers and those looking to draft new legislation.[29]

Following the assassinations of civil rights leader King and presidential candidate Robert F. Kennedy, the **1968 Gun Control Act** was passed. The law banned mail-order sales, restricted certain high-risk people from purchasing guns, and prohibited the importation of military surplus firearms.

Both major political parties supported stricter gun laws, and in particular the ban on mail-order sales of rifles. In 1968, the Republican Party platform included "enactment of legislation to control indiscriminate availability of firearms."[30]

Testifying to Congress before the passage of the Gun Control Act, the NRA's Franklin Orth said, "We do not think that any sane American, who calls himself an American, can object to placing into this bill the instrument which killed the president of the United States." Some elements of the legislation, he said, "appear unduly restrictive and unjustified in their application to law-abiding citizens, but the measure as a whole appears to be one that the sportsman of America can live with."[31]

The Republican Party platform of 1972 reflected the desire for gun control, with platform writers calling to "intensify efforts to prevent criminal access to weapons." It provided for the "Enactment of legislation to control indiscriminate availability of firearms, safeguarding the right of responsible citizens to collect, own and use firearms for legitimate purposes, retaining primary responsibility at the state level, with such federal laws as necessary to better enable the states to meet their responsibilities."[32]

But by 1976, the political winds were beginning to change, and the gun debate would never again be the same.

In a widely covered coup, the NRA leadership was ousted at its 1977 annual convention and replaced by a slate of those who were more politically motivated. The NRA's motto, "Firearms Safety Education, Marksmanship Training, Shooting for Recreation," literally came down from the front of its building and, that same year, its newly opened, monolithic headquarters in Fairfax, Virginia, bore the words, "The Right of the People to Keep and Bear Arms Shall Not Be Infringed."[33]

The **Republican Party** platform too changed in 1976, simply saying, "We support the right of citizens to keep and bear arms. We oppose federal registration of firearms."

Despite this, after the assassination attempt on President Reagan in 1981, Congress passed the **Brady Handgun Violence Prevention Act of 1993** that, which amended the Gun Control Act, requiring holders of FFLs to conduct a background check and establish waiting periods. The president's would-be assassin had purchased his small handgun at a pawnshop.

Gun lobbying efforts successfully placed a ten-year sunset clause in the **1994 Assault Weapons Ban** that prohibited the sale of 118 different weapons and magazines carrying more than ten rounds. The act failed to define the term "assault weapon" and had no impact on any firearms already owned.

With the influx of NRA lobbying money filling their campaign war chests, members of Congress passed no significant gun safety legislation in the succeeding twenty-five years. Though estimates exceeded $200 million in NRA spending since 1989, a mere $23 million was dedicated to the November 2020 federal races. As the NRA faces its own spending scandals and abuses by its executives, another advocacy lobbying organization began to appear. Gun Owners of America spent an estimated $880,000 on the election in an effort to flex its political muscle.[34]

Congress did provide liability protection for the industry. In 2005, Congress passed the **Protection of Lawful Commerce in Arms Act**, which prevents firearms manufacturers and licensed dealers from being held liable for negligence when crimes are committed with their products.

In addition, the **1996 Dickey Amendment** pulled $2.6 million from the Centers for Disease Control and Prevention's budget, the amount spent on firearms-related research the previous year. The amendment carried a stipulation that no funds be made available for injury prevention and control research or to advocate or promote gun control. Arkansas Republican Representative Jay Dickey had successfully attached the amendment to an omnibus spending bill, virtually assuring its passage.

It was a "chilling message," Dickey later wrote in a 2012 *Washington Post* op-ed explaining his regret for bringing the amendment. He had been the "point man" for the NRA, he explained, and NRA executives were angry over their failure to suppress comprehensive research revealing the danger of guns in the home, a study published in the *New England Journal of Medicine.*[35]

The research found that residents with a gun in the home faced a 2.7-fold greater risk of homicide and a 4.8-fold greater risk of suicide.[36] In the editorial, Dickey conceded that "as a consequence, US scientists cannot answer the most basic question: What works to prevent firearms injuries? We don't know whether having more citizens carry guns would decrease or increase firearm deaths; or whether firearm registration and licensing would make inner-city residents safer or expose them to greater harm."[37]

A total ban on research has been somewhat lifted by a reinterpretation of the Dickey amendment, but, even as of this writing, no funding can be used to advocate for gun control or gun safety measures. And the NRA maintains a list of legislative wants that would provide further protection for gun owners, gun sellers, and gun manufacturers.

The 1990s had its share of school, university, concert hall, shopping mall, and business shootings, so I won't detail them here except to share two thoughts.

First, it's worth noting that nearly all the guns used in these shootings were legally purchased, as I noted in chapter 3. The Sandy Hook shooter used a weapon purchased legally for him by his mother, and they had gone shooting as a way to get him out of the house. The Virginia Tech shooter purchased two handguns legally after instant background checks had been completed—one at a nearby pawnshop for $571 and the other online for $267.[38]

Second, semiautomatic or assault-style weapons were used in the deadliest shootings—Pulse, Sandy Hook, Las Vegas, San Bernardino, and Aurora. The Sandy Hook shooter fired 155 rounds in seven and a half minutes as he moved around the building. The shooter at Pulse fire 211 rounds. The Las Vegas shooter fired more than 1,000 rounds.

Estimates on the number of these types of weapons puts the count in the millions, begging us to ask, *What are the real solutions compared to the desired solutions?*

CURRENT SUPREME COURT LAW

Today, the ultimate guidance on individual gun rights granted by the Second Amendment is the landmark case *District of Columbia v. Heller*, as significant when it was decided as was *Brown v. Board of Education* or *Roe v. Wade*.[39]

The *Heller* case involved a Washington, DC, law that severely restricted the ability to own a handgun and required any gun to be registered and, if maintained in the home, to be either disassembled or protected with a trigger lock.

The decision in *Heller*, written by Justice Antonin Scalia, did away 100 years of limiting precedence to expressly find that the Second Amendment grants individuals a right to have a handgun in their home. The Court ruled that the Second Amendment was not just a right to be invoked for militia or military service but also an individual right that could be used for "traditionally lawful purposes, such as self-defense within the home."[40]

Led by those supporting a legal philosophy called originalism, the Court put its own meaning to the language. "We conclude that nothing in our precedents forecloses our adoption of the original understanding of the Second Amendment," the majority opinion stated.

Often quoted by gun advocates and referred to as justifying an absolute right to carry a gun, the case specifically says the opposite: "Like most rights, the right secured by the Second Amendment is not unlimited," the Court wrote. "Although we do not undertake an exhaustive historical analysis today of the full scope of the Second Amendment, nothing in our opinion should be taken to cast doubt on longstanding prohibitions on the possession of firearms by felons and the mentally ill, or laws forbidding the carrying of firearms in sensitive places such as schools and government buildings, or laws imposing conditions and qualifications on the commercial sale of arms."

Most important perhaps to future challenges of new legislation, the *Heller* decision listed what it might consider "presumptively lawful" regulations that could be passed by federal or state legislatures. "We also recognize another important limitation on the right to keep and carry arms," the Court went on to explain, citing *United States v. Miller*, 307 U.S. 174 (1939). "*Miller* said, as we have explained, that the sorts of weapons protected were those 'in common use at the time.' [citation omitted] We think that limitation is fairly supported by the historical tradition of prohibiting the carrying of 'dangerous and unusual weapons.'"[41]

In November 2021, the US Supreme Court heard oral arguments in *New York State Rifle & Pistol Association Inc. v. Bruen*, Docket 20-843, with a ruling expected mid-year 2022 on whether the state's denial of the petitioner's application for a concealed carry license violated his Second Amendment rights. The court has signaled, however, the ruling is likely to be limited in its scope and not the panacea either side desires.

Legislative efforts will continue on both sides of the gun debate and perhaps bring the right case back before the Supreme Court in the future. But legal scholars would agree that the rejection of ten other gun-related cases in the Court's 2020 term signaled to state courts and legislatures that the language in *Heller* and *Bruen* will provide sufficient guidance, at least for now.

A NOTE ABOUT RACE

As it happened, just a few weeks before my law school class on the Second Amendment was scheduled to begin, the country's temperature rose dramatically after the knee-to-the-neck killing of George Floyd, a Black man, during an arrest by four Minneapolis police officers.

Now, I debated with myself, *do I add an extensive discussion about guns and racial injustices to this two-weekend Zoom seminar?* I did not.[42]

Perhaps that was a mistake, since one frustrated student later wrote in an evaluation that "the real issues with gun violence and associated gun laws are the race relations." But in retrospect, this student's comments actually reinforced my decision to not expand the race discussion. Gun violence requires an appreciation of the history of how we got to where are today. Race is part of the equation in mass killings, to be sure, but no less relevant than socioeconomic inequalities and other factors.[43]

In a limited way, we did discuss the role race played in the passage of some of the laws restricting gun ownership, particularly in a historical context. Blacks were prohibited from owning guns for nearly a century, and some of the actions of the Black Panther movement of the 1960s highlighted the widespread frustration engendered by a system that allowed Whites to openly carry while Blacks could not. Black Panthers exercised rights afforded them by open-carry gun laws to provide security for others, and the swift legislative changes that resulted vividly demonstrate the double standard applied.

The Black Lives Matter movement as well as the protests and riots in the summer and fall of 2020 after the death of George Floyd exemplify how much cannot be covered in these few words. But this is a start.

Chapter Twelve

Helping Survivors and the Families of Victims

Once the shooting stops, nothing is more important than helping survivors and the families of victims.

"If you do it well, it helps people on the road to coping," the former FBI Assistant Director Kathryn Turman explained in an interview for the FBI.[1] "If you do it badly, it's just another set of chains that people have to drag behind them—bad memories of how they were treated or they didn't get what they needed."

Doing it well requires comprehending the impact on victims and survivors and knowing how to help. This chapter provides a brief overview of what services are available, as well as an interview, in her own words, with the most seriously injured survivor of the Virginia Tech shooting.

VICTIM SERVICES COME OF AGE

Unless you have used them, you probably are unaware of the labyrinth of services available to crime victims and their families. As a state prosecutor I never worried about it because I just asked the clerk to call someone to my courtroom. It's embarrassing to admit that now.

As an FBI special agent, I focused on the criminals and spent little time thinking of the victims. That changed for me when I worked a five-state fraud case in Wisconsin where we recovered money a con man had taken from dozens of small business owners. He went to jail, but the most important part in his punishment was the $100,000-plus fine he paid right near Christmastime. When that money was returned to them, some of his victims told us it kept them from closing their businesses for good. It made me truly appreciate the impact on victims.

In the 1980s and 1990s, programs to help victims began popping up across the United States. They initially focused resources at the scene of a crisis, connecting people to mental health services and providing financial support. Many were court-centric, helping people fill out forms and providing emotional support at court appearances. In time, nearly every jurisdiction handling criminal cases had developed some sort of companion program to support crime victims and their families.

In 1988, the parent of all victim services was established with the creation of the Department of Justice's (DOJ) Office for Victims of Crime (OVC), which was mandated by amendments to the 1984 Victims of Crime Act.[2]

Today, virtually every state and most counties have services available for victims and families affected by crime. The best way to find your local services is to check out county and state websites and follow the links to a handful of useful clearinghouses. The primary resources are the National Center for Victims of Crime and the Center for Victim Research, the latter funded through the DOJ's OVC.[3] Administrators of crime victim programs also can reach out to the federal clearinghouses for support.[4] They offer free training and resources for those who work with crime victims.[5]

Each group verifies information posted, preventing the revictimization of people whose names and information may be out in the public. Companion advocate organizations support victims' rights, and scores of helpful links can be found for confidential helplines, legal referrals, and other direct services. The National Hotline for Crime Victims,1-855-484-2846, can help you find the right connection. For example, there is a hotline specifically for parents of murdered children, 1-888-818-7662.

THE DEPARTMENT OF JUSTICE AND THE FBI

The long-term success of the FBI's victim services program was sealed when serendipity put Turman, then the head of the Victim Witness Assistance Unit in the US Attorney's Office for the District of Columbia, together with Robert Mueller, the future FBI director.

The two were part of the dozens who worked years to manage the complex trial and aftermath of the two terrorists charged with the bombing and death of all those aboard a Pan Am jet that exploded over Lockerbie, Scotland, in 1988. For the eight-month trial in the Netherlands, Turman orchestrated both in-person and remote access viewing of the trial for victim families, connecting video feeds to viewing sites in DC, New York, London, and Scotland.

Within a year, Mueller was named Director of the FBI, and he asked Turman to join him, setting up what became the FBI's Victim Services Division

(VSD). Turman set about to professionalize the victim specialist role, requiring advanced degrees for her team as well as additional training. By 2006, the FBI's 100-plus crime victim specialists were making referrals at times to the National Center for Victims of Crime, aligning federal and state services to provide a more seamless effort.[6]

From the start, Turman wanted the FBI's efforts to closely support the immediate needs of victims. Her teams responded along with investigators to support victims, such as those in often-neglected Native American communities.

In addition, she devised novel ways to maintain open-ended communication with victims and their families. This included setting up a private web page for more than 10,000 victims of the September 11, 2001, terrorist attacks that has given victims and their families access to services and accurate information about investigative efforts through the years.

By 2015, the 170-member team had developed rapid deployment capabilities and brought on two comfort dogs, which, not surprisingly, are very popular. It is these teams that join state and local resources at the scene of a mass shooting or other large tragedy. The teams bring as many victim specialists as needed to fill slots to sustain support for days, or even weeks, as they help set up a Family Assistance Center.

The FBI and Pennsylvania State University also developed a free, online training course for anyone who might need to provide a death notice, called *"We Regret to Inform You . . ."* which provides the right language for such a sensitive situation.[7]

In communities with strong victim services programs, such as Colorado, less support is needed. In other areas, particularly rural communities or where special needs exist, FBI manpower and a surge of assistance serve fragile communities with limited resources, sometimes for months.

When the 2016 Pulse nightclub shooting in Orlando occurred during a Latin Night celebration, the FBI sent scores of victim specialists in support, both Spanish-speaking agents and members of the FBI's LGBTQ Advisory Committee, to assist at the scene where forty-nine were killed and fifty-three injured.

Turman's advice is based on years of experience. During the past fifteen years, the FBI has responded to about thirty mass casualty situations, providing care for an estimated two million victims, including the tens of thousands counted after the complex terrorist attacks on September 11, 2001. When providing support, expect a diverse victim population, she says. Count on helping an average of ten people for every victim. Look for the walking wounded around you, physically and mentally, and deliver only unequivocal, accurate information to the families.

FAMILY ASSISTANCE CENTERS

Depending on the number of potential victims and the fluidity of the situation, first responders in unified command turn to victim services experts to set up a Family Assistance Center (FAC) near the scene. State, county, and local agencies may use a slightly different term for the centers, but the tasks performed there are universal.

Teams operating these FACs are often full-time professionals, or trained volunteers, dealing solely with victims, survivors, and their families. All are trained to provide a number of immediate essential services including

- Offering a safe, private location for survivors and victim family members to be reunited and get critically important information.
- Providing accurate information from unified command—a particularly important thing to remember in this era of instant-but-often-inaccurate social media–invented speculation.
- Performing death notifications or assisting law enforcement as they provide death notifications.
- Providing or referring to crisis counseling.
- Identifying potential locations where victims have been transported—critically important when gunshot victims are unidentified or unconscious.
- Informing and supporting families at hospitals.

In situations with mass casualties, it is not unusual for a half-dozen hospitals to be engaged—as in the case of the Boston Marathon bombing and the theater and high school shootings in Colorado. This could require family members to drive to different hospitals to get information and force them to challenge federal and local privacy laws blocking disclosure of information. FAC teams make all those calls and work to keep a running list of victims, survivors, family members, and people looking for loved ones.

Teams also help to protect the privacy of those inside the FAC from well-meaning outsiders. When tragedy strikes, faith leaders and others are often drawn to the location to offer their prayers, blankets, flowers, food, and other support. Those services are needed, FAC experts say, but not necessarily in those moments when the tragedy is still unfolding, unless those offering help have training. Turman once told me, pretty much all they immediately require is comfort, cold water, and Kleenex; above all, people in an FAC need information and to make tough decisions. Everything else can wait, she said.

FINANCIAL ASSISTANCE

Providing the financial safety net for all of this victim care is the federal Crime Victims Fund, which had a balance of more than $6 billion in 2020.[8] Overseen by the DOJ's OVC, millions of dollars are transferred annually to support state, local, and territorial victim service programs.

States have programs to administer the distribution of federal funds as well as manage local funding. All of the money goes to pre-approved expenses, such as crime-related medical and dental expenses, counseling costs, funeral or burial expenses, and lost wages.[9]

As with federal funding, no tax dollars are used. Federal and state programs are paid for with fines, fees, forfeited bail, and special assessments imposed on convicted criminals, as well as gifts and donations.

The National Association of Crime Victim Compensation Boards estimates compensation programs pay approximately $500 million annually to more than 200,000 victims and their families.[10] Though compensation is generally capped by statute for each service, the limits are generous, and the help comes at a critical time. If you need to find your state's website, look to the National Association of Crime Victim Compensation Boards' website to find a link.[11]

In Virginia, for example, there is currently a $10,000 cap for funeral expenses; $1,000 for crime scene cleanup; $35,000 for lost wages; and even a $35,000 limit for someone who loses someone who has been providing them support. Applicants also can seek money for prescriptions and transportation, including mileage, cabs, or bus fare, to travel to court appearances.

The FBI provides emergency funds that can be used for travel expenses and temporary housing for families affected by violence. Covered costs are as varied as you can imagine. For businesses and organizations seeking to use their limited funds wisely, these resources are invaluable.

After the Sandy Hook shooting, funds were used to buy a suit for the father of one victim when we learned he didn't have one to wear to his son's funeral. Oftentimes, money is used to provide flights for up to two family members, even from a foreign country. This can support victims, such as students ensnarled in a shooting on their campus or victims of another tragedy.

It's common for family members to be housed when tragedy strikes far from home. I even recall a cat being taken in and cared for when the panicked owner ended up in the hospital after the Boston bombing—an act of kindness I think more than a financial commitment. Victim specialists are very caring people, dealing with others who are suffering through the worst times of their lives.

MAKE A PLAN

Gone are the days of leaving survivors and families to their own devices. Now first responders have confidence that experienced, trained teams are at the ready. Knowing how to tap into available resources immediately requires every business, school, and organization to identify ahead of time whom to call.

The best news is that all the information you need is readily available to put a game plan in place. Everybody can, right now, locate available federal and local resources, make contact lists, and pre-designate who will coordinate with federal and local victim assistance coordinators if disaster strikes. Plans also can include pre-locating potential FAC locations you can share with first responders. Pick these locations, and touch base with the owners, offering them the same service in return.

To see where you might fit, and how resources are integrated to provide long-term support, consider this flowchart of services provided by OVC; see figure 12.1, "Victims of Crime Act." It breaks down the federal statute and describes the tiered system designed to provide long-term support for survivors and the families of victims.[12] Just a note about helping children deal with trauma.

Many excellent sources are available so ask the professionals to recommend some. Here are two: Talking to your children about school shootings, produced by the American Psychological Association, www.apa.org/topics/gun-violence-crime/school-shooting, and a similarly titled piece from The National Child Traumatic Stress Network – Talking to Children About the Shooting, www.nctsn.org/sites/default/files/resources//talking_to_children_about_the_shooting.pdf?fbclid=IwAR2P7HCZj6-AGt4rZThFEJmNy-B1iqBU1y6KjWYcY8OlumG37yE2_RnlW6p4.[13]

A SURVIVOR'S PERSPECTIVE

Kristina Anderson was a nineteen-year-old sophomore sitting in a French class at Virginia Tech University when a shooter burst into her classroom, shooting 17 of 19 people in the room. Twelve died. She and six other students survived.

Today she runs her own organization, the Koshka Foundation for Safe Schools, http://koshkafoundation.org/, joined by fellow French student and survivor Heidi Miller and others dedicated to forging connections between survivors and causes, improving campus safety, and empowering student activism.

Her thoughts are a retrospective reflection for first responders and other survivors. I have paraphrased my questions and, with her permission, edited her comments lightly for clarity; the words are hers.

Victims of Crime Act
Rebuilding Lives through Assistance and Compensation

U.S. Attorneys

U.S. Attorneys' Offices, federal courts, and the Federal Bureau of Prisons collect criminal fines, forfeited bail bonds, penalties, and special assessments, which are deposited into the Crime Victims Fund.

Crime Victims Fund

The Crime Victims Fund (the Fund), established by the Victims of Crime Act of 1984 (VOCA), is a major funding source for victim services throughout the United States and its territories. Millions of dollars collected are deposited into the Fund annually and support the state victim assistance and compensation program efforts. Since 1986, $4.8 billion in VOCA victim assistance funds and $1.8 billion in compensation funds have been awarded.

Office for Victims of Crime

VOCA is administered by the Office for Victims of Crime (OVC) within the Office of Justice Programs, U.S. Department of Justice. OVC distributes victim assistance and compensation funds to states and U.S. territories, in accordance with the Victims of Crime Act. OVC may also use funds for demonstration projects, program evaluation, compliance efforts, training and technical assistance services, and other related activities.

States and Territories

VOCA administrators distribute VOCA victim assistance and compensation grants. All states and territories, including the Northern Mariana Islands, Guam, and American Samoa, receive annual VOCA victim assistance grants, which are awarded competitively to local community-based organizations that provide direct services to crime victims. Similarly, all states, the District of Columbia, the U.S. Virgin Islands, and Puerto Rico receive VOCA compensation grants after satisfying criteria set forth in VOCA and OVC program rules.

Public and Private Organizations

Victim Assistance

Organizations (called "subrecipient programs") use the VOCA victim assistance funds to provide direct services—such as crisis intervention, emergency shelter, transportation, and criminal justice advocacy—to crime victims free of charge. Victim advocates in these programs inform victims about the eligibility requirements of compensation and assist victims with the required paperwork.

Victim Compensation

State programs (sometimes called commissions or boards) distribute compensation directly to victims, who must satisfy eligibility requirements.

Crime Victims

Victim Assistance

VOCA and the Crime Victims Fund help victims rebuild their lives by supporting programs that provide services directly to victims, such as crisis intervention, emergency shelter, emergency transportation, counseling, and criminal justice advocacy.

Victim Compensation

Victim compensation helps victims rebuild their lives by reimbursing victims for costs in the immediate aftermath of crime, such as crime-related medical costs, mental health counseling, funeral and burial costs, and lost wages or loss of support. Victim compensation is used as a payment of last resort and is paid when other financial resources (e.g., private insurance and worker's compensation) do not cover the loss.

| COLLECTIONS > | DEPOSITS > | DISBURSEMENTS > | STATE ADMINISTRATION > | DIRECT SERVICES > | REBUILT LIVES |

THE NATIONAL CENTER FOR
Victims of Crime
www.ncvc.org·1-800-FYI-CALL

Office for Victims of Crime
OVC
"Putting Victims First"

SPONSORED BY: U.S. DEPARTMENT OF JUSTICE ★ OFFICE OF JUSTICE PROGRAMS ★ OFFICE FOR VICTIMS OF CRIME

Figure 12.1. Victims of Crime Act
Office for Victims of Crimes, Department of Justice

You call yourself a survivor. *How is that different from* victim?

I think it's important to remember the weight and impact that words can have, and we should be careful not to quickly revert to *victim* when talking about mass trauma survivors. The word "victim," to me, places the individual back at the scene of the incident, and it disempowers the person. There is lack of control I associate with "victimhood," which is exactly what happened in the trauma in the first place. For me, the ability to choose the word *survivor* means that I've learned something from the event and hopefully overcome it and come out stronger. Everyone should have the right to decide for themselves if they prefer *victim* or *survivor*, and those labels may also evolve over time.

Can you describe what happened after the shooting stopped and when police first arrived?

It was suddenly very quiet after a very long eleven or twelve minutes of shooting. I'm lying on the floor. I can't speak just because of where I've been shot, and the first thing, I heard an officer say, "We have a lot of blacks in here." As a civilian, I didn't understand that he was referring to triage codes. We don't know what yellow, green, and all that means, but to hear that was very bizarre.

The officer stood over me, in the back of the room, and he initially said "Yellow" and then switched it to "Red." I panicked at that point, because going from yellow to red can't be a good sign. And at this point, I felt a very deep sense of coldness, as though an ice bucket was dropped on my head. During the shooting I never thought that I was actually going to die, but suddenly I wanted to be taken out of there, as quickly as possible.

I think I just thought that as long as I held onto my other bargain, which was being very still and quiet, someone, probably law enforcement, would come in there and save us. I thought this thing would end. I remember thinking, *Why did you just change yourself so quickly, and what is red?* So, I had a lot of confusion and internal questions because he wasn't explaining what he saw, he wasn't addressing me, he wasn't talking to me, he was just, you know, calling . . .

They didn't speak to you at that point?

No, not that I remember. I think the responding officers were trying to figure out who was alive, and who needed medical attention most urgently. I would say, please try to acknowledge us, even if you have to step over us. There is so much fear on our end, and for someone to pause for a second and acknowledge, say "I see you, I'm coming back for you," is very empowering.

Acknowledge them, even if you, if it's a second to say I see you, you've been shot, I'm going to come back for you, my name is Jared. Keep saying your name to us; that may be all we remember in the end. There's this sense of, I think, connection and humanity in that. That was very hopeful. You're giving us hope at that point in a time when we don't know what's going on.

Can you give them any other advice?

Speak to us, acknowledge us, and get us out of the building, or place, as quickly as possible. The longer we spend inside the space, the more memories, sights, and smells are accumulated, which may contribute to more trauma going forward.

After the event, during recovery, for first responders, I recommend whenever you feel comfortable doing so, to reconnect with the survivors. Allow us a chance to thank you, under better circumstances. I know that this can be potentially a little awkward, and law enforcement are sometimes nervous about approaching survivors, because they think it will somehow remind us of the terrible event. In truth, the person who was there on the scene may be the only one who can truly understand or relate to what happened.

And try not to talk too much about our injuries without addressing what's happening. Triage codes are great, but realize as you talk about the room and what you're seeing. Maybe not talk about the deceased or the crime scene; we can remember that, and that can be very traumatizing. If you're describing someone's really horrible injuries, that might stay with me for the next ten years because PTSD in survivors [is a] very, very real things—on both ends, both on our [end] and for law enforcement. No one will ever hold it against you, but realize that there have been examples of, if they're discussing triage and you're saying *We're going to leave this person* . . . they're going to hear that kind of language . . . and that can be traumatizing.

Officers moved you from the classroom to the hallway. Do you remember that?

Once they moved me to the hallway, I'm kind of hunched on the wall, and I started to fall asleep again. They would tap my face, to try to get me to wake up. And I remember feeling very frustrated because I just wanted to fall asleep I was in so much pain and tired. They called me everything but my actual name; obviously they didn't know my name. It was almost like they were like bugging me, disturbing me, but no one was telling me what was happening or why I needed to be awake. I remember just a lot of confusion and a little bit of annoyance and fear. Now I understand they were just trying to keep me awake, but at the time I just felt like everyone was speaking about or over me but never directly to me.

What was it like to finally get out of the building?

I had this overwhelming sense of gratitude once I [arrived at] the base of the building, because it looked different, it felt different, it felt like I was being saved. And so, at the door leading outside of Norris Hall was where we finally exited; as the officer handed me off, the only thing I said the entire time, I told the officer, "Thank you." And he, Patrick, remembers that. And I could not have told you there was a shooting because I was in so much shock. I couldn't have told you that I was even physically shot. But I knew this man was taking me from a place of very, very bad to a safe place.

And the ride to the hospital?

I was put into the ambulance with Derek, one of the EMTs. I remember that ride; it's one of the strongest memories I have. I remember him very well because the entire time he tried to keep me awake, so he would hit my face and he would repeatedly say, "What is your name?" "What is your major?" "Your eyes are so pretty."

Again, I couldn't speak because I was in a lot of pain. I remember thinking, *Shut up*, honestly, because I was so annoyed at this point that this man kept trying to wake me up because all I wanted to do was fall asleep. And I didn't think that I was actually dying, but I wanted this thing to end, and I didn't understand why he just wasn't letting me fall asleep. I know now that he was trying to keep me awake and alive. Any of that additional information might have made me a little bit calmer, because it's such an abnormal situation to put yourself though that any knowledge or other piece of information about my family or my injuries would have been, I hope, helpful. But again, who really knows?

Did you get counseling?

I did not seek help until about eight months after the shooting when I started having more intense triggers. I would be afraid for my safety in a few different situations, in public. I felt as though, in some ways, I didn't want to appear sad or [as] though I was in mourning months still after the shooting.

So, for me to be able to sit down with a person whom I trusted, in a very private space, who was in no way related to the incident, was extremely helpful. I was able to talk through all the crazy things you don't really want to articulate casually to your friends or family always because it makes you sound like you're insane.

My time in therapy and counseling was extremely helpful because it provided a space for someone to validate what I was experiencing, to remind me these reactions are totally normal. And to hear someone go back and say, *Well, this is PTSD, essentially, and here's why you're having this, and by the way, that's totally normal.*

Do you talk to other shooting survivors?

I do. I initially reached out to a survivor from Columbine High School. We talked about being afraid of loud noises, and generally [talked about] coping mechanisms. For me, it was just incredibly helpful and eye-opening to meet someone else who had experienced what I had and could understand. I felt much less alone in my experience as a survivor, back in the real world. Sam and I still keep in touch, and since then, I've also reached out to people in other communities who have experienced a school shooting. There are so many questions that arise in the aftermath: *How do you approach therapy? How do you tell new friends, or family members, about the trauma?* These are some of the things we talk about.

I have survivors from other shootings seek me out. I have family members who have lost people in other shootings seek me out. That sometimes puts me in a tailspin, in putting me back in my own trauma, because a lot of times the things they come to me with are things that I have experienced as well. And the hard part is, I know from my own personal experience, that there isn't one magic bullet. I can tell them that it's just going to suck for a long time and that they have to take some course of action. There's not really a game plan for surviving a school shooting. All I can say is, you have to do something. Unfortunately, whatever that is. It may be therapy, the way I went through it, or writing a book or [picking] up a non-profit's missions. You have to acknowledge those thoughts and those demons in some capacity, and that's very hard.

You said you find support talking to the first responders?

Yes—conversations over coffee or in a bar. I've had a lot of just one-on-one dinners and conversations at their homes, and to hear that they also carry these things is—it's just heartfelt. It makes you feel like you're not alone.

Do you have any advice for survivors, including those first responders?

The scariest thing about all of these shootings, I think, is the control piece. We go through our lives thinking that I could have gone to the door faster, or that I could have alerted the teacher, or that we could have done something to change the outcome of that terrible day. I would suggest that both survivors and first responders, as best as possible, try not to ask the "What if?" questions after an event and take the time to find a counselor [whom] they really trust and connect with. We can't hold on to just what happened in that space. Really, we were doing the best we can, and I'm sure that they all were, right? And for me, what it was, what was the most helpful [part] of therapy was realizing that I was having normal reactions to an abnormal situation.

And, speaking with other people, who also responded.

To an officer who responds to a school shooting, and afterward lives with that, I think I would say, give yourself space, give yourself a break. You responded pretty well in the immediacy, right? Active shooter response—you get there, you take them out, everything works with the rescue task force and everything else. Understand that while, yes, you did go in, there's absolutely no fault in what happened. You are not to blame for the loss of life or the injuries sustained, or, god forbid, if another officer was shot or killed. There's a third party—there's a very evil individual on that other end—and that's where the cause and effect is.

Did you use victim assistance resources?

The victims' assistance fund was extremely helpful in the first few years afterward because they helped with medical bills, counseling—which was extremely therapeutic. Counseling is very expensive, and so I was able to go, I think, like, once a week for two years more or less . . . and that made the difference night and day.

What didn't I ask you?

Yes—people often ask how they can help survivors and communities that recently experienced a mass shooting event. While it's tempting to send items such as blankets, toys, or food, sometimes this becomes an additional workload for the community to process. Virginia Tech received literally thousands of cards, paintings, et cetera. There's so many hidden costs in dealing with these things that it sometimes becomes a burden on the families as well, so I would encourage people to make contributions, as they're able to, to local charities. Thankfully, my hospital covered our bills and all that, but other people have issues like long-term care that need financial assistance. So, skip the cheese plate and just send money.

Did it change you?

Yes, it did. The truth is, Virginia Tech, while it was a horribly and unfortunately well-planned attack, we all know it really could happen anywhere. We all know, in reality, there is no logic or reason why he picked that day and that classroom and that building. People will sometimes ask, *When did you get over it*, and I don't think you can; I think it's a lot to ask of anyone.

And today?

It's made me be much more grateful and appreciative for things we can sometimes take for granted, such as seemingly small moments with family. I've realized that we never quite know how long we have on earth, so it's up to us to ensure we're doing something meaningful with this precious opportunity. I have a hard time accepting any kind of overwhelming sympathy or empathy from the whole thing, because the way that I look back at it is that I survived, right? Out of eighteen students, I lived. I have nothing to complain about in this world.

Chapter Thirteen

What's Happening?

On September 11, 2001, shortly after the second plane hit the Twin Towers in New York, my phone rang in my FBI office in Milwaukee, Wisconsin. It was a friend who told me, as she gulped back tears, that she just wanted me to know that she loved me and knew I likely only had that minute to talk.

As the terrorism supervisor for the Wisconsin field office, I didn't know if our nation was on the brink of a war. The stress was tangible.

I hadn't experienced anything like this before. Orders quickly came in from headquarters to make sure we were all armed and carrying all our equipment; cars were filled with gasoline, supplies and personnel located. Some personnel just wanted to go home. Everyone wanted to check in with family. No one knew what the next hours might bring.

Those of us working were the fortunate ones because we were busy. My family and friends in Michigan and Chicago, and millions of others around the nation, sat frozen in place, watching television, with no idea what to do or how our country might respond to the unfolding nightmare.

If you are old enough to remember the September 11, 2001, terrorist attacks, you may recall this feeling of helplessness. As the days turned to weeks and then months, I heard this over and over again from friends, family, and neighbors.

Most of us know what to expect when a fire, tornado, power outage, or traffic accident occurs. We aren't happy, but we understand why it's happening and what others are doing to fix the situation. This is true even when the fire department doesn't have time to talk to onlookers or police are busy at an accident scene. In the same way, knowing answers to some of the most common questions will reduce your level of inevitable stress if you are involved in a shooting.

With that in mind, I've pulled together answers to the questions I and other first responders hear most frequently. The question-and-answer format should assist in understanding the chronology of a shooting incident. This is what might be going through your mind if you are involved in a shooting or other incident involving targeted violence, from the time you might hear gunshots to the time you engage with first responders.

I think I still hear gunshots. What should I do?
- If safe to do so, run. Flee the area so you cannot be a target. If you cannot run, hide in the safest place you can find, preferably with cover and concealment.
- Remember your Run. Hide. Fight.® training: Stay quiet. Keep those around you quiet; turn off your cell phone. Turn out nearby lights. Pull shades; lock and block doors as best you can; look around for what you could use to attack an intruder just the way you might attack a home invader threatening your family.

I'm locked down. How long should I stay here?
- Wait for police to find you; be patient. It may be an hour or more as police methodically go through the entire building "clearing" each room; they will find you. Don't open a door until you are sure it is the police.

The kids and adults with me are freaking out, and it's making me worry. What can I do?
- Be the calm; calm is contagious. Start with one person, and recruit them to help you keep others calm. In an emergency everyone needs something to do. Remind yourself and others that the most dangerous time period during these incidents is often over in minutes and then it becomes a waiting game for police to come and get you out safely.
- With children, make a game of seeing who can be the quietest for the longest time or, if safe to do so, share stories, pray, count ceiling tiles, or anything. Rely on your training, and urge others to do the same.

Why aren't police coming to get the hurt people around me?
- They are, but it takes time. Law enforcement has to stop the threat first; they may pass by the injured, but others are coming to render aid. Emergency medical responders are trained to come in behind police to assist. Do what you can to help the injured. Pack fabric into bleeding wounds. Apply tourniquets tighter than you think you should.

I'm injured. Who can help me?
- You are your best advocate. Adrenaline will be coursing through your body and will help you to save yourself. Take care of yourself. Pack your wound to stop your bleeding. Use a rope, cord, or, if nothing else, strips of a shirt or a belt to stop your arm or leg from bleeding.
- Believe earnestly that you will survive. The power of positive thinking isn't just a phrase; it has been proven to work. If you are alone, try to move to

where others are present or where others can help you if you lose conscious-
ness. Remain sitting up if you can. Keep awake, and tell others how they can
help you. Talking to people helps keep you conscious.

How can I help someone who is injured?
- Don't worry you will hurt someone by moving them if they are injured; that's
  old-school advice. If a person is unconscious, turn them on their side if you
  can. Keep them warm. The ground is cold, so don't move them there if there is
  a place off the ground where they can stay. Huddle with them, and share your
  body heat. Cover them with any coats, blankets, or even floor rugs.
- Learn how to use a tourniquet, and understand cutting off the blood circulation on an arm or leg will make the person cry out in pain; let them. You will
  save their life.
- Pack wounds with fabric, any fabric you have, and push it in and in and in
  and in. More will fit in than you think. You want to stop the bleeding inside.
  Then press down as hard as you can to stop the bleeding, and don't stop until
  emergency medical personnel tell you to or someone else takes over.
- If you have a car and no medical personnel are around, spend a brief amount
  of time to try to stabilize a person who is bleeding, and then get them to an
  emergency room. The faster someone gets to surgery or needed medical care,
  the more likely they will survive.

I know how to get away to safety. What should I know before I go?
- Keep your hands visible and empty. Don't be alarmed when you see officers
  with rifles, shotguns, or handguns. Know that officers will shout commands
  and may have individuals move to the ground as they stabilize the scene. Follow law enforcement instructions, and evacuate in the direction from which
  they came unless instructed otherwise.

I ran away when the shooting started. What should I do?
- Make sure you are in a safe location. Don't go back where the shooting might
  be ongoing no matter whom you think you left behind. Call 911 first to let
  them know you are safe and what you know. You might be able to help them
  with critical details. News travels fast; contact a family member or friend so
  people know you are safe. Absent checking in to say you are safe, hold off on
  posting on social media live or static; there'll be enough time for that later. If
  you were at school or a work location, is there someone you should contact to
  let them know you are okay?

I left, but I'm still scared. What should I do?
- It's okay to still be scared even if you are physically safe; it's a natural response. Know each person deals with trauma in their own way and in their
  own time; there is no correct way to respond. Many immediate and long-term
  resources are available for free for survivors and the families of victims. Others who have gone through similar traumas have very close support groups
  you can connect with, if and when you are ready.

Can I talk about what I saw to the media?
- Yes, if you like, but you do not need to and should consider that you will likely be very upset. People who know you may be watching, and this may be the first time they see you. What you say and do on social media and with the news media is public and permanent. Once your name is released, the media can track you down—and not only you but your family and friends. Remember, you don't want people hearing about their loved ones because you are talking about them on livestream.

FIRST RESPONDERS' DUTIES

Police, firefighters, and other first responders are well-schooled in the duties that involve the response and recovery at the scene and elsewhere. This includes working with panicked family and friends, supporting survivors who may still be at the scene, and even working with the public, the media, and government officials.

Here are some of the most common questions asked about first responders:

What are those first arriving police and fire officials doing?
- Arriving officers are first concerned with scene security. Their priority is to seek out and end any threats. If anyone potentially is still shooting, you will hear law enforcement say they need to first end the threat by finding and stopping the shooter.

Are police shooting to wound a person?
- *Neutralize* does not mean discuss, fire warning shots, or shoot to wound. It means try to find and kill a shooter, unless the shooter voluntarily lays down their weapons and surrenders. If a shooter already has killed or tried to kill people by firing a weapon, police are facing a person willing and able to kill again. They will most often respond with equal force.
- Society relies on police to protect innocent people caught in the crossfire, and officers train to be as accurate as possible, shooting at the center mass of a person. Shooting to wound may be common in old Westerns, but it isn't realistic, and it isn't how law enforcement is trained, both for their own safety and the safety of the public. If an officer tries to shoot at an arm or leg and misses, that bullet is going past the intended target and could hit someone behind a shooter.

Why does it take so long to get the real details on what is happening?
- Shootings are often over in minutes. The brief duration seems to surprise everyone because there is no time to get ready. Most people have never experienced something like this and want to know what's happening immediately. This frustration is based, in part, on misplaced expectations. People are used to seeing news reports that provide hard and fast details about how many shooters were involved, how many people are dead, and the hospital where

the injured are being taken. Facts are the one sure thing everyone welcomes. Expectations are too often set by dramatized, made-for-television and movie tragedies: in less than an hour, events need to happen and get wrapped up neatly with a bow, and the stars need to be standing in a bar drinking a beer.

- Real incidents are messy and take a long time to manage. Information released prematurely can be inaccurate. Everything is in flux, so explaining what is actually happening is very much a minute-by-minute proposition. *Messy* is the most common word used by responders at the scene. I'd liken it to asking responders to work with a bucket of marbles on a hillside. Available workforce and resources for law enforcement, fire departments, and city hall will be stretched beyond planned limits. You just keep trying to catch the marbles rolling downhill and put them back on the top.

Why do we have to have our hands up when we are the innocent survivors just trying to flee?

- On scene, officers must quickly assess the size and scope of the threat and establish a perimeter. Anyone inside the perimeter is a suspect until the shooter or shooters are properly identified. Anyone outside that perimeter must stay out. Even if someone tells an officer that the shooter has killed themselves, that is not enough information for the officer to responsibly act on. Although an officer may find one person who appears to have committed suicide, law enforcement can never assume the threat has abated until they've conducted a more thorough search of the scene.
- One reason for this is that shooters often come to the scene with multiple guns and plenty of ammunition. A shooter might discard an empty weapon around where people have been killed. What if there is more than one shooter involved? In the same way, law enforcement never assumes that people fleeing the scene are all innocent. Some shooters have successfully fled the scene by blending into the panicked and scattering people around them.
- Police must make split-second decisions about whether to shoot to kill anyone who appears to threaten their life or the lives of others. Hands are the biggest risk to an officer, and hands raised high and visible—not holding a cell phone—assure an officer you are not a threat. This is why training for citizens, even children, must include telling them to swiftly and clearly show hands.

Do police go inside a building right away?

- The first officer arriving has been trained to go inside and to the shooter, even if the officer is alone. Prior to the Columbine High School shooting, departments routinely trained their officers to contain the scene and wait for backup or wait for a trained tactical team to arrive. Now police are trained to go in as soon as possible. Each officer has to assess the best way to enter and look for the shooter. Arriving police create response teams, even if they are from different departments. The next arriving officers then form another team. Subsequent teams are doing the same, and some may be supporting medical personnel or bringing injured people out for medical assistance.
- Depending on the circumstances, an officer may wait for a second or even third arriving officer. A single officer may decide to wait because they know

another officer is moments away or because they may not have enough ammunition or the right equipment, such as a ballistic vest or helmet.

How is a call to 911 helpful if I am trapped in a room or have fled the scene?
- The emergency system phone operators—those answering 911 calls—are
  highly trained to triage and relay information to officers on the scene to
  help them determine where a shooter may be, who the shooter is, and what
  a shooter may be wearing and even to resolve contradictory information. To
  aid in this triage effort, it's important for everyone involved or at the scene
  to try to share what they know by calling 911. Don't assume police already
  know what you know.

Are first responders worried about bombs?
- Experience has taught first responders to look for secondary threats right
  from the start, though they also will move past a potential bomb if they need
  to get to a shooter to stop the killing. The shooter at the movie house in Aurora, Colorado, left scores of homemade explosive devices in his apartment,
  hoping to distract police with an initial explosion he hoped would cause the
  death of as many people as possible. The Columbine High School shooters
  had set homemade bombs inside the school, hoping to collapse the roof over
  the cafeteria.
- The initial pass through an area is not considered "clearing" the scene, because officers are just looking for the direct threats—someone holding a gun
  or a knife, or an explosive device. Training on spotting explosives is important
  but not always done. Initial responders missed an improvised explosive device
  in a bag at the 2015 terrorist shooting in San Bernardino, California, where
  fourteen people were killed and another twenty-four injured. The follow-up
  teams found it.

Why do some responding officers run past wounded people?
- Officers moving through the entire affected area need to ensure they can
  safely move the injured, so their first priority is to fall into teams and move in
  predictable patterns to stop the shooter. Officers are noting where the injured
  are and will either return or send help. If you see an officer pass by, that is
  the time to get up and run out to safety if you can, keeping your hands where
  law enforcement can see them. Civilians often freeze, waiting for someone
  to give them permission to flee. No permission is required. Get out—if and
  when you can.

I heard the shooter is dead. Why don't paramedics just go get the wounded?
- The areas where the officers are moving are considered "hot" zones. Rescue
  officials, such as paramedics, emergency medical technicians, and others,
  generally won't enter a "hot" zone with the officers until officers determine
  a particular area is free of potential threats. Then, the area is considered a
  "warm" zone. Even in a warm zone, law enforcement must provide protection
  for any medical team members moving to help the wounded, because they
  are not armed themselves. Additional responding fire and emergency medical

personnel will stay out of the hot zone and typically avoid warm zones too, staying in areas designated as safe or "cold" zones.

- In recent years, some first responders have created hybrid teams to provide faster medical assistance within the warm zone. How effective are they? We don't know because of limited current data available. No record system in the United States actually exists to determine if gunshot victim survival rates are different when better or faster treatment occurs.

What are first responders doing outside?
- The next people arriving are those responsible for initiating a *unified command*—the term used for a central location for police, fire, government, and other officials to coordinate the response and recovery efforts.
- Their first priorities are to establish an adequately wide perimeter, call for mutual aid from other law enforcement and other first responders in surrounding communities, and assess other threats, such as potential secondary threats at that scene or at other scenes, such as the shooter's car and home or apartment.
- Unified command officers also establish staging areas to quickly create designated areas for all the resources that inevitably will pour into the scene. Understanding these staging areas also can help guide you if you are looking for help or to locate one of the decision makers from your company, school, or organization.
- First responders are extensively schooled in organizing incidents by function categories, such as logistics, operations, and planning. To civilians, these translate into areas to manage the people, the things, and the responsibilities that come with any incident.
- In mass casualty or active shooter situations, first responders will set up six or seven separate staging areas almost immediately, taking over buildings and spreading out over a pretty big territory. This is why no one is allowed to get too close to the scene. In addition, caring for the injured and protecting the privacy of those involved is paramount. Citizen gawkers are not welcome, and it seems everybody is a social media streamer these days. While this can create frustration for concerned family and friends, there is another way concerned citizens can get information that I'll discuss below.
- If you are one of the designated decision makers for an affected business, property owner, school, or religious organization, you may need to be in or speaking with those in unified command. You may have things they need urgently, including access to keys, building schematics, utility shutoffs, closed-circuit video tapes, employee lists, and other resources necessary to resolving threats and get businesses back up and running.
- The unified command team is making the decisions about when and what to say to the news media, another reason affected entities want to be involved. Initially, unified command may be the hood of a car where these individuals gather, but in mass casualty incidents or major tragedies, police and fire often bring in larger command vehicles to allow people to work outside the elements, in private, 24-7, and in a safe location.

What are the other staging areas?

- *Witness interview areas* allow witnesses to be moved away from the chaos and given privacy. Other times, witness names and contact information, as well as a gauge of their involvement, are recorded at a witness interview location near the scene so law enforcement can reach out to them at a later time.
- *Casualty collection areas* are reserved as an initial staging area for the wounded, whether they are carried or walked from the scene. Here, medically trained personnel triage victims to identify, treat, and transport the most seriously wounded. Coordinators advise hospitals of incoming patients and evaluate whether hospitals are prepared to handle additional wounded and the most acutely injured.
- Many times, individuals fleeing a scene under their own power go to a hospital on their own, which can overtax emergency rooms. In overwhelming circumstances, casualty collection takes a back seat. This occurred at the Aurora theater shooting, when, out of sheer necessity, police transported as many people to the hospital as were taken by ambulance. During the Pulse nightclub shooting in Orlando, dozens of victims were carried or traveled on their own to the hospital six blocks away.
- *Tactical response teams and other law enforcement staging areas* create a ready pool of available law enforcement officers to support decisions made in unified command. The staging area helps to sort through who is needed and who can be sent away for other duties. Tactical teams are often used to do a methodical clearing of buildings because they are wearing the best ballistic protection, should an armed shooter who has secreted themselves be discovered.
- The dramatic rise in active shooter incidents in the United States over the past twenty years has resulted in law enforcement officers responding as if there has been an all-hands call—that is, a call that all officers should respond to. When a shooting occurred at a Navy Yard building in Washington, DC, it was impossible for commanders to give the all-clear and turn the building from a warm zone to a cold zone because so many armed officers had run inside. In all, 117 officers, from most of the twenty-some law enforcement agencies in and around the District of Columbia, were inside the building and had to be ordered out.
- A *Family Assistance Center* is a location out of the public eye where survivors can be reunified with their family and friends and where overwhelmed family members can go to safely ask for assistance finding their missing loved ones. Those coordinating the local, state, and federal resources for victims are the unsung heroes of these terrible incidents. I discussed Family Assistance Centers in chapter 12.
- An *air landing pad* is useful in rural or congested areas, like where I am in the Washington, DC, area. Though infrequently used prior to the 1990s, these flight-for-life efforts are now commonplace. When roads were clogged with police cars, fire trucks, and regular traffic, medical helicopters were put to good use in the Navy Yard shooting in Washington, DC.

- *News media staging* at these locations is necessary because the media oftentimes are faster than anyone else to arrive. Media staging areas need to include a press conference location separated from the public, large enough for cameras and reporters, and a place for media satellite trucks.

What are all the other officers doing at the scene?
- These scenes require plenty of personnel. They need additional personnel for later shifts, to search a shooter's car or home, and to cover other responsibilities. The FBI's evidence collection effort at the Navy Yard building took three weeks to complete. The FBI's response involved 552 investigators, evidence collectors, tactical officers, technical experts, command staff, and more. Their response to the shooting at Fort Hood in Texas similarly required 175, just in FBI support.

Why do police worry about the news media in an emergency?
- The most effective way to get accurate information to the public is via the news media. Probably the most neglected but most necessary task is establishing media staging sites—one for news or press conferences and for media satellite trucks and vehicles.
- A good location for press conferences is often set up, at least initially, not far from the location of the incident because the media and unified command will be nearby. Failure to set up this staging area quickly during the 2013 shooting at Los Angeles International Airport resulted in two locations and confusion at the scene, the chief in charge told me later. Relaying accurate information clears up errors, whether brought on by ignorance, opportunistic troublemakers, or the well-intended sharing of erroneous rumors.

Chapter Fourteen

Don't Go It Alone

When a Google search for active shooter turns up 100 million initial hits, where do you look for the best information?

Start here. For convenience, you can also find these on a PDF list on my web sites at: www.katherineschweit.com and www.schweitconsulting.com.

This chapter includes many sites that will continue to provide the latest resources and research. If you are looking for something not included here, don't forget to go back to the endnotes from each chapter, which are filled with scads of additional resources. Not every resource is listed, but this is a start.

The increase in active shooter incidents has created a pop-up industry over the last decade, some of it built on fear. The hawkers offer specialized equipment to safeguard buildings and doors, detect intruders and gunshots, and train people in gun use, martial arts, and the art of survival. Many of these might be a good match for your security program.

It's sometimes difficult to sort the wheat from the chaff. Very good products are mixed within; any of these might be something you need, but how do you know? Look first to the government and not-for-profit agencies and then look to some of the most reliable resources.

In addition to these sites, check the websites for local and neighboring police and fire departments, town and city officials, and local emergency management teams. The governors' offices in most states coordinate the disbursement of federal funds during an emergency, including for victims' families and survivors. They all have robust websites.

Once you get to the sites I will list below, simply type in keywords such as *active shooter*, *threat assessment*, *template*, and *emergency operations guides*. This will lead you not only to sample policies and emergency operations guides but also to information on opportunities to sign up for live training, webinars, and seminars already recorded or scheduled in the future.

All government publications are in the public domain, and so using the material exactly as you find it, or parts of the material, is perfectly legal and not a copyright violation because it is does not hold a copyright. You do not need to seek written permission to do this. I mention this detail here because I am so often asked if permissions need to be granted.

The one caveat: you cannot use a government seal or symbol without permission, absent perhaps placing it on a training PowerPoint slide inside a presentation to indicate, for example, that you have looked to these agencies for resources. This includes a Federal Bureau of Investigation (FBI) seal or badge, a US Secret Service (USSS) seal or badge, or any of the other seals representing departments or offices of the US government. A violation occurs if the use appears to show endorsement of, or collaboration with, a federal agency. In those cases, it's better not to use it.

Some of my favorite go-to materials from the links below:

- In 2020, the FBI released four short training films demonstrating Run. Hide. Fight.®, which can be used freely. The 30-second to four-minute films are shot in a house of worship and in a bar.
- The White House released a first-ever series of all-agency "Guides to De-veloping High Quality Emergency Operations Plans," located on several agency sites. Initially tailored to schools, universities, and houses of wor-ship, subsequent guides have been released for businesses, airports, and health care facilities.
- In 2017 the FBI released "A Study of Pre-Attack Behaviors of Active Shooters in the United States Between 2000 and 2013." The study explores the motivations and backgrounds of sixty-seven shooters by reviewing police reports and evaluating personal interviews of those closest to the shooter. It's the second in a four-part study still underway studying inci-dents and shooters. The first part is "A Study of Active Shooter Incidents in the United States Between 2000 and 2013."
- The FBI's experts from the Behavioral Analysis Unit (BAU) and the Of-fice of Partner Engagement shepherded an extraordinary group of world experts through discussions in prevention, eventually releasing "Making Prevention a Reality: Identifying, Assessing, and Managing the Threat of Targeted Violence." The group concluded that "engaging a multidisci-plinary team for threat assessments is perhaps the single most important thing a community or organization can do to further its prevention efforts."

FIRST PLACES TO VISIT

The primary location for government-generated information can be found on the **Ready.gov** site: www.ready.gov/active-shooter.

The **FBI** initiates all things active shooter on a single site that is easy to find if you go to fbi.gov and search *active shooter resources*. Look here: www.fbi.gov/about/partnerships/office-of-partner-engagement/active-shooter-resources and www.fbi.gov/survive. The study posted there, "A Study of Active Shooter Incidents in the United States Between 2000 and 2013," is so heavily relied upon that the Government Printing Office has it in their annual catalogue, and Amazon sells a Kindle edition if you need it.

The **US Department of Justice's Office of Justice Programs** coordinates research and resources as well as information about research that is underway. Its **National Institute of Justice** funds grants for academic, nonprofit, and faith-based organizations and even individuals who want to conduct research. Look here: www.ojp.gov.

The **Bureau of Justice Assistance** grants are awarded for innovative, evidence-based strategies and collaborative efforts by state, local, tribal, private, and public entities seeking ways to prevent crime and protect communities. Look here: www.bja.gov.

For victim and survivor assistance and planning, turn to the **Office for Victims of Crime** site with resources to help you find a local program, contact a helpline, find a compensation program, and learn more. Look here: www.ovc.gov/help/index.html. The FBI also provides an overview and resources. Look here: www.fbi.gov/resources/victim-services.

The **US Department of Homeland Security** (DHS) has a seemingly endless number of links, training materials, and resources translated into nine languages. Start here: www.dhs.gov/cisa/active-shooter-preparedness. Training is also available at www.dhs.gov/cisa/private-citizen.

Publications are available such as "Mass Gatherings: Take Charge of Your Personal Safety," at www.cisa.gov/sites/default/files/publications/Mass%20Gatherings%20-%20Take%20Charge%20of%20Your%20Personal%20Safety.pdf. Take note, the capital letters in this citation are required.

They also offer a fill-in-the-blank active shooter emergency planning guide and template: www.cisa.gov/publication/active-shooter-emergency-action-plan-guide and www.cisa.gov/sites/default/files/publications/active-shooter-emergency-action-plan-template-112017-508.pdf.

You must request access to this additional site from DHS, www.dhs.gov/cveas-portal, which is available for people with job-related duties, a public service interest, or those who work with programs that support people affected by active shooters. Send an email to get access.

The **Federal Emergency Management Agency** is the leader in this area at DHS. Scads of training for individuals, businesses, and other groups is available through DHS, online and live. Look here: training.fema.gov/.

The **USSS**, a part of DHS, does research at its **National Threat Assessment Center**. Their most recent publication discusses "Mass Attacks in Public Spaces—2018." Look here: www.secretservice.gov/node/2553.

A nearly twenty-year-old USSS report on how to establish a threat assessment team, put together with the **US Department of Education** (ED), is still relevant today: "The Final Report and Findings of the Safe School Initiative: Implications for the Prevention of School Attacks in the United States." Look here: www2.ed.gov/admins/lead/safety/preventingattacksreport.pdf.

ED's Readiness and Emergency Management for Schools Center (REMS center) not only has materials on active shooter response but also extensive materials on prevention programs that speak to bullying prevention and other ways to support individuals rolled into a subject called Psychological First Aid for Schools at rems.ed.gov/K12PreparingForActiveShooter.aspx.

The **US Department of Health and Human Services** (HHS) can get you started if you work on, or are responsible for, emergency matters in a health care setting. Start here: asprtracie.hhs.gov/technical-resources/resource/1952/active-shooter-planning-and-response-in-a-healthcare-setting. For guides in the development of emergency operations plans, look here: www.phe.gov/Preparedness/planning/Documents/active-shooter-planning-eop2014.pdf.

The **Substance Abuse and Mental Health Services Administration** within HHS focuses on behavioral health, including reducing mental illness in America's communities. They have published recommendations to support crisis intervention teams and provide mental health resources for schools. Look here: www.store.samhsa.gov.

The **National Council for Behavioral Health** is one of the best and most expansive resources you'll find. Don't let the organizational name confuse you. The National Council released "Mass Violence in America: Causes, Impacts and Solutions" in 2019, shortly after the shootings in El Paso, Texas, and Dayton, Ohio. Several years in the making, the report examines the reasons, contributing factors, and actionable solutions surrounding mass violence in America through the lens of behavioral health. It offers a detailed public health model of prevention and has specific recommendations for community leaders, legislators, government agencies, law enforcement, and school officials. It's often ignored and undervalued for its quality content. An extensive resources list and reference materials at the end of the 96-page document touch on a wide swath of topics, so you can find just what you are looking for, whether it's help with bereavement or victim counseling, establishing threat assessment teams, guns and mental health research, advice on media management, or current position papers on best practices. See, www. thenationalcouncil.org/ and www.thenationalcouncil.org/press-releases/ following-tragic-shootings-in-el-paso-and-dayton-new-report-recommends-wide-range-of-actionable-solutions-to-reduce-mass-violence/.

Finally, one of the oldest, but still valuable resources, is a product from the **USSS, ED**, and the **FBI**, titled "Campus Attacks: Targeted Violence Affecting Institutions of Higher Education," at rems.ed.gov/docs/CampusAt tacks_201004.pdf.

Several organizations provide reliable support and information, too. A few of the most important are named here, including these organizations created by parents whose children were killed in school shootings. All three of these, and more, are run by dedicated teams who are working to prevent the next shooting.

Safe and Sound Schools at www.safeandsoundschools.org/.
I Love You Guys Foundation at www.iloveuguys.org/.
Safe Schools for Alex at www.safeschoolsforalex.org/.

National Center for School Safety at www.nc2s.org/.
The National Center (NC2S) is a federally funded clearinghouse for all things having to do with school safety; it crosses over, and is supported by, several other public and private organizations, including some listed below as well as the University of Michigan, Michigan State University, the University of Virginia, the National Council on Behavioral Health, Sandy Hook Promise, Schweit Consulting LLC, and national school superintendent and principal organizations. Created in 2018 and funded by the US Department of Justice, Office of Justice Programs, Bureau of Justice Assistance, NC2S resources bring rigorous academic research together with practical experience and best practices.

Safe2Tell.org at safe2tell.org/.
Susan Payne and her team created Safe2Tell.org initially to build an anonymous place for parents, students, teachers, school administrators, and law enforcement to share information and leave tips. The impetus was both the Columbine High School massacre and the staggering reality that 80 percent or even 90 percent of the time, someone other than the attacker knew violence was going to happen but failed to report it.

Train4Safety.org at train4safety.com/.
Creators of Train 4 Safety believe even the youngest can be better prepared but know that often disaster preparedness is designed only for adults. Disaster affects everyone, even preschoolers. The mission of Train 4 Safety is to use fun and engaging stories to teach children how to stay safe and be prepared.

Everytown for Gun Safety at everytown.org/.

Everytown for Gun Safety advocates for issues centered on gun safety and gun access. The heart of the organization centers on a **Moms Demand Action** component advocating within their own community. The organization was created in 2014 when Mayors Against Illegal Guns and Moms Demand Action for Gun Sense in America came together to address gun violence.

American Red Cross at www.redcross.org.

The Red Cross has a free active shooter PowerPoint slide deck of training materials you can review on your own and provide to your family, organization, business, or school at www.readyrating.org/Resource-Center/ Active-Shooter/acat/1/tag/active-shooter-training. You can also find extensive materials and courses in English and Spanish to train yourself, your congregation, or your employees in first aid, AED use, and CPR.

National Safety Council at www.nsc.org/.

The 100-year-old Council advocates reducing risk at work, in homes, in communities, and on the road. The Council site is filled with tools and resources to share and educate the reader. Look here: www.nsc.org. Free active shooter presentations and other materials are available here: https:// www.nsc.org/safety-training/workplace/emergency-preparedness. The site is so thorough they even have the advertisement flyer so you can post it in lunchrooms and on bulletin boards to announce the training.

City of Houston's Mayor's office, the originators of the training film *Run. Hide. Fight.*®, has resources in six languages, with plenty of materials for kids and adults alike. Look here: www.readyhoustontx.gov.

Notes

CHAPTER ONE

1. Megan Slack, "President Obama Speaks on the Shooting in Connecticut," December 14, 2012, https://obamawhitehouse.archives.gov/blog/2012/12/14/president-obama-speaks-shooting-connecticut.

2. Tom Cohen, "Wiping Away Tears, Obama Mourns Children Killed in School Shooting," CNN News, updated December 15, 2012, accessed September 30, 2020, https://www.cnn.com/2012/12/14/us/obama-school-shooting/index.html.

3. He did not know at the time that all six adult victims in the school were women.

4. "President Obama's Remarks on New Gun Control Actions, Jan. 16, 2013 (Transcript)," *Washington Post,* accessed September 30, 2020, https://www.washingtonpost.com/politics/president-obamas-remarks-on-new-gun-control-proposals-jan-16-2013-transcript/2013/01/16/528e7758-5ffc-11e2-b05a-605528f6b712_story.html; see also "White House: Gun Violence Reduction Executive Actions," accessed September 30, 2020, *Washington Post,* http://apps.washingtonpost.com/g/documents/politics/white-house-gun-violence-reduction-executive-actions/248/ and "White House Gun Violence Fact Sheet," *Washington Post,* accessed September 30 2020, http://apps.washingtonpost.com/g/documents/politics/gun-violence-fact-sheet/247/.

5. "Now Is the Time to Do Something about Gun Violence," accessed September 30, 2020, https://obamawhitehouse.archives.gov/issues/preventing-gun-violence; see also "Remarks by the President at Sandy Hook Interfaith Prayer Vigil," December 16, 2012, accessed September 30, 2020, https://obamawhitehouse.archives.gov/the-press-office/2012/12/16/remarks-president-sandy-hook-interfaith-prayer-vigil.

6. David Nakamura, "Biden Vows White House Action on Gun Control," *Washington Post*, January 9, 2013, accessed September 30, 2020, https://www.washingtonpost.com/news/post-politics/wp/2013/01/09/biden-vows-white-house-action-on-gun-control/?arc404=true.

7. The same year, the *American Journal of Public Health* released an exhaustive look at thirty-three years of data on suicides and gender, as well as other data,

concluding a strong relationship exists between suicide rates in men and women and the higher level of gun ownership in a state. "Higher gun ownership was associated with higher suicide rates by any means among male, but not among female, persons," researchers concluded. "For male persons, policies that reduce firearm ownership will likely reduce suicides by all means and by firearms. For female persons, such policies will likely reduce suicides by firearms." Michael Siegel and Emily F. Rothman, "Firearm Ownership and Suicide Rates Among US Men and Women, 1981–2013," *American Journal of Public Health* (July 2016), https://ajph.aphapublications.org/doi/abs/10.2105/AJPH.2016.303182.

8. Gun suicides, according to the Centers for Disease Control and Prevention, account for nearly half of all suicides in the United States. See Siegel and Rothman, "Firearm Ownership and Suicide Rates," 1316.

9. "America's Gun Culture in Charts," BBC World News, August 5, 2019, accessed September 30, 2020, https://www.bbc.com/news/world-us-canada-41488081.

10. John Haitiwanger, "Las Vegas Shooting Recovery Will Cost at Least $600 Million," Yahoo News, accessed September 30, 2020, https://finance.yahoo.com/news/las-vegas-shooting-recovery-cost-205522945.html; see also Jaeah Lee and Julia Lurie, "The True Cost of Gun Violence: Our Methodology," *Mother Jones*, April 15, 2015, accessed September 30, 2020, https://www.motherjones.com/politics/2015/04/methodology-gun-violence-data-ted-miller.

11. J. Peter Blair and Katherine W. Schweit, "A Study of Active Shooter Incidents in the United States Between 2000 and 2013," Federal Bureau of Investigation 2014, accessed September 30, 2020, https://www.fbi.gov/file-repository/active-shooter-study-2000-2013-1.pdf/view; see also ISBN-10: 1542689511 and ISBN-13: 978-1542689519; see also https://bookstore.gpo.gov/products/study-active-shooter-incidents-united-states-between-2000-and-2013" and Amazon.com Services LLC, ASIN: B076C86CQK.

12. Those killings included thirteen at Fort Hood in Killeen, Texas, and another individual at a recruiting center in Little Rock, Arkansas.

13. My FBI colleague Christopher Combs and I joined the overworked VP team and about a dozen on the Emergency Management Planning team, which included Jeff Afman from the Federal Emergency Management Agency (FEMA), Kevin Horahan from Health and Human Services (HHS), Calvin Hodnett from Justice's Community Oriented Policing Services, Donald Lumpkin from the Department of Homeland Security (DHS), and David Esquith and Madeline Sullivan from the Department of Education (ED). Combs, shortly after, was assigned other executive duties and the task was left for me to manage.

14. United States Department of Justice, "Attorney General Holder Recognizes Department Employees and Others for Their Service at Annual Awards Ceremony," October 15, 2014, accessed September 30, 2020, https://www.justice.gov/opa/pr/attorney-general-holder-recognizes-department-employees-and-others-their-service-annual-1 (Recipients: Supervisory Special Agent Michael McElhenny; Resource Planning Office Special Advisor Kathryn M. Crotts; Critical Incident Response Group Supervisory Special Agent Katherine W. Schweit; Public Affairs Specialist Andrew C. Ames; from the Department of California Highway Patrol, Lieutenant David William Knoff).

15. National Council for Behavioral Health, "Mass Violence in America: Causes, Impacts and Solutions," August 2019, accessed September 30, 2020, https://www.thenationalcouncil.org/wp-content/uploads/2019/08/Mass-Violence-in-Amer ica_8-6-19.pdf.

16. William Wan and Carolyn Y. Johnson, "Coronavirus May Never Go Away, Even with a Vaccine," *Washington Post*, May 27, 2020, accessed September 30, 2020, https://www.washingtonpost.com/health/2020/05/27/coronavirus-endemic/.

17. Chapter 9 provides more detail about the origins of Run. Hide. Fight.®, which originated in Houston as a federally supported emergency preparedness program of the same name.

18. Only 7 percent of United States law enforcement agencies have more than one hundred sworn officers, and 86 percent have fewer than fifty.

19. Meghan Keneally and Luis Martinez, "Devin Kelley's History Shows Series of Violent Incidents before Texas Church Shooting," November 8, 2017, accessed December 4, 2021, https://abcnews.go.com/US/devin-kelleys-history-shows-series-violent-incidents-textas/story?id=50985889.

20. Mike Lupica, "Lupica: Morbid Find Suggests Murder-Obsessed Gunman Adam Lanza Plotted Newtown, Conn.'s Sandy Hook Massacre for Years," *New York Daily News*, March 25, 2013, https://www.nydailynews.com/news/national/lupica-lanza-plotted-massacre-years-article-1.1291408?print.

CHAPTER TWO

1. John Peter Blair, Terry Nichols, David Burns, and John R. Curnutt, *Active Shooter Events and Response* (Boca Raton, FL: CRC, 2013); see also ISBN-13: 978-1466512290; ISBN-10: 1466512296.

2. Blair and Schweit, "A Study of Active Shooter Incidents," appendix B.

3. Blair produced no academic research at the time, for which he added my name, but several years later he, M. Hunter Martaindale, and William L. Sandel did rely on the FBI study as the basis for their thoughtful view of policy implications on workplace violence; see https://alerrt.org/research-projects.

4. Blair and Schweit, "A Study of Active Shooter Incidents." (The FBI's methodology for its research is detailed in appendix B, and each of the 160 incidents is identified in appendix A.)

5. Investigative Assistance for Violent Crimes Act of 2012, 6 U.S.C. 455, 18 U.S.C. 2332f.

6. Basia E. Lopez, Danielle M. Crimmins, and Paul A. Haskins, "Advancing Mass Shooting Research to Inform Practice," *National Institute of Justice Journal* (April 6, 2020), accessed September 30, 2020, https://nij.ojp.gov/topics/articles/advancing-mass-shooting-research-inform-practice.

7. Lopez, Crimmins, and Haskins, "Advancing Mass Shooting Research."

8. Jerome P. Bjelopera, Erin Bagalman, Sarah W. Caldwell, Kristin M. Finklea, and Gail McCallion, "Public Mass Shootings in the United States: Selected Implications for Federal Public Health and Safety Policy," Congressional Research Service,

March 18, 2013, accessed September 30, 2020, https://fas.org/sgp/crs/misc/R43004. pdf; see also Robert J. Morton, "Serial Murder: Multi-Disciplinary Perspectives for Investigators," Federal Bureau of Investigation, 2005, accessed September 30, 2020, https://www.fbi.gov/stats-services/publications/serial-murder; but see Protection of Children from Sexual Predators Act of 1998, 18 U.S.C. 51, Sec. 1111, defining serial killings as three or more killed, not less than one, in the United States.

9. Bjelopera et al., "Public Mass Shootings in the United States."

10. Blair and Schweit, "A Study of Active Shooter Incidents."

11. Federal Bureau of Investigation, accessed September 30, 2020, https://www. fbi.gov/about/partnerships/office-of-partner-engagement/active-shooter-resources.

12. "A Study of Active Shooter Incidents in the United States Between 2000 and 2013," https://bookstore.gpo.gov/products/study-active-shooter-incidents-united-states-between-2000-and-2013 and Amazon.com Services LLC, ASIN: B076C-86CQK.

13. Some ask whether the term "active shooter" should also apply to incidents committed with knives, bombs, or cars. These incidents are even rarer and can skew research efforts involving firearms. This is also why many researchers, including those at the FBI, exclude gang and domestic violence shooting in their methodology. Gangs and domestic violence research efforts abound. The FBI's goal was to do research on incidents that only fit into this uniquely frightening public phenomenon, and the methodology is provided in detail in its study. See Blair and Schweit, "A Study of Active Shooter Incidents," appendix B.

14. The FBI continued its annual tallies, but we were left wanting a downturn. In the nine years since that research was released, this country now averages about one shooting every week. For US-based incidents, the FBI counted twenty annually in 2014, 2015, and 2016. The number rose to thirty in 2017, 2018, and 2019. See US Department of Justice, Federal Bureau of Investigation, "Quick Look: 277 Active Shooter Incidents in the United States from 2000 to 2018," 2019, accessed September 30, 2020, https://www.fbi.gov/about/partnerships/office-of-partner-engagement/ active-shooter-incidents-graphics.

15. Blair and Schweit, "A Study of Active Shooter Incidents," 9.

16. James Silver, Andre Simons, and Sarah Craun, "A Study of the Pre-Attack Behaviors of Active Shooters in the United States Between 2000 and 2013," Federal Bureau of Investigation, June 2018, accessed September 30, 2020, https://www.fbi. gov/file-repository/pre-attack-behaviors-of-active-shooters-in-us-2000-2013.pdf.

17. The Department of Education categorizes colleges and universities under one category: Institutions of Higher Education.

18. "Quick Look: 277 Active Shooter Incidents."

19. US Secret Service, National Threat Assessment Center Research and Publications, "Mass Attacks in Public Spaces—2019," report, August 2020, accessed September 30, 2020, https://www.secretservice.gov/protection/ntac.

20. Bjelopera et al., "Public Mass Shootings in the United States."

21. Brady Campaign to Prevent Gun Violence, https://www.bradyunited.org.

22. National Council for Behavioral Health (NCBH), "Mass Violence in America: Causes, Impacts and Solutions," National Council Medical Director Institute (MDI)

report, August 2019, accessed September 30, 2020, https://www.thenationalcoun cil.org/wp-content/uploads/2019/08/Mass-Violence-in-America_8-6-19.pdf, v; and Sophia Majlessi, "Following Tragic Shootings in El Paso and Dayton, New Report Recommends Wide Range of Actionable Solutions to Reduce Mass Violence," MDI NCBH press release, August 6, 2019, accessed September 30, 2020, https:// www.thenationalcouncil.org/press-releases/following-tragic-shootings-in-el-paso-and-dayton-new-report-recommends-wide-range-of-actionable-solutions-to-reduce-mass-violence/.

23. Chuck Ross, "CNN Slashes School Shooting Stats Claim by 80 Percent," *Daily Caller*, November 6, 2014, accessed September 30, 2020, http://dailycaller. com/2014/06/11/cnn-slashes-school-sooting-stts-claim-by-80-percent.

24. John Gramlich, "What the Data Says (and Doesn't Say) about Crime in the United States," Pew Research Center, November 20, 2020, https://www.pewresearch. org/fact-tank/2019/10/17/facts-about-crime-in-the-u-s/; see also "Crime," https:// news.gallup.com/poll/1603/crime.aspx; and Art Swift, "Americans' Perceptions of U.S. Crime Problem Are Steady," Gallup, November 9, 2016, accessed September 30, 2020, https://news.gallup.com/poll/197318/americans-perceptions-crime-problem-steady.aspx. (Since 1993, Gallup has surveyed Americans about violence, finding in nearly every year that 60 to 70 percent of Americans believe there is more violent crime in the United States compared to the year before. In eighteen of twenty-two Gallup surveys conducted between 1993 and 2018, at least six in ten Americans said there was more crime in the United States. Another noted group, the Pew Research Center, found similar patterns in a check of registered voters in late 2016, with 57 percent of the people surveyed saying crime had gotten worse in the United States since 2008.)

25. Pew Research Center, "A Divided and Pessimistic Electorate," November 10, 2016, accessed September 30, 2020, https://www.people-press.org/2016/11/10/a-di vided-and-pessimistic-electorate/#voters-said-there-has-been-scant-progress-across-most-areas.

26. Federal Bureau of Investigation, "2019 Crime in the United States," report, accessed September 30, 2020, https://ucr.fbi.gov/crime-in-the-u.s/2019/preliminary-report/home.

27. Michael Jetter and Jay K. Walker, "The Effect of Media Coverage on Mass Shootings," IZA Institute of Labor Economics, discussion paper, October 2018, accessed September 30, 2020, http://ftp.iza.org/dp11900.pdf.

28. Jetter and Walker, "The Effect of Media Coverage on Mass Shootings."

29. Sherry Towers, Andres Gomez-Lievano, Maryam Khan, Anuj Mubayi, and Carlos Castillo-Chavez, "Contagion in Mass Killings and School Shootings," July 2, 2015, accessed September 30, 2020, https://journals.plos.org/plosone/ article?id=10.1371/journal.pone.0117259.

30. Miles Kohrman and Katherine Reed, "Coverage of Mass Shootings Threatens Public Safety. Let's Fix It," *Columbia Journalism Review* (August 14, 2019), accessed September 30, 2020, https://www.cjr.org/united_states_project/mass-shoot ing-contagion-guidelines-the-trace.php.

31. Kohrman and Reed, "Coverage of Mass Shootings Threatens Public."

32. Holly Honderich, "Why So Many US 'Mass Shooting' Arrests Suddenly?" BBC World News, August 23, 2019, accessed September 30, 2020, https://www.bbc.com/news/world-us-canada-49439539.

33. Kasey Cordell, "The News Coverage of Columbine Helped Turn the Tragedy into an International Phenomenon," *5280 Magazine*, April 2019, accessed September 30, 2020, https://columbine.5280.com/the-news-coverage-of-columbine-helped-turn-the-tragedy-into-an-international-phenomenon/.

CHAPTER THREE

1. Morton, "Serial Murder; Multi-Disciplinary Perspectives."

2. Silver, Simons, and Craun, "A Study of the Pre-Attack Behaviors of Active Shooters." See also James L. Knoll IV and Ronald W. Pies, "Moving Beyond 'Motives' in Mass Shootings," *Psychiatric Times* 36, no. 1 (January 13, 2019), accessed September 30, 2020, https://www.psychiatrictimes.com/view/moving-beyond-motives-mass-shootings.

3. American Psychological Association, "Resolution on Violent Video Games," August 2015, accessed September 30, 2020, https://www.apa.org/about/policy/violent-video-games.

4. Christina Gough, "Distribution of Video Gamers Worldwide in 2017, by Age Group and Gender," August 9, 2019, Statista, accessed September 30, 2020, https://www.statista.com/statistics/722259/world-gamers-by-age-and-gender.

5. Christina Gough, "Number of Video Gamers Worldwide in 2020, by Region (in Millions)," August 28, 2020, accessed September 30, 2020, https://www.statista.com/statistics/293304/number-video-gamers. (Video gaming is a hobby enjoyed by young and old across the globe. Figures in 2020 showed that there were almost 1.5 billion gamers in the Asia Pacific region, making it the largest region for video gaming worldwide. In total, there were an estimated 2.7 billion gamers across the globe in 2020.)

6. Silver, Simons, and Craun, "A Study of the Pre-Attack Behaviors of Active Shooters."

7. Blair and Schweit, "A Study of Active Shooter Incidents."

8. Silver, Simons, and Craun, "A Study of the Pre-Attack Behaviors of Active Shooters."

9. US Secret Service, National Threat Assessment Center, "Mass Attacks in Public Spaces."

10. Silver, Simons, and Craun, "A Study of the Pre-Attack Behaviors of Active Shooters." See also Knoll IV and Pies, "Moving Beyond Motives."

11. National Council for Behavioral Health, "Mass Violence in America."

12. Silver, Simons, and Craun, "A Study of the Pre-Attack Behaviors of Active Shooters."

13. Everytown for Gun Safety, "Guns and Violence Against Women: America's Uniquely Lethal Intimate Partner Violence Problem," October 17, 2019, accessed

September 30, 2020, https://everytownresearch.org/reports/guns-intimate-partner-violence.

14. Shannan N. Catalano, PhD, "Intimate Partner Violence: Attributes of Victimization, 1993–2011," Bureau of Justice Statistics, November 21, 2013, accessed September 30, 2020, https://www.bjs.gov/index.cfm?ty=pbdetail&iid=4801.

15. FBI, "Quick Look: 277 Active Shooter Incidents."

16. Blair and Schweit, "A Study of Active Shooter Incidents."

17. Silver, Simons, and Craun, "A Study of Pre-Attack Behaviors of Active Shooters."

18. Silver, Simons, and Craun, "A Study of Pre-Attack Behaviors of Active Shooters."

19. US Department of Justice, Federal Bureau of Investigation, "Quick Reference Guide: A Study of Pre-Attack Behaviors of Active Shooters in the United States Between 2000 and 2013," 2018, accessed September 30, 2020, https://www.fbi.gov/file-repository/pre-attack-behaviors-of-active-shooters-2000-2013-quick-reference-guide.pdf/view.

20. Martha Griffith and Scott Sonner, "Sparks Shooter Was a Typical Kid, Not a Loner, Friend Says," *Nevada Appeal*, October 35, 2013, https://www.nevadaappeal.com/news/government/sparks-shooter-was-a-typical-kid-not-a-loner-friend-says/.

21. Siobhan McAndrew, "Sparks School Shooting: No One Can Understand How the Gentle Boy Committed an Act of Ultimate Violence," *Reno Gazette Journal*, November 10, 2013, accessed September 30, 2020, https://www.rgj.com/story/news/2014/03/23/sparks-school-shooting-jose-reyes-parents-worked-to-raise-son-right/6619079.

22. Sparks Police Department, "Sparks Middle School Shooting Police Report," October 21, 2013, accessed September 30, 2020, http://www.documentcloud.org/documents/1159662-sparkspolicereport.html, 87.

23. Sparks Police Department, "Sparks Middle School Shooting," 86.

24. Sparks Police Department, "Sparks Middle School Shooting," 108; see Staff reports, "Sparks Middle School Shooting: Report Highlights," *Reno Gazette-Journal*, May 13, 2014, accessed September 30, 2020, https://www.rgj.com/story/news/crime/2014/05/13/sparks-middle-school-shooting-report/9050153/.

25. Sparks Police Department, "Sparks Middle School Shooting," 498–499, 506.

26. Sparks Police Department, "Sparks Middle School Shooting," 498–499, 1209–1210.

27. Sparks Police Department, "Sparks Middle School Shooting," 108–109.

28. Sparks Police Department, "Sparks Middle School Shooting," 108–109.

29. National Council for Behavioral Health, "Mass Violence in America."

CHAPTER FOUR

1. National Council for Behavioral Health, "Mass Violence in America."

2. Frederick S. Calhoun and Steve W. Weston, *Threat Assessment and Management Strategies: Identifying the Howlers and Hunters*, second edition (Boca Raton,

FL: CRC, 2016), ISBN-13: 978-1498721844, ISBN-10: 1498721842, 27; see also Frederick S. Calhoun and Steve W. Weston, *Contemporary Threat Management: A Practical Guide for Identifying, Assessing and Managing Individuals of Violent Intent* (Specialized Training Services, 2003).

3. Frederick S. Calhoun and Steve W. Weston, "Perspectives on Threat Management," *Journal of Threat Assessment and Management* 2, nos. 3–4 (2015), 258–267, http://dx.doi.org/10.1037/tam0000056.

4. Timothy R. Levine, "Truth-Default Theory (TDT): A Theory of Human Deception and Deception Detection," *Journal of Language and Social Psychology* 33, no. 4 (May 23, 2014): 378–392, doi:10.1177/0261927x14535916. ISSN 0261-927X.

5. Malcolm Gladwell, *Talking to Strangers: What We Should Know about the People We Don't Know* (New York: Little, Brown, 2019).

6. Silver, Simons, and Craun, "A Study of the Pre-Attack Behaviors of Active Shooters."

7. Melina Druga, "MTI Examines Effectiveness of 'See Something, Say Something' Programs," Homeland Preparedness News, December 17, 2018, accessed September 30, 2020, https://homelandprepnews.com/stories/31768-mti-examines-effectiveness-of-see-something-say-something-programs/#:~:text=The%20Mineta%20Transportation%20Institute%20(MTI,and%2014%20percent%20of%20attacks.

8. Brian Michael Jenkins and Bruce R. Butterworth, "Terrorist Vehicle Attacks on Public Surface Transportation Targets," Mineta Transportation Institute, September 2017, https://transweb.sjsu.edu/research/Terrorist-Vehicle-Attacks-Public-Surface-Transportation-Targets.

9. Silver, Simons, and Craun, "A Study of the Pre-Attack Behaviors of Active Shooters."

10. Derek Hawkins, "Teen Arrested in L.A. School Shooting Threat Had List of Students and Access to AR-15, Police Say," *Washington Post*, November 23, 2019, accessed September 30, 2020, https://www.washingtonpost.com/nation/2019/11/23/teen-arrested-la-school-shooting-threat-had-list-students-access-ar-police-say/.

11. Peter Langman and Frank Straub, "A Comparison of Averted and Completed School Attacks from the Police Foundation Averted School Violence Database," US Department of Justice, Office of Community Oriented Policing Services, February 2019, 8, https://www.policefoundation.org/publication/a-comparison-of-averted-and-completed-school-attacks-from-the-police-foundation-averted-school-violence-database/.

12. Silver, Simons, and Craun, "A Study of Pre-Attack Behaviors of Active Shooters," 9–13.

13. Molly Amman, Matthew Bowlin, Lesley Buckles, Kevin C. Burton, Kimberly F. Brunell, Karie A. Gibson, Sarah H. Griffin, Kirk Kennedy, and Cari J. Robins, "Making Prevention a Reality: Identifying, Assessing, and Managing the Threat of Targeted Attacks," US Department of Justice, Federal Bureau of Investigation, February 2017, accessed September 30, 2020, https://www.fbi.gov/file-repository/making_prevention_a_reality.pdf/view, 28.

14. Amman et al., "Making Prevention a Reality," 8–11, 90.

15. Erin Miller, "Global Terrorism Database Coding Notes: Las Vegas 2017," START (Study of Terrorism and Responses to Terrorism), December 7, 2018, accessed September 30, 2020, https://www.start.umd.edu/news/global-terrorism -database-coding-notes-las-vegas-2017. (Law enforcement records from the Las Vegas Metro Police Department include two witnesses' reports stating that the assailant made references indicating a political goal shortly before the attack in Las Vegas—in particular that "somebody has to wake up the American public and get them to arm themselves" because the United States government would "confiscate guns." While not addressing or refuting these accounts, the Federal Bureau of Investigation Behavioral Analysis Unit ultimately determined that "there was no single or clear motivating factor" for the attack. Due to this conflicting information, we included the attack in the GTD and classified it as "doubt terrorism proper.")

CHAPTER FIVE

1. One clearinghouse on upstander training that works with communities, law enforcement, and schools is Not In Our Town (NIOT), https://www.niot.org/, which has a companion organization, Not In Our School, https://www.niot.org/nios, accessed September 30, 2020. (Free videos, tips, and training resources are available on request.)

2. Terry Dickson, "McIntosh County Schools Reopen with Heavy Police Presence a Day After Closure Because of Online Threat," *Jacksonville Florida Times-Union*, September 6, 2013, accessed September 30, 2020, https://www.jacksonville.com/ article/20130906/NEWS/801247068.

3. Vincenz Leuschner, Rebecca Bondü, Miriam Schroer-Hippel, Jennifer Panno, Katharina Neumetzler, Sarah Fisch, Johanna Scholl, and Herbert Scheithauer, "Prevention of Homicidal Violence in Schools in Germany: The Berlin Leaking Project and the Networks Against School Shootings Project (NETWASS)," April 13, 2011, accessed September 30, 2020, https://onlinelibrary.wi ley.com/doi/epdf/10.1002/yd.387, 61–67.

4. The follow-on study will examine the nature of tips and follow-up actions taken by reviewing multiple years of tip data from the same ARS (anonymous reporting system) in a different US school district and state. With a longitudinal approach and by analyzing ARS data in multiple states, this research is an important first step in validating the use of ARSs in educational contexts.

5. Robert A. Fein, Bryan Vossekuil, William S. Pollack, Randy Borum, William Modzeleski, and Marisa Reddy, "Threat Assessment in Schools: A Guide to Managing Threatening Situations and to Creating Safe School Climates," Department of Education and United States Secret Service, May 1, 2002, accessed September 30, 2020, https://www.govinfo.gov/app/details/ERIC-ED466013, 33.

6. Robert A. Fein, Bryan Vossekuil, William S. Pollack, Randy Borum, William Modzeleski, and Marisa Reddy, *Threat Assessment in Schools: A Guide to Managing Threatening Situations and to Creating Safe School Climates* (Washington, DC:

United States Secret Service and United States Department of Education, 2002), https://www.amazon.com/Threat-Assessment-Schools-Threatening-Situations/dp/1482696592.

7. Robert A. Fein, Bryan Vossekuil, William S. Pollack, Randy Borum, William Modzeleski, and Marisa Reddy, "The Final Report and Findings of the *Safe School Initiative*: Implications for the Prevention of School Attacks in the United States," United States Secret Service and United States Department of Education, June/July 2004, Washington, DC, https://www2.ed.gov/admins/lead/safety/preventingattack sreport.pdf.

8. School Threat Assessment Consultants LLC, "Training in School-Based Threat Assessment," accessed September 30, 2020, https://www.schoolta.com/.

9. School Threat Assessment Consultants LLC, "Forms for the Comprehensive School Threat Assessment Guidelines," accessed September 30, 2020, https://www.schoolta.com/s/Forms-for-Comprehensive-School-Threat-Assessment-Guide lines-8-9-19.docx.

10. Mike Marsee, "Threat Assessment Model Catching On in Kentucky Schools," *Kentucky Teacher*, December 3, 2019, accessed September 30, 2020, https://www.kentuckyteacher.org/features/2019/12/threat-assessment-model-catching-on-in-ken tucky-schools/.

11. Stephen Sawchuk, "What Schools Need to Know About Threat Assessment Techniques," *Education Week*, September 3, 2019, accessed September 30, 2020, https://www.edweek.org/ew/articles/2019/09/04/what-schools-need-to-know-about -threat.html.

12. Sawchuk, "What Schools Need to Know." See also Melissa Diliberti, Michael Jackson, Jana Kemp, and Rachel Hansen, "Crime, Violence, Discipline, and Safety in U.S. Public Schools: Findings From the School Survey on Crime and Safety: 2015–16, First Look" (NCES 2017-122), US Department of Education, National Center for Education Statistics, accessed September 30, 2020, https://nces.ed.gov/pubs2017/2017122.pdf.

13. Donna Michaelis, "The Value of Threat Assessment Teams," *Notes from the Field*, November 12, 2019, US Department of Justice, National Institute of Justice, accessed September 30, 2020, https://nij.ojp.gov/topics/articles/value-threat-assess ment-teams.

14. US Department of Justice, Federal Bureau of Investigation, "Health Insurance Portability and Accountability Act (HIPAA) Privacy Rule: A Guide for Law Enforcement," accessed September 30, 2020, https://www.fbi.gov/file-repository/hipaa-guide.pdf/view.

15. US Department of Justice, Federal Bureau of Investigation, "Family Educational Rights and Privacy Act (FERPA): A Guide for First Responders and Law Enforcement," accessed September 30, 2020, https://www.fbi.gov/file-repository/ferpa-guide.pdf/view.

CHAPTER SIX

1. Amman et al., "Making Prevention a Reality." See also School Threat Assessment Consultants LLC, "Forms."

2. Lina Alathari, Ashley Blair, Catherine Camilletti, Steven Driscoll, Diana Drysdale, Jeffrey McGarry, and Amanda Snook, "Enhancing School Safety Using a Threat Assessment Model: An Operational Guide for Preventing Targeted School Violence," US Secret Service, July 2018, accessed September 30, 2020, https://www.cisa.gov/sites/default/files/publications/18_0711_USSS_NTAC-Enhancing-School-Safety-Guide.pdf. See also "Enhancing School Safety Using a Threat Assessment Model: An Operational Guide for Preventing Targeted School Violence," Cybersecurity & Infrastructure Security Agency, US Secret Service, accessed September 30, 2020, https://www.cisa.gov/publication/enhancing-school-safety-using-threat-assessment-model-operational-guide-preventing.

3. School Threat Assessment Consultants LLC, "Forms."

4. School Threat Assessment Consultants LLC, "Training."

5. School Threat Assessment Consultants LLC, "Training."

6. Maddie Hanna, "Finger Shoot from 6-year-old Causes Threat Assessment in Philadelphia Suburban School," *Pittsburgh Post-Gazette*, February 16, 2020, accessed September 30, 2020, https://www.post-gazette.com/news/education/2020/02/16/Finger-shoot-from-6-year-old-causes-threat-assessment-in-Philadelphia-suburban-school/stories/202002160023.

7. Kristen Taketa, "What Should Schools Do When a Second-Grader Makes a Threat?" *Los Angeles Times*, January 2, 2020, accessed September 30, 2020, https://www.latimes.com/california/story/2020-01-02/assessing-school-threats-elementary-grades.

8. Pew Research Center, "Public's Mood Turns Grim; Trump Trails Biden on Most Personal Traits, Major Issues," June 30, 2020, https://www.pewresearch.org/politics/2020/06/30/publics-mood-turns-grim-trump-trails-biden-on-most-personal-traits-major-issues/.

9. Pew Research Center, "Public's Mood Turns Grim." See also Charles Duhigg, "The Real Roots of American Rage: The Untold Story of How Anger Became the Dominant Emotion in Our Politics and Personal Lives—and What We Can Do About It," *Atlantic* (January/February 2018), https://www.theatlantic.com/magazine/archive/2019/01/charles-duhigg-american-anger/576424/.

CHAPTER SEVEN

1. Ke Wang, Yongqui Chen, Jizhi Zhang, and Barbara Oudekerk, "Indicators of School Crime and Safety 2019," (NCES 2020-063/NCJ 254485), July 2020, National Center for Education Statistics, US Department of Education, US Department of Justice, Office of Justice Programs, Bureau of Justice Statistics, accessed September 30, 2020, https://nces.ed.gov/pubs2020/2020063.pdf.

2. National Center for Educational Statistics, "Indicator 13: Students Carrying Weapons on School Property and Anywhere and Students' Access to Firearms," July 2020, accessed September 30, 2020, https://nces.ed.gov/programs/crimeindicators/ind_13.asp.

3. US Department of Justice, Federal Bureau of Investigation, "2017: Crime in the United States: Burglary," accessed September 30, 2020, https://ucr.fbi.gov/crime-in-the-u.s/2017/crime-in-the-u.s.-2017/topic-pages/burglary; and see table 23, "Offense Analysis: Number and Percent Change: 2016–2017," https://ucr.fbi.gov/crime-in-the-u.s/2017/crime-in-the-u.s.-2017/tables/table-23.

4. National Center for School Safety, accessed September 30, 2020, https://www.nc2s.org/.

5. US Department of Homeland Security, Federal Emergency Management Agency (FEMA), "Multihazard Emergency Planning for Schools Site Index," accessed September 30, 2020, https://training.fema.gov/programs/emischool/el361tool kit/siteindex.htm#item4; see also "Developing Procedures and Protocols," https://training.fema.gov/programs/emischool/el361toolkit/developingproceduresprotocols.htm; "Guide for Developing High-Quality School Emergency Operations Plans," https://www.fema.gov/media-library-data/20130726-1922-25045-3850/rems_k_12_guide.pdf; and various at https://www.ready.gov/. See also Interagency Security Committee, "Best Practices for Planning and Managing Physical Security Resources: An Interagency Security Committee Guide," December 2015, accessed September 30, 2020, https://www.cisa.gov/sites/default/files/publications/isc-planning-managing-physical-security-resources-dec-2015-508.pdf.

6. Katie Peters, "RELEASE: Virginia Tech Massacre Cost Taxpayers and Public University at Least $48.2 Million," Center For American Progress, April 12, 2012, accessed September 20, 2020, https://www.americanprogress.org/press/release/2012/04/12/15681/release-virginia-tech-massacre-cost-taxpayers-and-public-university-at-least-48-2-million/.

7. Dana Goldstein, "Do Police Officers Make Schools Safer or More Dangerous?" *New York Times*, June 12, 2020, accessed September 30, 2020, https://www.nytimes.com/2020/06/12/us/schools-police-resource-officers.html.

8. Dewey Cornell, "Briefing on Capitol Hill on March 23, 2018: Purpose and Foundation for Threat Assessments in Schools," C-SPAN, July 16, 2018, accessed September 30, 2020, https://www.c-span.org/video/?c4740361/user-clip-dewey-cornell-briefing.

9. University of Virginia, "Virginia Secondary School Climate Study," Youth Violence Project, accessed September 30, 2020, https://curry.virginia.edu/faculty-research/centers-labs-projects/research-labs/youth-violence-project/virginia-secondary.

10. National Center for School Safety.

11. US Department of Justice, Community Oriented Policing Services, "Supporting Safe Schools," accessed September 30, 2020, https://cops.usdoj.gov/supporting safeschools.

12. Jennifer E. Cobbina, Matthew Galasso, Mary Cunningham, Chris Melde, and Justin Heinze, "A Qualitative Study of Perception of School Safety among Youth in a High Crime City," *Journal of School Violence* 19, no. 3 (October 14, 2019):

277–291, DOI:10.1080/15388220.2019.1677477, http://doi.org/10.1080/15388220.2
019.1677477.

13. A. W. Geiger, "18 Striking Findings from 2018," Pew Research Center, December 13, 2018, accessed September 30, 2020, https://www.pewresearch.org/fact-tank/2018/12/13/18-striking-findings-from-2018/.

CHAPTER EIGHT

1. Hartford Institute for Religious Research, "Fast Facts about American Religion," accessed September 30, 2020, http://hirr.hartsem.edu/research/fastfacts/fast_facts.html.

2. National Restaurant Association, "National Statistics," accessed September 30, 2020, https://restaurant.org/research/restaurant-statistics/restaurant-industry-facts-at-a-glance.

3. US Small Business Administration, "2018 Small Business Profile," accessed September 30, 2020, https://www.sba.gov/sites/default/files/advocacy/2018-Small-Business-Profiles-US.pdf.

4. Blair and Schweit, "A Study of Active Shooter Incidents."

5. Live Nation's security person Carol Haave was watching the concert and became just another potential victim when the shooting started at its Las Vegas festival in 2017, prompting the company to reevaluate the following year and hire a team of professional security experts.

6. US Small Business Administration, "2018 Profile."

7. US Department of Labor, Occupational Safety and Health Administration, "Workplace Violence," accessed September 30, 2020, https://www.osha.gov/SLTC/workplaceviolence/. See also Neckerman Insurance Services, "Workplace Violence Costs Employers More than $120 Billion Each Year," March 19, 2012, accessed September 30, 2020, https://neckerman.com/workplace-violence-costs-employers-more-than-120-billion-each-year/.

8. Detis T. Duhart, "Violence in the Workplace, 1993–99," Special Report from the National Crime Victimization Survey, US Department of Justice, Bureau of Justice Statistics, December 2001, accessed September 30, 2020, http://www.bjs.gov/content/pub/pdf/vw99.pdf.

9. Lorraine Sheridan, Adrian C. North, and Adrian J. Scott, "Stalking in the Workplace," *Journal of Threat Assessment and Management* 6, no. 2 (June 2019): 61–75, accessed September 30, 2020, at http://dx.doi.org/10.1037/tam0000124.

10. US Department of Homeland Security (USDHS), Federal Emergency Management Agency (FEMA), "Faith-Based Community Preparedness," accessed September 30, 2020, https://www.fema.gov/emergency-managers/individuals-communities/faith-preparedness.

11. US Department of Homeland Security, Federal Emergency Management Agency, "Guide for Developing High-Quality Emergency Operations Plans for Houses of Worship," June 2013, accessed September 30, 2020, https://www.dhs.gov/

sites/default/files/publications/Developing_EOPs_for_Houses_of_Worship_FINAL. PDF.

12. USDHS, FEMA, "Guide for Developing High-Quality Emergency Operations Plans for Houses of Worship," 28.

13. USDHS, FEMA, "Faith-Based Community Preparedness."

14. US Department of Homeland Security, "Protecting Houses of Worship," November 8, 2019, accessed September 30, 2020, https://www.youtube.com/watch?v=i PhOH0C7cio&list=PLyTgR4PDHXBnnl7dd-MyGV3oqq6GalOIb&index=8.

15. City of Fairfax, "Model Emergency Operations Plan for Houses of Worship," *TIME*, March 2014, accessed September 30, 2020, http://www.fairfaxva.gov/Home/ ShowDocument?id=7314.

16. City of Fairfax, "Model Emergency Operations Plan."

17. Melissa Chan, "Here's How Much Closing Schools for a Terror Threat Cost L.A.," December 16, 2015, accessed September 30, 2020, https://time.com/4151902/ los-angeles-school-closures-cost/.

18. Larry Barszewski, "Broward Pays More than $500,000 Returning Abandoned Belongings Following Airport Shootings," *South Florida Sun Sentinel*, December 8, 2017, https://www.sun-sentinel.com/local/broward/fl-sb-fort-lauderdale-airport-shooting-financial-costs-20171206-story.html.

19. Kimberly Larsen, "Workplace Violence: Paranoid or Prepared?" Mediate, https://www.mediate.com/articles/larsen.cfm#:~:text=The%20Cost%20to%20 Employers&text=This%20figure%20includes%20monetary%20costs,verdicts%20 averaging%20about%20%243%20million.

20. Richard A. Oppel Jr., "MGM Agrees to Pay Las Vegas Shooting Victims Up to $800 Million," *New York Times*, October 3, 2019, https://www.nytimes. com/2019/10/03/us/mgm-las-vegas-shooting-settlement.html.

21. Sean Burns, "Promoter, Hotel Targeted in New Law Vegas Massacre Lawsuit," *Ticket News*, October 17, 2017, https://www.ticketnews.com/2017/10/ promoter-hotel-sued-las-vegas-massacre/.

22. US Department of Labor, Occupational Safety and Health Administration, https://www.osha.gov/laws-regs/standardinterpretations/2003-12-18-1.

23. US Department of Labor, Occupational Safety and Health Administration, "OSHA Archive: Workplace Violence," https://www.osha.gov/archive/oshinfo/pri orities/violence.html.

24. Larsen, "Workplace Violence: Paranoid or Prepared?"

25. US Department of Labor, Occupational Safety and Health Administration, "Emergency Preparedness Response: Getting Started: Evacuation & Shelter-in-Place," https://www.osha.gov/SLTC/emergencypreparedness/gettingstarted_evacua tion.html.

26. Beatrice Dupuy, "Building City Halls with Active Shooter Situations in Mind," August 13, 2016, *Minneapolis Star Tribune*, accessed September 30, 2020, https://www.startribune.com/building-city-halls-with-active-shooter-situations-in-mind/390049631/.

27. Silver, Simons, and Craun, "A Study of the Pre-Attack Behaviors of Active Shooters," 9.

28. Tony Miller, "How to Build an Effective Threat Assessment Team," Security Enterprise Services, February 1, 2013, accessed September 30, 2020, https://www.securitymagazine.com/articles/83982-how-to-build-an-effective-threat-assessment-team.

29. Fein et al., "Threat Assessment in Schools: A Guide."

30. US Department of Justice, Federal Bureau of Investigation, "Crisis Communications Quick Reference Guide," accessed September 30, 2020, https://www.dhs.gov/sites/default/files/publications/fbi-crisis-communications-trifold-reference-guide.pdf.

31. Experior Group, "Red Ball Drills®," accessed September 30, 2020, http://redballdrills.com/.

32. US Department of Justice, Federal Bureau of investigation, "Active Shooter Resources," accessed September 30, 2020, www.fbi.gov/survive.

33. US Department of Justice, Federal Bureau of Investigation, "Developing Emergency Operations Plans: A Guide for Business," March 2018, accessed September 30, 2020, https://www.fbi.gov/file-repository/active-shooter-guide-for-businesses-march-2018.pdf/view.

34. Cody Mulla, "Guidance on Threat Assessment Teams," ASIS International, January 1, 2019, accessed September 30, 2020, https://www.asisonline.org/security-management-magazine/articles/2019/01/guidance-on-threat-assessment-teams/.

35. ASIS International, "Featured Resources: Soft Target, Active Shooter," accessed September 30, 2020, https://www.asisonline.org/publications--resources/security-topics/active-shooter.

36. ASIS International, "Workplace Violence and Active Assailant—Prevention, Intervention, and Response Standard," (e-book), accessed September 30, 2020, https://store.asisonline.org/workplace-violence-prevention-and-intervention-standard-e-book.html.

37. US Department of Health and Human Services, Centers for Disease Control and Prevention, National Institute for Occupational Safety and Health, "NIOSH Emergency Preparedness and Response Program," August 2019, accessed September 30, 2020, https://www.cdc.gov/niosh/docs/2019-149/default.html#:~:text.

38. Security Executive Council, "Strategic Master Plan for Corporate Security and KPIs: The Process," accessed September 30, 2020, https://www.securityexecutivecouncil.com/spotlight/?sid=31324.

39. US Department of Health and Human Services, "Mass Violence," accessed September 30, 2020, https://asprtracie.hhs.gov/mass-violence.

CHAPTER NINE

1. Paul M. Reeping, Sara Jacoby, Sonali, Rajan, and Charles C. Branas, "Rapid Response to Mass Shootings: A Review and Recommendations," *Criminology & Public Policy* (December 16, 2019), accessed September 30, 2020, https://onlinelibrary.wiley.com/doi/full/10.1111/1745-9133.12479.

2. Metropolitan Transportation Authority, "MTA Security Campaign," accessed September 30, 2020, http://www.mta.info/mta-security-campaign.

3. City of Houston, Office of Emergency Management, "Run. Hide. Fight.® | Surviving an Active Shooter Event," accessed September 30, 2020, https://www.houstonoem.org/run-hide-fight-surviving-an-active-shooter-event/, and "Active Shooter Brochure Main Practice," accessed September 30, 2020, https://www.houstontx.gov/police/pdfs/brochures/english/Active_Shooter_Brochure_Main_Practice_2013.pdf. See also US Department of Justice, Federal Bureau of Investigation, "Active Shooter Event Quick Reference Guide," accessed September 30, 2020, https://www.fbi.gov/file-repository/active-shooter-event-quick-reference-guide_2015.pdf/view; "Ready: Attacks in Crowded and Public Spaces," https://www.ready.gov/active-shooter; and Cybersecurity & Infrastructure Security Agency, "Active Shooter Preparedness," accessed September 30, 202, https://www.cisa.gov/active-shooter-preparedness.

4. US Department of Defense, Defense Health Agency and the American College of Surgeons, "STOP THE BLEED," accessed September 30, 2020, https://www.stopthebleed.org.

5. The STOP THE BLEED® logo and phrase is a registered trademark of the United States Department of Defense and cannot be used without permission. The American College of Surgeons has authorized use of the STOP THE BLEED® logo and phrase.

6. While grant funding was used for the Run. Hide. Fight.® video, the City of Houston maintains a copyright on it; so you don't need permission to show it for training, but the City specifically grants no permission to edit the video, copy the script, or use the video to make a profit.

7. City of Houston, Office of Emergency Management, "Run. Hide. Fight.® | Surviving."

8. US DOJ, FBI, "Active Shooter Quick Reference Guide." See also Cybersecurity & Infrastructure Security Agency, "Active Shooter Preparedness," and "Guide for Developing High-Quality School Emergency Operations Plans," accessed September 30, 2020, https://www.fbi.gov/file-repository/rems-k-12-guide-508.pdf/view. See also US Department of Homeland Security, Federal Emergency Management Agency, "Training and Education," accessed September 30, 2020, https://www.fema.gov/emergency-managers/national-preparedness/training; "Faith-Based Community Preparedness," https://www.fema.gov/emergency-managers/individuals-communities/faith-preparedness#. (Joining ED executives in the sign-off with the White House were the Department of Justice and its FBI; the Department of Homeland Security and its Federal Emergency Management Agency (FEMA); and the Department of Health and Human Services (HHS). HHS has released specific, additional information for health care facilities, the FBI has released specific guidance for businesses, and DHS and FEMA have released specific, additional guidance for everybody, including valuable materials for faith-based organizations.)

9. The STOP THE BLEED® logo and phrase are registered trademarks of the United States Department of Defense and cannot be used without permission. The American College of Surgeons has authorized use of the STOP THE BLEED® logo and phrase.

10. STOP THE BLEED®, "Resource Hub," accessed September 30, 2020, https://www.stopthebleed.org/resources-poster-booklet; see American College of Surgeons, "Terms of Use," https://www.facs.org/terms-of-use; the website and all contents are copyrighted 1996–2020 by the American College of Surgeons (ACS), Chicago, IL 60611-3295, all rights reserved.

11. STOP THE BLEED®, "Class Search," accessed September 30, 2020, https://cms.bleedingcontrol.org/class/search.

12. American College of Surgeons, "New Trauma Study Results Show Tourniquet Practice Adopted from the Military Saves Lives and Limbs in Civilians," press release, March 9, 2018, accessed September 30, 2020, https://www.facs.org/media/press-releases/2018/tourniquet040418; see also Pedro G. R. Teixeira, Carlos V. R. Brown, Brent Emigh, Michael Long, Michael Foreman, Brian Eastridge, Stephen Gale, Michael S. Truitt, Sharmila Dissanaike, Therese Duane, John Holcomb, Alex Eastman, Justin Regner, and the Texas Tourniquet Study Group, "Civilian Prehospital Tourniquet Use Is Associated with Improved Survival in Patients with Peripheral Vascular Injury," *Journal of the American College of Surgeons* 226, no. 5 (May 2018), accessed September 30, 2020, DOI: https://doi.org/10.1016/j.jamcollsurg.2018.01.047, https://www.journalacs.org/article/S1072-7515(18)30101-7/abstract; and, John F. Kragh Jr., Michelle L. Littrel, John A. Jones, Thomas J. Walters, David G. Gaer, Charles E. Wade, and John B. Holcomb, "Battle Casualty Survival with Emergency Tourniquet Use to Stop Limb Bleeding," *Journal of Emergency Medicine* 41, no. 6 (December 2011), accessed September 30, 2020, https://pubmed.ncbi.nlm.nih.gov/19717268/.

13. Lorne H. Blackbourne, David G. Baer, Brian J. Eastridge, Bijan Kheirabadi, Stephanie Bagley, John F. Kragh Jr., Andrew P. Cap, Michael A. Dubick, Jonathan J. Morrison, Mark J. Midwinter, Frank K. Butler, Russ S. Kotwal, and John B. Holcomb, "Military Medical Revolution: Prehospital Combat Casualty Care," *Journal of Trauma and Acute Care Surgery* 73, no. 5 (December 2012), accessed September 30, 2020, https://pubmed.ncbi.nlm.nih.gov/23192058/.

14. Bulletin of the American College of Surgeons, "The Hartford Consensus III: Implementation of Bleeding Control," July 1, 2015, accessed September 30, 2020, https://bulletin.facs.org/2015/07/the-hartford-consensus-iii-implementation-of-bleeding-control/. See also American College of Surgeons, "New Trauma Study Results ."

15. Bulletin of the American College of Surgeons, "The Hartford Consensus III."

16. Bulletin of the American College of Surgeons, "The Hartford Consensus III."

17. American College of Surgeons, "New Trauma Study Results."

18. Teixeira et al., "Civilian Prehospital Tourniquet Use."

19. Tyler Kingkade, "Active Shooter Drills Are Meant to Prepare Students. But Research Finds 'Severe' Side Effects," NBC News, September 3, 2020, accessed September 30, 2020, https://www.nbcnews.com/news/us-news/active-shooter-drills-are-meant-prepare-students-research-finds-severe-n1239103.

20. Everytown for Gun Safety, "The Impact of Active Shooter Drills in Schools: Time to Rethink Reactive School Safety Strategies," September 3, 2020, accessed September 30, 2020, https://everytownresearch.org/report/the-impact-of-active-shooter-drills-in-schools/.

21. Everytown, "Impact of Active Shooter Drills in Schools."

22. Everytown, "Impact of Active Shooter Drills in Schools."

23. Everytown, "Impact of Active Shooter Drills in Schools," Executive Summary, 1.

24. Evie Blad and Madeline Will, "'I Felt More Traumatized Than Trained': Active-Shooter Drills Take Toll on Teachers," *Education Weekly* (March 24, 2019), accessed September 30, 2020, https://www.edweek.org/ew/articles/2019/03/24/i-felt-more-traumatized-than-trained-active-shooter.html.

25. Dan Frosch, "'Active Shooter' Drills Spark Raft of Legal Complaints: Critics Say Simulation Exercises Can Traumatize Those Taking Part," *Wall Street Journal*, September 4, 2014, accessed September 30, 2020, https://online.wsj.com/articles/active-shooter-drills-spark-raft-of-legal-complaints-1409760255.

26. Police1, "Ind. Teachers Hit by Pellets in Training Drill Sue Police," Associated Press, August 27, 2020, accessed September 30, 2020, https://www.police1.com/school-safety/articles/ind-teachers-hit-by-pellets-in-training-drill-sue-police-VEFZbT99gEsw6yNa/; see also Mitchell Willetts, "Teachers 'Executed' in Shooter Drill Sue Indiana Sheriff's Office for Trauma, Injury," *Miami Herald*, August 25, 2020, accessed September 30, 2020, https://www.yahoo.com/news/teachers-executed-shooter-drill-sue-220814776.html.

27. Sylvia Varnham O'Regan, "The Company Behind America's Scariest School Shooter Drills," *Trace/Huff Post*, December 13, 2019, accessed September 30, 2020, https://www.thetrace.org/2019/12/alice-active-shooter-training-school-safety/.

28. Mahita Gajanan, "Alaska's Students Will Be Taught How to Evade a School Shooter," *TIME*, August 28, 2016, accessed September 30, 2020, https://time.com/4469968/alaskas-alice-student-school-shooter-evade/#:~:text=Training%20for%20the%20ALICE%20program,training%20renewal%2C%20the%20ADN%20reported.

29. Champe Barton, "ALICE Is Overstating the Effectiveness of Its Active Shooter Trainings," *Trace*, January 8, 2020, accessed September 30, 2020, https://www.thetrace.org/2020/01/alice-training-institute-school-shooting-examples/.

30. "History of the Clery Act: Fact Sheet," EveryCRSReport.com, October 20, 2014, https://www.everycrsreport.com/reports/R43759.html#:~:text=Additional%20amendments%20to%20the%20Clery,emergency%20response%20and%20evacuation%20procedures. See also H.R.4137—Higher Education Opportunity Act, 110th Congress (2007–2008), https://www.congress.gov/bill/110th-congress/house-bill/4137?q=%7B%22search%22%3A%5B%22cite%3APL110-315%22%5D%7D&s=1&r=1.

31. Everytown, "Impact of Active Shooter Drills in Schools."

32. Jeffco Public Schools, accessed September 30, 2020, http://www.jeffcopublicschools.org.

33. I Love U Guys Foundation, "The Standard Response Protocol (SRP) for K-12 Schools," accessed September 30, 2020, https://iloveuguys.org/programs/standard-response-protocol-for-k-12/.

34. Everytown for Gun Safety, "Keeping Our Schools Safe: A Plan for Preventing Mass Shootings and Ending All Gun Violence in American Schools," May 19, 2020, accessed September 30, 2020, https://everytownresearch.org/report/a-plan-for-preventing-mass-shootings-and-ending-all-gun-violence-in-american-schools/.

CHAPTER TEN

1. For those trapped above floor 91, the plane impact destroyed stairwells and escape routes.

2. Jason D. Averill, Dennis S. Mileti, Richard D. Peacock, Erica D. Kuligowski, N. Groner, Guylene Proulx, Paul A. Reneke, and Harold E. Nelson, "Occupant Behavior, Egress, and Emergency Communication. Federal Building and Fire Safety Investigation of the World Trade Center Disaster (NIST NCSTAR 1-7)," National Institute of Standards and Technology, National Construction Safety Team Act Reports, paper, December 1, 2005, accessed September 30, 2020, https://www.nist.gov/publications/occupant-behavior-egress-and-emergency-communication-federal-building-and-fire-safety-0, xxiv.

3. Averill et al., "Occupant Behavior, Egress, and Emergency Communication (NIST NCSTAR 1-7)," 144–147.

4. City of Houston, Office of Emergency Management, "Run. Hide. Fight.® | Surviving."

5. Andres Viglucci, Kyra Gurney, Manny Navarro, Carli Teproff, and Martin Vassolo, "How Killer's Path through a School Left 17 Dead in Six Short Minutes of Terror," *Miami Herald*, February 17, 2018, accessed September 30, 2020, https://www.miamiherald.com/news/local/community/broward/article200661169.html.

6. CNBC, "Surveillance Video from Seattle Pacific University Shooting," CBS News, June 15, 2016, accessed September 30, 2020, https://www.youtube.com/watch?v=kc9ZeHIGphk; see also Mike Carter, "Dramatic Video Shows Hero Disarming Shooter at Seattle Pacific University in 2014," *Seattle Times*, June 14, 2016, accessed September 30, 2020, https://www.seattletimes.com/seattle-news/crime/dramatic-video-shows-hero-disarm-shooter-at-seattle-pacific-university-in-2014/.

7. Blad and Will, "'I Felt More Traumatized Than Trained.'"

8. Train 4 Safety Press, "Even the Youngest Can Be Better Prepared: Disaster Affects Everyone, Even Children. We Use Fun and Engaging Stories to Teach Children How to Stay Safe and Be Prepared," accessed September 30, 2020, http://train4safety.com/.

9. Sesame Street in Communities, "Traumatic Experiences," accessed September 30, 2020, https://sesamestreetincommunities.org/topics/traumatic-experiences/; see also Sesame Street in Communities, "I Can Feel Safe," accessed September 30, 2020, https://sesamestreetincommunities.org/activities/i-can-feel-safe/.

10. Ready Houston, "Elementary School Overview," accessed September 30, 2020, http://www.readyhoustontx.gov/school-ready/elementary-school/; see also "Request Preparedness Materials," accessed September 30, 2020, https://www.houstonoem.org/request-preparedness-materials/; and Ready Houston, "Are You Ready?" accessed September 30, 2020, http://www.readyhoustontx.gov, and "Ready Heroes Performance," accessed September 30, 2020, http://www.readyhoustontx.gov/school-ready/elementary-school/watch-and-listen/.

11. Averill et al., "Occupant Behavior, Egress, and Emergency Communication (NIST NCSTAR 1-7)," 88.

CHAPTER ELEVEN

1. John Gramlich, "What the Data Says about Gun Deaths in the U.S.," Pew Research Center, August 16, 2019, accessed September 30, 2020, https://www.pewre search.org/fact-tank/2019/08/16/what-the-data-says-about-gun-deaths-in-the-u-s/.

2. Statista Research Department, "Weapon Types Used in Mass Shootings in the United States Between 1982 and February 2020," July 31, 2020, accessed September 30, 2020, https://www.statista.com/statistics/476409/mass-shootings-in-the-us-by-weapon-types-used/.

3. Doug Cameron and Cara Lombardo, "Vista Outdoor Aims to Exit Several Brands, Including Firearms," *Wall Street Journal*, May 1, 2018, accessed September 30, 2020, https://www.wsj.com/articles/vista-outdoor-aims-to-exit-several-brands-including-firearms-1525183300.

4. Everytown for Gun Safety, "Virginia at a Glance," accessed September 30, 2020, https://everytown.org/state/virginia/.

5. Brad Kutner, "Virginia Governor Signs Package of Gun-Control Bills," Courthouse Service News, April 10, 2020, *Courthouse News Service,* accessed September 30, 2020, https://www.courthousenews.com/virginia-governor-signs-package-of-gun-control-bills/.

6. Kutner, "Virginia Governor Signs Package."

7. Sabrina Tavernise and Robert Gebeloff, "How Voters Turned Virginia from Deep Red to Solid Blue," *New York Times*, November 9, 2019, accessed September 30, 2020, https://www.nytimes.com/2019/11/09/us/virginia-elections-democrats-re publicans.html.

8. Virginia Governor, "Governor Northam Signs Historic Gun Safety Legislation into Law," April 10, 2020, accessed September 30, 2020, https://www.governor.virginia.gov/newsroom/all-releases/2020/april/headline-856016-en.html.

9. Kathleen Schuster, "8 Facts about Gun Control in the US," DW Akademie, January 20, 2020, accessed September 30, 2020, https://www.dw.com/en/8-facts-about-gun-control-in-the-us/a-40816418.

10. Mark Duggan, Randi Hjalmarsson, and Brian A. Jacob, "The Effect of Gun Shows on Gun-Related Deaths: Evidence from California and Texas," National Bureau of Economic Research (NBER)," working paper, October 2008, DOI: 10.3386/w14371, http://www.nber.org/papers/w14371; and "The Short-Term and Localized Effect of Gun Shows: Evidence from California and Texas," *Review of Economics and Statistics* 93, no. 3 (August 2011): 786–799, accessed September 30, 2020, https://www.mitpressjournals.org/toc/rest/93/3.

11. J. A. Shepperd, J. E. Losee, G. C. Pogge, N. P. Lipsey, L. Redford, and M. Crandall, "The Anticipated Consequences of Legalizing Guns on College Campuses," *Journal of Threat Assessment and Management* 5, no. 1 (2018): 21–34, accessed September 30, 2020, https://doi.org/10.1037/tam0000097.

12. US Constitution, Second Amendment, 1791.

13. Nelson Lund and Adam Winkler, "The Second Amendment," National Constitution Center, accessed September 30, 2020, https://constitutioncenter.org/interactive-constitution/interpretation/amendment-ii/interps/99.

14. Chelsea Hansen, "Slave Patrols: An Early Form of American Policing," National Law Enforcement Museum (blog), July 10, 2019, accessed September 30, 2020, https://lawenforcementmuseum.org/2019/07/10/slave-patrols-an-early-form-of-american-policing/. See also Sally E. Hadden, *Slave Patrols: Law and Violence in Virginia and the Carolinas* (Cambridge: Harvard University Press, 2002), ISBN 9780674012349.

15. Many states that didn't already have individual rights to gun ownership passed them in successive years, setting up future debates about federal statutes.

16. Statista Research Department, "Largest Armies in the World by Active Military Personnel 2020," accessed September 30, 2020, https://www.statista.com/statistics/264443/the-worlds-largest-armies-based-on-active-force-level/.

17. Keith Wood, "Top 10 Gun Movies on Netflix," *Guns&Ammo*, April 2, 2015, accessed September 30, 2020, https://www.gunsandammo.com/editorial/top-10-gun-movies-netflix/249470.

18. American Psychological Association (APA), "Report of the APA Commission on Violence in Youth," 1993, accessed September 30, 2020, https://www.apa.org/pubs/info/reports/violence-youth, 22.

19. US Department of Justice (DOJ), Federal Bureau of Investigation (FBI), "Active Shooter Resources," accessed September 30, 2020, https://www.fbi.gov/about/partnerships/office-of-partner-engagement/active-shooter-resources.

20. US DOJ, FBI, "Active Shooter Resources."

21. "Jordan Klepper, Good Guy with a Gun," *Daily Show with Trevor Noah*, February 10, 2015, two parts, accessed September 30, 2020, http://www.cc.com/video-clips/xqleli/the-daily-show-with-trevor-noah-jordan-klepper--good-guy-with-a-gun-pt--1 and http://www.cc.com/video-playlists/kw3fj0/the-opposition-with-jordan-klepper-welcome-to-the-opposition-w--jordan-klepper/w2bq3a.

22. Rand Corporation, Gun Policy in America, The Effects of Laws Allowing Armed Staff in K–12 Schools, April 22, 2020. www.rand.org/research/gun-policy/analysis/laws-allowing-armed-staff-in-K12-schools.html (accessed, December 10, 2020).

23. American Bar Association, "Opposition to Arming of School Personnel (19M106A)," Standing Committee on Gun Violence, Civil Rights and Social Justice Section, Criminal Justice Section, and Commission on Domestic & Sexual Violence, Report to the House of Delegates, January 28, 2019, accessed September 30, 2020, https://www.americanbar.org/groups/public_interest/gun_violence/policy/19M106A/.

24. United States v. Miller, 307 U.S. 174 (1939).

25. Warren Commission Report, "JFK Assassination Records, Chapter 4: The Assassin," accessed September 30, 2020, https://www.archives.gov/research/jfk/warren-commission-report/chapter-4.html#purchase.

26. UPI, "J. Edgar Hoover: Black Panther Greatest Threat to U.S. Security," United Press International, July 16, 1969, accessed September 30, 2020, https://www.upi.com/Archives/1969/07/16/J-Edgar-Hoover-Black-Panther-Greatest-Threat-to-US-Security/1571551977068/.

27. Thomas Hartman, *The Hidden History of Guns and the Second Amendment* (Oakland: Berrett-Koehler, 2018), 79.

28. Ibid.

29. Jill LaPore, *These Truths: A History of the United States* (New York: W. W. Norton, 2018), 678.

30. University of California, Santa Barbara, The American Presidency Project, accessed December 4, 2021, https://www.presidency.ucsb.edu/documents/republican-party-platform-1968.

31. Adam Winkler, *Gunfight: The Battle over the Right to Bear Arms in America* (New York: W. W. Norton, 2011), 253.

32. University of California, Santa Barbara, The American Presidency Project, "National Political Party Platforms," accessed September 30, 2020, https://www.presidency.ucsb.edu/documents/presidential-documents-archive-guidebook/party-platforms-and-nominating-conventions-3.

33. Winkler, *Gunfight*, 63–68.

34. Louis Jacobson, "Counting Up How Much the NRA Spends on Campaigns and Lobbying," *PolitiFact*, Poynter Institute, October 11, 2017, accessed September 30, 2020, https://www.politifact.com/article/2017/oct/11/counting-up-how-much-nra-spends/.

35. Jay Dickey and Mark Rosenberg, "We Won't Know the Cause of Gun Violence until We Look for It," *Washington Post*, July 27, 2012, accessed September 30, 2020, https://www.washingtonpost.com/opinions/we-wont-know-the-cause-of-gun-violence-until-we-look-for-it/2012/07/27/gJQAPfenEX_story.html.

36. Arthur L. Kellermann, Frederick P. Rivara, Norman B. Rushforth, Joyce G. Banton, Donald T. Reay, Jerry T. Francisco, Ana B. Locci, Janice Prodzinski, Bela B. Hackman, and Grant Somes, "Gun Ownership as a Risk Factor for Homicide in the Home," *New England Journal of Medicine* 329 (October 7, 1993), https://www.nejm.org/doi/full/10.1056/NEJM199310073291506.

37. Dickey and Rosenberg, "We Won't Know."

38. National Police Foundation, "Mass Shootings at Virginia Tech," August 2007, https://www.policefoundation.org/critical-incident-review-library/mass-shootings-at-virginia-tech/, and April 16, 2007, http://www.policefoundation.org/wp-content/uploads/2016/08/Mass-Shootings-at-Virginia-Tech.pdf.

39. District of Columbia v. Heller, 554 U.S. 570 (2008), 53–54; Brown v. Board of Education of Topeka, 347 U.S. 483 (1954); and Roe v. Wade, 410 U.S. 113 (1973).

40. District of Columbia v. Heller, 53–54.

41. District of Columbia v. Heller, 53–55. ("We therefore read *Miller* to say only that the Second Amendment does not protect those weapons not typically possessed by law-abiding citizens for lawful purposes, such as short-barreled shotguns.")

42. We did discuss that Black men are more likely to die by guns in homicides whereas White men are more likely to die by guns in suicides. See Corinne A. Riddell, Sam Harper, Magdalena Cerdá, and Jay S. Kaufman, "Comparison of Rates of Firearm and Nonfirearm Homicide and Suicide in Black and White Non-Hispanic Men, by U.S. State," *Annuals of Internal Medicine* 168, no. 10 (May 15, 2018): 712–720, accessed September 30, 2020, https://scholar.google.com/citations?user=3y2op6AAAAAJ#.

43. APA, "Report on Violence in Youth," 23.

CHAPTER TWELVE

1. Steve Lewis, "Inside the FBI: An 'Empathetic Pioneer': Architect of Victim Services Division Retires," transcript, Federal Bureau of Investigation, June 30, 2020, accessed September 30, 2020, https://www.fbi.gov/news/podcasts/inside-the-fbi-an-empathetic-pioneer-063020.

2. Victim Rights, Compensation, and Assistance, 34 U.S. Code 201.

3. US Department of Justice, Office for Victims of Crime, Office of Justice Programs, "Center for Victim Research," accessed September 30, 2020, https://victimresearch.org/.

4. US Department of Justice, Office for Victims of Crime, Office of Justice Programs, "Victims of Crime Act (VOCA) Administrators," accessed September 30, 2020, https://ovc.ojp.gov/program/victims-crime-act-voca-administrators/welcome.

5. National Center for Victims of Crime, "Aiding Crime Victims Through eLearning," accessed September 30, 2020, https://education.victimsofcrime.org/.

6. National Center for Victims of Crime, "About the National Center," https://victimsofcrime.org/about/.

7. Penn State University and the Federal Bureau of Investigation, "We Regret to Inform You," 2014, accessed September 30, 2020, https://www.deathnotification.psu.edu/.

8. US Department of Justice, Office for Victims of Crime, Office of Justice Programs, "Crime Victims Fund," accessed September 30, 2020, https://ovc.ojp.gov/about/crime-victims-fund.

9. Victim Connect, Nation Center for Victims of Crime, "Financial Assistance," accessed September 30, 2020, https://victimconnect.org/resources/financial-assistance/. See also Donna Engel, "Legal Matters: Each State Has Compensation Fund for Victims of Crime," *Carroll County Times*, October 20, 2017, https://www.baltimoresun.com/maryland/carroll/opinion/cc-lt-engle-102217-story.html.

10. National Association of Crime Victim Compensation Boards, "Crime Victim Compensation: An Overview," accessed September 30, 2020, http://www.nacvcb.org/index.asp?bid=14.

11. National Association of Crime Victim Compensation Boards, "Victim Compensation Programs Help Victims Cope with the Costs of Violent Crime," accessed September 30, 2020, http://www.nacvcb.org/index.asp?sid=1.

12. US Department of Justice, Office for Victims of Crime, Office of Justice Programs, "Victims of Crime Act: Rebuilding Lives through Assistance and Compensation," accessed September 30, 2020, http://ncdsv.org/images/VOCA_RebuildLives AssistCompChart_2009.pdf.

13. The following chart and others are available for download off the resources tab on my websites at www.katherineschweit.com and www.schweitconsulting.com.

Index

atypical behavior, 37, 58
Austin, Texas, 101

baseline behavior, 58
BATF. *See* US Department of Justice
Beal, Heather L., 142, 145
Before. During. After., Schweit, 11
Behavioral Analysis Unit. *See* US
    Department of Justice, Federal
    Bureau of Investigation
Behavioral Threat Assessment Center.
    See US Department of Justice,
    Federal Bureau of Investigation
behaviors of concern, def., 46, 52, 57
Bennett, Steven B., 35, 135
Betts, Andrew, 148–49
Biden, Joseph R., President of the
    United States and former Vice
    President, 2, 150, 155
Biden team, 17
Bill of Rights, 153–54
Black Lives Matter movement, 164
Black Panther Party, 158, 160, 164
Blair, J. Pete, 19
Bloomberg, Michael, 152
Bobrow, Bob, xvii
Borum, Randy, 69
Boston Marathon bombing, 168–69
Bousson, Allison Adams, xvii
Brady Campaign to Prevent Gun
    Violence, 25
Brady Campaign to Stop Gun Violence,
    152
Brady Handgun Violence Prevention
    Act of 1993, 161
Brady, James, 159
British Broadcasting Corporation, 24
brittle, def., 56
Brody, Farrell, xvii
Brown v. Board of Education, 159
buckle up for safety, buckle up, 6
Bundy, Ted, 32
Bureau of Justice Statistics, 26
Burns, David, 19
bystander, def., 51

Calhoun, Frederick S., 48, 71
California State Capitol march of 1967,
    160
Campos, Fay, xvii
*Campus Attacks: Targeted Violence
    Affecting Institutions of Higher
    Education*, 191
Captain Kirk, 155
Cascades Park, 117
Castillo-Chavez, Carlos, 28
Castleberry, Jerry, 19
casualty collection, 184
Centers for Disease Control and
    Prevention, 8, 115, 125, 149, 161
Centers for Disease Control and
    Prevention, National Institute for
    Occupational Safety and Health,
    115
Center for Victim Research, 166
Chicago, 95
Chicago Tribune, 1
Civil War, 154
Clery Act, 130
Clint Eastwood, 156
CNN, 14, 25
Coalition to Stop Gun Violence, 152
Colorado, Attorney General, 67
Columbia Journalism Review, 28
Columbine generation, 145
Columbine locks, 92
Combs, Christopher, xvii
concealment, def., 140
Confederacy, 151
Congressional Research Service, CRS,
    21, 25, 29
Connecticut State Police, 15
contagion effect and the media's
    responsibility, 26–29
contextually inappropriate behavior, 58
Cook County State's Attorney Office, 2
Cook, Julia, 145
copycat, 27. *See also* contagion effect
Cordell, Kasey, 28
Cornell, Dewey G., 71, 81, 95
Coulombe, Maribeth, xviii

About the Author

Ms. Katherine Schweit is a licensed attorney and retired Federal Bureau of Investigation special agent who spent nearly five years as the executive responsible for the FBI's active shooter efforts. After the tragedy at Sandy Hook Elementary School, she joined the select group in Washington, DC, working on violence prevention with then–Vice President Joseph Biden and his team. She was an author of the FBI's seminal research, "A Study of 160 Active Shooter Incidents in the United States Between 2000 and 2013," and was part of the crisis team responding to incidents including the shootings at the Holocaust Memorial Museum, the Pentagon, and the Navy Yard in the Washington, DC, area. She is the executive producer of the award-winning film, *The Coming Storm*, widely used in security and law enforcement training in the United States and relied upon by the Department of State worldwide. This work earned her a second US Attorney General's Award.

Before joining the FBI, Ms. Schweit was an assistant state's attorney in Chicago. Before opening her own consulting firm, Schweit Consulting LLC, she was the director for security training at a Fortune 300 company. A one-time print journalist, she has published extensively, including opinion pieces in the *New York Times* and Chicago's *Daily Herald*. She is a recognized expert in active shooter matters, crisis response, workplace violence, and corporate security policies and often provides on-air television commentary after mass shootings. She regularly speaks at professional, government, and private organization events. She is a member of the Association of Threat Assessment Professionals, the International Association of Chiefs of Police, and the International Association for Healthcare Security and Safety and is a Certified Compliance and Ethics Professional. She is currently a member of the adjunct faculty at DePaul University College of Law and Webster University. She lives in Virginia, outside of Washington, DC.

CPSIA information can be obtained
at www.ICGtesting.com
Printed in the USA
BVHW032047270622
640785BV00002B/2